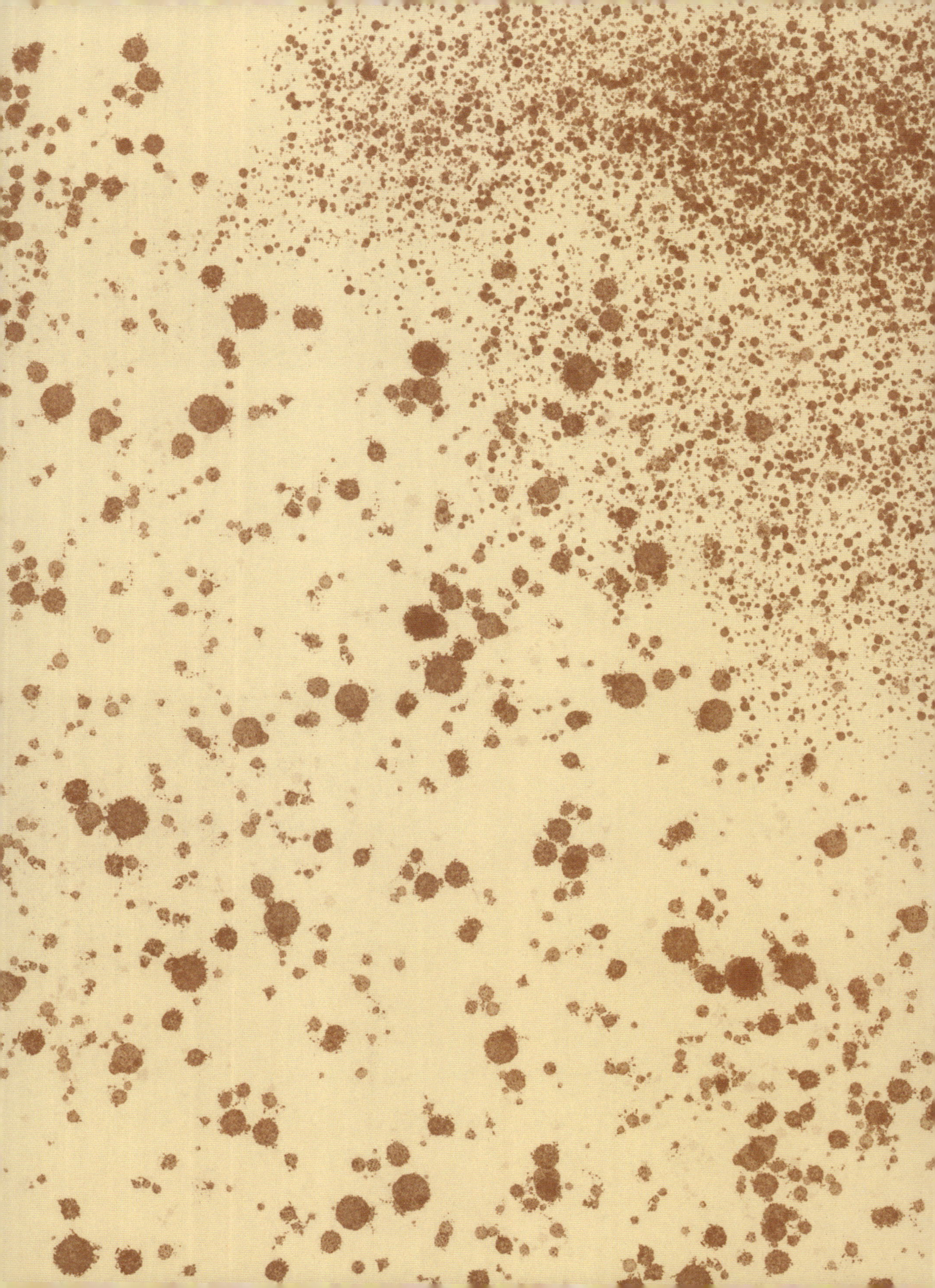

CHOCOLATE
baking

CHOCOLATE *baking*

THE ULTIMATE GUIDE TO CAKES, COOKIES, DESSERTS AND PASTRIES

EDD KIMBER

Photography by Matthew Hague

Quadrille

INTRODUCTION

When I think back on why I became a baker, I realise the answer lies inside a slice of homemade chocolate cake, a cake made with love to celebrate a birthday. I was very lucky growing up, as I had parents that regularly cooked and, more importantly, baked from scratch. Some of my earliest memories might seem a little clichéd – standing on a kitchen stool rolling out pastry with my mum to make mince pies at Christmas and weighing ingredients for our regular Sunday lunch apple crumble – but they remain incredibly significant. I can close my eyes and instantly recall the cake made for my seventh birthday, a simple chocolate one decorated with Smarties, Disney decals and train-themed candles. I can also vividly remember the time my twin brother and I, being looked after by my sister, ended up hidden beneath the kitchen table licking chocolate cake batter from the bowl. What I am trying to say is that this book is a love letter, a lifetime in the making. From the birthday cakes of my childhood to the comfort food of my adulthood, chocolate has always been the flavour I've turned to more than any other.

Chocolate's popularity is unquestioned, but as an ingredient it is frequently misunderstood and the techniques used to bake with it are often viewed with trepidation. My aim with this book is to show you not only how to avoid common pitfalls but how to rescue problems. Sometimes we follow recipes blindly, not understanding the whys or hows, which leaves us frustrated when things go wrong. At the first restaurant kitchen I worked in, I was put to work making a spectacular chocolate dessert based around a simple ganache. The chef instructed me to make the ganache in a way I had never seen before, but when I asked the reasoning behind it I was told that's just how it's done. The vagueness of this rubbed me the wrong way, I like to know the why, to understand the mechanics of the how. Because of this experience, and others like it, I have always tried to champion the home baker, to give detail in my recipes, to hold the reader's hand through the process, so they have the knowledge and confidence to feel comfortable in the kitchen, and the best chance of success. Look, chocolate is an expensive ingredient, it's the least I can do.

To demonstrate my love for chocolate, but also to show how incredibly adaptable it is, the recipes in this book, and the flavours used with it, vary wildly. And there's a recipe for each and every occasion, no matter what you're in the mood to make. Sometimes the chocolate flavour is front and centre, sometimes it plays a supporting role, but each recipe is a celebration of this very special ingredient. My hope is that, over the years, this book becomes covered in stains from cocoa powder spills and splashes of melted chocolate, the pages dog-eared where they mark family favourites, from the chocolate cake you've become known for to the dessert your kids ask you to make at least once a week. The book encompasses everything from cakes and cookies to tarts and pies, ice cream and sorbet to breads, buns and croissants. Chocolate is an ingredient that can be paired with so many different flavours, so you'll find recipes that are both new and exciting, but because it so often needs no other adornment, I've also included recipes for a classic chocolate cake, brownies and the best chocolate chip cookies you'll ever make.

This book is all about celebrating my favourite ingredient and I hope you get as much joy from the recipes as I did from writing them.

A CHOCOLATE PRIMER

WHAT IS CHOCOLATE?

We all know what chocolate is, right? But do you know the difference between cacao and cocoa, what cocoa liquor is or what cocoa nibs are? Let me tell you the story of how your chocolate bar came to be.

Chocolate starts out as a fruit, grown on the theobroma cacao tree, a word that translates as 'food of the gods'. The trees typically flourish in what is referred to as the cacao belt, an area 20 degrees north and south of the equator, the hot tropical climate providing the perfect growing conditions of ample rainfall but also shade from rainforest.

Although it originated in the Amazon basin, the cacao tree is now cultivated in more than 50 countries around the world, though 50% of production takes place in just two, Ivory Coast and Ghana. It is a difficult crop, prone to disease, which is part of the reason why chocolate has risen in price recently; another being the challenges stemming from climate change.

When a cacao pod is harvested, it is cut open to reveal white fleshy pulp surrounding the cacao beans. This pulp is often discarded, but it can be turned into a drink or eaten like a fruit. It has an almost tropical fruit flavour and is utterly delicious. Some bean-to-bar producers are now also using it to sweeten their chocolate bars instead of sugar.

Once harvested, the beans are fermented, which is when the flavour of chocolate begins to develop. They are then dried, to prevent mould from developing. At this point, they are shipped to the end processor, the chocolate maker. For many years, chocolate was always made thousands of miles away from the farms on which the cacao grew, divorcing the end product from the original farmer, but there is now a burgeoning number of cacao farmers who also make chocolate from the beans they grow.

When they arrive at the chocolate maker, the beans are roasted. The heat and length of this process being determined by the chocolate maker and the flavour profile they want to achieve. At a basic level, the longer and hotter the roast, the more the acidity is rounded out. If you buy a cheaper bar of chocolate, you'll often find its colour is almost black, which is a result of the beans being roasted to such a degree that the imperfections are hidden, leaving you with one-note, less-interesting chocolate (the colour is also influenced by the 'dutching' process). As with coffee beans, a lighter roast allows the unique flavour of the cacao to shine through, whilst roasting it more heavily results in a more generic flavour profile.

Once dried, the beans go through another process, called cracking and winnowing, where they are broken apart and the papery outer shells, known as cocoa husks are separated from the inner part of the bean, known as nibs. The husks are often discarded but can be used to make a cocoa tea, as a mulch or fertiliser, or turned into animal feed.

The nibs are then ground into a thick paste, known as cocoa liquor, which is used either in the chocolate-making process or put into a press that separates most of the fat (cocoa butter) from the dry solids. These solids are broken up to make cocoa powder and the cocoa butter is used to make white chocolate. To make chocolate the cocoa liquor is combined with sugar and refined into a smooth finished product. Finally, the chocolate is tempered, a process that involves precise heating and cooling, which ensures that the finished product is smooth, shiny and, when broken, has a satisfying snap. It also slightly increases the melting point of the chocolate, meaning it doesn't melt as easily when handled.

A BRIEF HISTORY LESSON

It was the Spanish conquistadors who gave Europeans their first taste of cacao in the mid 16th century, but prior to its transatlantic journey it bore very little resemblance to the confection we enjoy today.

It is widely accepted that cacao originated in the Amazon basin, with the most recent evidence revealing that cacao can be traced at least as far back as 3300 BCE, due to recent archaeological discoveries in Peru. Through trading, cacao migrated north to Latin America and found a home with the Olmecs of southern Mexico, who were believed to have imbibed a cacao-based drink during important ceremonies. It is, however, the Mayans, whose Mexican civilisation was at its peak c.250–900 CE, who get the most credit for our love of cacao. Their written histories reveal an incredible level of reverence for the beans, which they roasted over fire, ground into a paste and used to make a thick, frothy drink, the original hot chocolate. Don't be confused, though, this drink was nothing like the beverage we consume today as the cacao beans were ground with maize and mixed with water and spices such as allspice and chilli powder. The Mayans, and later the Aztecs (who ruled in Mexico from 1325–1521 CE), also used cacao beans as currency.

Cocoa remained primarily a beverage until 1847, when the British chocolatier, J.S. Fry, made the first moulded bar of chocolate. Thirty years later, Swiss chocolatier Daniel Peter added milk powder, creating the first form of milk chocolate. If you like chocolate because of its smooth, creamy, melt-in-the mouth texture, you have Lindt to thank for inventing conching, a prolonged process of mixing chocolate to refine the final texture and flavour.

In the 17th century, drinking hot chocolate had become a craze across Europe, the first chocolate house opening in London in 1657. Sadly, this love of cocoa came at huge human cost. Initially, the Spanish used a form of forced local labour to grow and harvest cacao, but as other European countries developed a taste for cocoa they, too, began to exploit the region, starting their own plantations and transporting African people, against their will, to work as slaves. With the formal abolishment of slavery (which occurred in the UK in 1834), chocolate production shifted to Africa, the presence of the right climate and an abundance of cheap labour meant industrialists could continue large-scale production while at the same time keeping their costs low. On the surface this was progress, the workers were now being paid, after all, but in reality it was indentured servitude, so just another form of exploitation.

I would love to be able to tell you that today the abuses in chocolate production are a thing of the past, but the actions of colonial powers and rich industrialists have had long-lasting impact. More than half the world's chocolate is produced in Central and Western Africa, where unfortunately exploitation is still rampant. The supply chain has been historically murky, with big manufacturers ignoring these issues or at the very least brushing them under the carpet whilst making millions in profit. Over the last decade or so, with mounting negative press attention and public pressure, the big five chocolate manufacturers have repeatedly acknowledged and publicly committed to assessing these issues, yet their target for doing so has moved ever further into the future with no fundamental changes yet to be made.

ETHICAL CHOCOLATE

If this issue matters to you – and it should – you can encourage ethical cacao production by choosing to buy chocolate from ethical manufacturers.

There are many certification schemes that chocolate makers can sign up to, such as Fairtrade and Rainforest Alliance, whose aims include ensuring farmers are paid a living wage. These schemes do not go nearly far enough and do little to eradicate enslaved labour from the supply chain. Some of the schemes have been developed by the big chocolate makers themselves, meaning the incentive for change may not be as strong as we'd hope for. Some of the most ethically produced chocolate isn't part of any of these schemes, instead it uses a simpler approach – Direct Trade. Here, the chocolate maker buys direct from the farmer (or a sourcing specialist). As a result the chocolate makers pay significantly higher prices to the farmers whilst encouraging, and helping with, the growth of high-quality cacao, good environmental practices and social sustainability of the farms.

PERFORMATIVE PERCENTAGES

Marketing by big chocolate companies has led us to equate high percentages, and specifically 70%, with quality, when in reality it has nothing to do with how good or bad a chocolate might be.

It can be argued that the higher the percentage the healthier the chocolate is, because it is made with less sugar, but the quality of chocolate has nothing to do with percentages. I've had incredible chocolate made with 40 and 50% cocoa and terrible chocolate made with 85% cocoa. All the percentage tells you is how much cocoa was used to make that particular chocolate, it tells you nothing about the quality of said cocoa.

Another reason why, in my opinion, 70% chocolate has become so prolific, is that the flavour profile is pleasing to a wide swathe of people. Dark enough to have a pronounced chocolate flavour, with just enough sugar to round out the bitterness and acidity and make it widely palatable. It is this balanced flavour profile that also makes it a popular percentage to use in baking.

CHOCOLATE VARIETIES

For a long time it was believed that all chocolate could be categorised into three varieties: criollo, trinitario and forastero. Recent research has revealed that this isn't the full picture and there are at least 10 different varieties. Some are very rare, with distinct flavour profiles. Others are hardy and so are prized by big chocolate manufacturers for their high yields and resistance to disease, their flavour profile being almost an afterthought. Varieties you may see listed on packaging include:

- **Criollo** A rare variety that makes up less than 5% of the world's production. It's said to have a delicate flavour, with floral and nutty notes.
- **Forastero** The most common variety, grown primarily in Western Africa, it makes up at least 80% of the world's production. Often described as having a strong cocoa flavour profile, it is less complex with a slight bitterness.
- **Trinitario** A hybrid of criollo and forastero, it makes up about 10% of the world's cocoa production. Popular with chocolate makers, it combines the robust flavour of forastero with the complexity of criollo, with fruity and floral notes.
- **Nacional** Another rare variety of cacao, grown in the coastal regions of Ecuador and accounting for just 1% of the world's production. It is said to have an intense floral and fruity flavour profile.

Knowing the variety can help us understand the flavour of the chocolate, but it shouldn't always be how we determine quality. Forastero is often viewed as the lowest-quality cacao but there are farmers growing this variety whose beans are turned into exceptional quality chocolate. The country in which it is grown, the soil composition and the climate can all directly impact the flavour of the cacao, as can the processing which turns cacao into chocolate. A recognition of this is why the traditional variety classification used to market chocolate has slowly started to fade away in favour of using the region as the primary descriptor.

If you're looking to buy chocolate with a specific flavour profile, don't worry about trying to remember which country's chocolate has the character you're looking for. Instead, trust the chocolate maker. Good-quality chocolate makers will almost always give you flavour notes, which can help you choose the chocolate you want to eat or bake with. Chocolate doesn't magically transform in the oven, so my advice is always to use a chocolate you love to eat. If it tastes good as a chocolate bar, it'll taste great as a baked treat.

USING CHOCOLATE IN THIS BOOK

Throughout this book I've listed chocolate in one of two ways. On most occasions, I give a guide percentage. This is so that you taste the recipe as it is designed to taste, with the correct balance of fat and sweetness. Drastically changing the percentage in these recipes can have a detrimental effect on the texture, sweetness and flavour, so to ensure a successful outcome it is advisable to stick to what's suggested. Where chocolate is used as a mix-in, such as chocolate chip cookies, I simply list 'dark' or 'milk' chocolate, leaving the choice of percentage up to you. In these recipes the percentage of cocoa used will only affect the sweetness and not the texture. I generally use a dark chocolate that is 65–75% cocoa content, a milk chocolate that has at least 40% cocoa content and white chocolate made with at least 30% cocoa butter. Ultimately, my best advice, especially when using chocolate as a mix-in, not as a building block ingredient, is to use a chocolate you love the taste of.

COCOA POWDER CONFUSION

Cocoa powder comes in two main forms: natural and dutched. Natural cocoa powder, which has a lighter colour with a bright, acidic flavour, is simply the dry cocoa solids that have been ground into a powder. Dutched cocoa is a deeper reddish-brown colour with a more roasted flavour profile. The solids have gone through an additional step, where it is processed with an alkaline solution. This process results in a cocoa powder that is more soluble in water and has a deeper flavour with reduced acidity.

ARE THEY INTERCHANGEABLE?

This depends on the recipe. Natural cocoa powder, as it is more acidic, is commonly recommended for recipes that use bicarbonate of soda (baking soda) as the primary form of leavening. The acidity of the cocoa reacts with the alkaline bicarbonate, allowing the bake to rise. Dutched cocoa powder, as it is more neutral, is usually found in recipes that use baking powder. Being a mixture of acid and alkaline, it doesn't need the additional acid to make the recipe rise. Natural cocoa powder has always been more popular in the US, whereas in Europe the reverse is true.

But what happens if you accidentally use the wrong form of cocoa? If the recipe relies on baking powder to leaven a cake, it will work with both forms, but the cake will be lighter if natural cocoa powder is used and the cocoa flavour will be more subtle. If it is made with dutched cocoa, the cake will be slightly fudgier and will have a deeper, more 'chocolatey' flavour. If a cake relies solely on bicarbonate of soda to rise, the recipe may need the acid of the natural cocoa powder to rise properly, which means that if it is made with dutched cocoa powder it is unlikely to rise as much as intended; it may also develop a soapy aftertaste as the bicarbonate of soda will lend the cake an alkaline flavour that isn't balanced by the acidity of natural cocoa powder.

The technical differences aren't an issue when the recipe doesn't rely on chemical leavening, as is the case when making genoise cakes, sauces and ice creams. Personally, my preference is to use dutched cocoa powder in almost all situations as I like its rich chocolate notes, but the choice is yours.

HOW TO TELL THE DIFFERENCE?

It can be confusing, standing in the baking aisle, trying to distinguish which cocoa powder you're looking at. Most brands usually declare it on the packaging if they're 'natural', but many dutched powders require a little detective work. You need to look for wording such as 'treated with an alkali' or even some form of the word 'dutched'. Once opened, though, you can tell by the colour of the powder. Natural cocoa is a very pale, light terracotta colour that can look a little grey and almost dusty. Dutched cocoa powder is a more concentrated reddish-brown colour.

WHAT'S THE DEAL WITH BLACK COCOA POWDER?

This style of cocoa powder is a form of dutched cocoa, which goes through a more intense version of the dutching process, resulting in a powder that is almost jet black in colour and devoid of any acidity. It is the least expressive of all cocoa powders, having a simple roasted flavour. If you've ever eaten an Oreo, this is the cocoa powder used to flavour these cookies.

You can use black cocoa powder whenever dutched cocoa is called for, but it is worth considering the potential change in flavour and texture this would cause, not just the dramatic change in colour. Good-quality dutched cocoa powder tends to have 20–22% fat content, whereas black cocoa is generally 10–11% fat. This may seem like little difference but it can result in a drier texture. To achieve the dramatic look of black cocoa without losing out on texture I often use one-third black cocoa and two-thirds regular dutched cocoa.

A BRIEF CHOCOLATE GLOSSARY

Baking Chocolate Baking chocolate, sometimes also called cooking chocolate, was a marketing term used mainly in the 1980s and 90s that has now fallen out of favour. It generally referred to a style of chocolate made with less cocoa butter than 'eating' chocolate; it was also often made with lower-quality cacao.

Bean-to-Bar A term that refers to a chocolate maker who makes chocolate from scratch, starting with the fermented and dried beans. There is also a small but growing number of tree-to-bar producers, farmers that grow the cacao as well as make the chocolate, controlling every step in the process.

Bittersweet and Semisweet A vague naming convention for dark chocolate used solely in the US. Both refer to what the rest of the world calls 'dark' chocolate, though semisweet tends to have a lower cocoa content than bittersweet.

Bloom When chocolate is untempered, or stored incorrectly, it can develop a 'fat bloom' of white or grey streaks which show that the cocoa butter has risen to the surface and is oxidising. 'Sugar Bloom', where the sugar is drawn to the surface leaving a gritty texture, is a similar issue but it occurs when the chocolate is stored in a cold and damp environment, such as a refrigerator. In both instances the chocolate is fine to eat but the texture may be subpar. They're perfectly fine to bake with.

Cacao vs Cocoa Confusingly, these terms are often used interchangeably and have no legal definition. Generally, however, cacao is used to refer to the products before roasting has occurred, i.e. the tree, pods and beans, and cocoa is used to refer to products after roasting, i.e. cocoa powder and cocoa nibs.

Cacao Beans The seeds of the cacao fruit. When the cacao pod is cracked open they are found encased in a white pulp which tastes like tropical fruit.

Cacao Pods The fruit of the cacao tree. Shaped like American footballs/rugby balls, they come in a variety of colours and can be anything from red, green, yellow or purple.

Callets/Wafers/Discs Oval or round discs of couverture chocolate sold by chocolate companies to enable pastry chefs to spend less time chopping.

Caramelised White Chocolate A type of white chocolate, sometimes known as roasted or blonde chocolate, that is heated so that the milk solids and the sugars caramelise, giving the simple sweetness of white chocolate a more caramel-based flavour profile.

Chocolate Chips Chocolate chips are made with a lower percentage of cocoa butter than other forms of chocolate. This means they hold their shape when baked in products like cookies. It also means the melted chocolate is more viscous, so they're not ideal for dipping or coating. Often made with low-quality cocoa, if you do like using chips, look for a version made by a quality chocolate producer. Personally, I generally avoid using them.

Cocoa Butter Cocoa nibs are made up of solids and fat, the latter accounting for just over half of the content.

Cocoa Nibs Cocoa nibs are broken-up pieces of the cacao bean that have gone through the process of fermenting, drying and roasting. Cacao nibs are the same product except they haven't been roasted. Once ground into a paste and mixed with sugar, the nibs then become finished chocolate.

Cocoa Powder Once cacao beans have been roasted, the nibs are ground into a paste called cocoa, or chocolate liquor/mass. This is then separated into fat, known as cocoa butter, and dry cocoa solids, which are broken up to become cocoa powder and cocoa butter. If the beans have not been roasted prior to pressing, this powder is referred to as cacao powder or raw cacao powder. Cocoa powder also comes in two varieties: 'natural' and 'dutched' see page 16.

Cocoa Solids/Percentage The percentage indicates how much cocoa has been used to make the chocolate. If a bar of dark chocolate is made with 70% cocoa, the remaining 30% should be sugar.

Compound Chocolate This type of chocolate, sometimes called 'coating chocolate', is made with fat other than cocoa butter and is generally considered to be low quality and not a true form of chocolate. Do not use this when a recipe calls for chocolate, as the recipe may not work as written.

Couverture Chocolate A term used to refer to chocolate made specifically for pastry chefs and chocolatiers, with more cocoa butter than chips or bars. Thinner and less viscous, it is perfect for coating and dipping.

Crémeux A ganache made with chocolate and crème anglaise.

Dark Chocolate Chocolate typically made with at least a 50% cocoa content. In some countries, the amount of cocoa solids in dark chocolate is determined by law. Often this is a much lower amount than we might think of as typical, sometimes as low as 35%.

Dark-Milk Chocolate This style of milk chocolate has a higher cocoa content than most milk chocolate but is still made with milk powder, meaning it has a rich chocolate flavour but also the creamy milky notes that you get with milk chocolate.

Direct Trade When the chocolate maker buys cacao beans directly from the farmer or a cooperative, not through an intermediary. It is also used to describe a more ethical form of chocolate production.

Ganache An emulsion of chocolate and liquid, most commonly cream.

Gianduja A type of chocolate made from cocoa, sugar and hazelnuts. The nibs and hazelnuts are roasted separately then combined with sugar and ground into a smooth paste. The high fat content means it is far softer than other forms of chocolate. Most likely you've seen it sold in individual foil-wrapped portions in Italian coffee shops.

Lecithin An ingredient mainly used by large-scale chocolate makers to reduce the viscosity of the chocolate so it passes through their machinery a little easier. The lecithin is normally derived from either sunflowers or soya.

Milk Chocolate Chocolate made with the addition of milk powder that typically contains 35% cocoa. In some countries there is a legal minimum for the cocoa content. In the UK, for example, it is 25%.

Single Origin A chocolate made with cacao from one particular farm or region. The term has no legal definition so there is no strict limit to the area that 'single origin' can refer to. Some bars of chocolate are referred to as 'single estate' to better define that the cacao came from one single farm, or estate.

Tempering A process in which chocolate is precisely heated and cooled, to give it its characteristic shine and snap. It also raises the melting point slightly so that it doesn't melt as quickly when handled.

Theobroma Cacao The botanical name of the cacao tree, from the Latin word 'theobroma', meaning food of the gods.

White Chocolate A controversial topic, as many people like to loudly declare this is not a real form of chocolate, to which I say, not so fast! It is a delicious and very creamy confection that has excellent uses in baking. At a minimum it should contain 20% cocoa butter, though the best versions are made with as much as 45%.

A FEW NOTES ON INGREDIENTS

Baking Powder A chemical leavener, made up of bicarbonate of soda (baking soda) and cream of tartar, a mild acid. The combination means it is a self-contained chemical leavener, so it requires no additional acid to activate its leavening power.

Bicarbonate of Soda Normally used alongside acidic ingredients, such as buttermilk or natural cocoa powder, to create a chemical reaction to allow recipes to rise. Known as baking soda in some countries.

Butter In this book I exclusively use unsalted butter that has a fat content of 82%.

Buttermilk When making chocolate cakes, buttermilk's tang and acidity work beautifully to elevate flavours and create perfectly moist recipes. The acidity also helps cakes to rise when combined with bicarbonate of soda (baking soda). Traditionally a low-fat dairy product, there are now some producers making 'whole' buttermilk. In the recipes that call for buttermilk, any version can be used. If you can't get hold of buttermilk you can substitute kefir, a fermented yoghurt drink, or plain yoghurt thinned with a little water.

Caster Sugar A refined white sugar with a fine texture. In the US, and in some other countries, it's also known as superfine or baker's sugar. If it's unavailable, white granulated sugar will work well in its place.

Coconut Oil This plant-based fat comes in two varieties: refined and unrefined (raw or extra virgin). The two styles are interchangeable from a technical standpoint, the only difference is in flavour. Unrefined has a strong coconut flavour and should be used when that is what is desired. If you want a vegan fat without any added flavour, use refined.

Cornflour A very fine, almost talc-like, powder that is known in the UK as cornflour and in the US as cornstarch. Used as a thickening agent, if you can't get hold of it, potato starch is generally the best alternative.

Cream Other than chocolate and butter, cream is probably the most-used ingredient in this book. I exclusively use 'whipping cream', which in the US is referred to as 'heavy whipping cream'. The name is immaterial, what is important is the fat content. You want a cream with a fat content of about 36%. If you're in the UK, you can also use double cream, which has a fat content closer to 50%, but be aware that your ganache may be more prone to splitting if you switch.

Cream Cheese I love cream cheese for its rich fatty texture, its gentle tang and creamy taste. I use it to make cream cheese frosting but also, occasionally, to make actual cakes. Whenever I call for this ingredient I am referring to the full-fat version, never a low-fat one. This is simply because the latter often have a very different texture that doesn't work as well in baking. I also tend to stick to branded versions as some supermarket ones can be watery, which means they also perform poorly.

Cream of Tartar A powdered acid that is commonly used in the making of meringues. It helps to balance the sweetness but also acts as a stabiliser and prevents the sugar from crystallising. If you don't have any, adding a few drops of lemon juice will produce similar results.

Demerara Sugar A coarse sugar with a golden hue. It is mainly used as a garnish to add sparkle and a light crunch. If it's unavailable, you can use turbinado, which is very similar.

Eggs This book uses UK size large eggs, which are also termed large in Australia and in the EU. These are eggs that weigh 63–73 g with their shell. In the US and Canada, this equates to an XL egg.

Espresso Powder A form of instant coffee that comes as a very fine soluble powder. I use it to add a strong coffee flavour to some bakes and also, in smaller amounts, to boost the roasted flavour of chocolate without adding a detectable coffee flavour.

Gelatine I prefer to use sheet gelatine, which is the most commonly available form of gelatine in the UK. I list gelatine by the number of sheets needed, not the weight. This is because gelatine sheets are designed to be universal, whatever the bloom/strength, i.e. one gold gelatine leaf will set the same amount of liquid as one platinum gelatine leaf. If sheet gelatine is unavailable, you can substitute with powdered gelatine using the following formula:

1 sheet of gelatine = 2 g powdered gelatine dissolved in 1 tablespoon water

Stir the powdered gelatine together with the water and leave for a few minutes until a paste has formed. Add this paste at the same time the recipe calls for the addition of the soaked gelatine leaf.

Golden Syrup A liquid sugar with a warm caramel flavour that is specific to the UK but also popular in most Commonwealth countries. In the US, it can be found online and, as it is a staple in British baking, I recommend buying some. It can be replaced with corn syrup, though this will add zero flavour, or, in most recipes, with honey.

Icing (Powdered) Sugar The finest form of sugar available which, depending on the brand and the country in which it is sold, may also be called 10x or confectioner's sugar. Most brands add something to prevent the sugar from clumping, such as a cornflour (cornstarch), but even so it will still need to be sifted before using.

Light Brown Sugar I prefer to use an unrefined muscovado variety of light brown sugar as it has slightly higher levels of molasses and a better flavour compared to refined versions. However, the recipes in this book will work with any form of light brown sugar.

Malted Milk Powder A favourite ingredient of mine when I want something to have cosiness and a real depth of flavour. In this book malted milk powder refers to commercial drink mixes such as Horlicks or Ovaltine, these two being my preferred brands. Make sure to use plain malted milk powder and not the chocolate variety.

Neutral Tasting Oil Some recipes call for the use of a vegetable or 'neutral tasting oil'. This is simply an oil, suitable for baking, that is flavourless. You can use grapeseed, canola or sunflower oil.

Nut Butter/Nut Paste In a couple of recipes I call for a nut paste, a term that describes a very smooth, runny paste made from 100% nuts. This should not be confused with praline paste, which is a similar product but made with the addition of caramelised sugar. Nut pastes, at least the better-quality versions, can be expensive, so an alternative is nut butter. If made with 100% nuts, this is a similar product, though it is a little coarser in texture. »»»

Nuts Nuts and chocolate are obvious bedfellows. To get the best out of them, don't let them sit in your kitchen cupboards for months, as they can go rancid. And always toast them before using (unless specifically told otherwise). As a general rule, I toast nuts on a rimmed baking tray (sheet pan) in an oven preheated to 180°C (160°fan/350°F) for 10–12 minutes. They should smell aromatic and nutty when ready. Even nuts that claim to have been roasted already will benefit from being toasted.

Peanut Butter Most baking recipes are tested using commercially made peanut butter, as that is what most people buy and have access to. If you want to use a 'natural' variety, the texture of the recipe may differ slightly from the one intended.

Plain (all purpose) Flour A wheat flour with a protein content of 9–10%, it is used for everything from pastry to cookies and cakes, basically everything except bread. If it's unavailable, use an unbleached flour with a comparable protein content. Known as all-purpose flour in some countries.

Salt I use two forms of salt, a fine sea salt and a flaked sea salt.

Skimmed Milk Powder A powdered form of milk, normally sold in the coffee aisle of the supermarket. It is sometimes referred to as non-fat milk powder.

Strong White Bread Flour A wheat flour with a protein content of 12–14%, perfect for making bread.

Vanilla In baking you'll most commonly use one of three styles of vanilla: pod, paste or extract. Vanilla pods, or beans, are the real deal and come with the biggest punch of flavour – and the biggest cost. I like to use them when the flavour is the main feature of a recipe. Vanilla bean paste is a sugar syrup made with ground-up pods and is the type of vanilla I use more than any other; it is punchy in flavour and more economical than vanilla pods. Vanilla extract is a flavouring made by soaking vanilla pods in water and ethyl alcohol. I use it as a seasoning, to add depth to a recipe, such as a butter cake or a cookie dough, when I don't necessarily want the full punch of flavour that adding a vanilla pod would give. If a recipe calls for vanilla pods and you don't have any you can add 2 teaspoons of vanilla bean paste or 1 tablespoon of extract in place of each pod. The flavour won't be exactly the same but it's an acceptable compromise. Never discard used pods, as they can be used to make flavoured sugars, or even homemade vanilla extract.

Wholemeal (Wholewheat) Flours In several recipes I suggest using wholemeal flour to add a nutty, toasty flavour that can't be got from refined white flour. Flours such as rye and einkorn are increasingly available but if you can't get hold of them you can substitute with an equal amount of plain (all-purpose flour), though the flavour, and potentially the texture, of the recipe will not be the same.

Yeast I almost exclusively use instant yeast, also known as dried fast-action yeast, for my bread recipes. The only exception being the recipe for croissants; to make this dough I prefer to use fresh yeast, which comes as a compressed cube, as it is more reliable when making low-hydration recipes such as croissant dough.

CHOCOLATE TECHNIQUES

Many of the techniques used in this book will be familiar to home bakers, but there are some that are specific to chocolate which may be less so. These are important to learn to ensure success each and every time.

MELTING

This might seem mightily obvious, but chocolate can be a fussy fellow at times, so it is worth going over this basic technique to ensure you don't run into problems. In a home kitchen you are likely to melt chocolate in one of two ways: using a bain-marie or a microwave.

BAIN-MARIE

With a bain-marie you place a heatproof bowl over a pan of barely simmering water, add the chocolate and heat it until melted. The benefit of this method is that the heat is gentle and the risk of scorching or burning the chocolate is minimal. The potential issue is that water can accidentally get into the chocolate, causing it to seize.

Tips

- Finely chop the chocolate to ensure even melting.
- Stir often to ensure even melting.
- Keep both the water level and the heat low. The water should never be allowed to touch the bowl and the heat should similarly be kept low, so the chocolate doesn't become too hot.
- Wipe the bottom of the bowl with a towel once the chocolate is melted, to remove the risk of water contaminating the melted chocolate.

MICROWAVE

Using a microwave to melt chocolate is probably my favourite method, as it is simple and creates the least washing up, a big bonus!

Tips

- Use short bursts of heat; microwaves are powerful machines, so to prevent scorching or burning, never heat the chocolate for more than 30 seconds at a time.
- If your microwave allows you to, select a lower wattage. It's better to go a little slower than to risk scorching your chocolate.
- To ensure an even melt and to prevent the chocolate overheating, make sure you give it a stir between each burst of heat, even if it doesn't seem to have melted at first.

WHAT TO DO IF YOUR CHOCOLATE SEIZES

Sometimes, a glossy bowl of melted chocolate can quickly seize into a grainy mess. An absolute nightmare! This is usually because of the addition of a small amount of liquid, although it can also occur when the chocolate has been overheated. Whilst you can't rewind the problem, you can still use the seized chocolate, just not as you intended. To rescue it, a hot liquid (such as water or cream) needs to be added, a little at a time, until the mixture is smooth. I tend to use this rescued chocolate to make a sauce or glaze.

GANACHE

A ganache is a combination of a liquid and chocolate to make an emulsion. Although the liquid is usually cream, it can also be anything from tea or coffee to fruit juices and even just water. At its simplest, a ganache is made by heating a liquid, pouring it over chocolate and then stirring the two together.

Ganaches appear throughout this book as they form the base of many fillings and glazes. There are several potential pitfalls to be avoided when making one, and it is a technique that people sometimes struggle with, but both the methods given below should ensure success every time.

BEFORE YOU START: A NOTE ON SPLIT GANACHE

The most likely issue you'll face when making any form of ganache is a mixture that splits into an oily mess. This is a problem that can easily be rectified (see opposite) but it is important to understand why it happens in the first place so you can avoid it recurring in the future.

One cause of a ganache splitting is heat. Too much and the emulsion breaks and the ganache splits. Another is an imbalance of chocolate and liquid. Not enough liquid can result in a grainy ganache. One of the reasons I use whipping cream, which has a fat content of 30–35%, is that the fat and water are well balanced. It is perfectly possible to make a successful ganache with double cream (which has a fat content of 48–50%), but it will be more prone to splitting. Sticking with whipping cream makes everything just that little bit easier.

HOW TO MAKE A GANACHE

This is my gold standard ganache method, but occasionally a recipe will deviate from it slightly. Use it as an all-purpose guide if you're ever making a ganache, but do follow the recipe as written if it suggests a different technique.

1. Finely chop the chocolate; when chocolate is in small pieces it melts more efficiently, needing less heat, which reduces the risk of the ganache splitting through overheating. Melt using either a bain-marie or a microwave (see page 24).
2. Bring your liquid to a bare simmer but don't let it come to a full boil. It should show the odd bubble around the edges but that's all. If the liquid is too hot, you risk the cocoa butter separating and the ganache splitting. However, if it does come to the boil, don't worry, just set it aside for a couple of minutes to cool down slightly before using.
3. Pour a third of the liquid over the melted chocolate and, working with a flexible spatula, start by stirring in tight circles in the middle of the bowl, ensuring the spatula stays in contact with the bottom of the bowl. Once the centre of the ganache mixture looks smooth you can start to work outwards, continuing to stir until the ganache forms a thick paste.
4. Add the remaining liquid in two additions, stirring to combine as soon as the liquid has been added. After the first, and possibly the second addition, the ganache may look a little grainy or even split, but continue to stir in the remaining cream. It should form a perfectly smooth ganache.
5. To emulsify a ganache, I like to use a stick blender, which is a sure-fire way to give it a perfectly smooth texture. To avoid aerating it, keep the blades of the blender beneath the surface of the ganache. This is most easily achieved if the ganache is in a jug.
6. A well-made ganache is a mixture with a very smooth texture that is incredibly glossy and almost elastic. If the finished ganache looks at all grainy or uneven it is likely split or on the verge of splitting (see opposite on how to rescue this).
7. If the ganache needs to firm up before using, cover it with cling film (plastic wrap) and store at room temperature (unless otherwise stated) until set.

THE SUPER SIMPLE GANACHE METHOD

If the method opposite feels just a bit too involved, there is a simpler, all-in-one way of making ganache where you just pour hot cream (or whatever liquid you're using) over the chocolate and allow the liquid's heat to melt it. This method will work just as well, but the ganache it forms can be a little more unstable and also more prone to splitting. To ensure success, follow the tips below.

1 Finely chop the chocolate; when chocolate is in very small pieces it melts more evenly.

2 Bring the liquid to a gentle simmer. Make sure the liquid is hot but not boiling. If it is too hot, a split ganache is more likely.

3 Once the liquid has been poured over the chocolate, leave for a couple minutes before stirring together with a spatula. This allows the chocolate to begin melting and the temperatures of the chocolate and liquid to closer align, which creates a better emulsion.

4 Using a flexible spatula, stir in tight circles in the centre of the bowl, making sure the spatula stays in contact with the bottom of the bowl. Once the centre of the ganache mixture looks smooth you can start to work outwards, continuing to stir until the ganache is smooth and silky.

5 If you have one, finish with a brief blend using a stick blender. To avoid aerating the mixture, keep the blades of the blender beneath the surface of the ganache. This is most easily achieved if the ganache is in a jug.

Images overleaf»

HOW TO RESCUE A SPLIT GANACHE

When a ganache breaks or splits, yes, it's an absolute pain, but all is not lost: most of the time this is an entirely fixable problem.

Use Force

A stick blender is not only my go-to piece of equipment when making a ganache, it is also my favourite bit of kit when rescuing a split one. If you previously opted to skip the blender in favour of using just a spatula, dig out one now. Put the ganache in a jug and use the blender to re-emulsify it, keeping the blades beneath the surface to avoid the mixture becoming aerated. If this remedy is going to work, the ganache will become shiny and smooth almost immediately.

Briefly Heat

If the ganache begins to split as it starts to cool, another option is to briefly reheat it. Gently heat the ganache using a bain-marie or a the microwave (see page 24) – you don't want it to come to a temperature of more than 38°C (100°F) – then re-emulsify it by stirring, as above, with a spatula or blending briefly with stick blender.

Add Water

Another answer is water. Yes, you read that right, water. Many people will have heard the advice that water and chocolate should never be combined, but that doesn't apply here. In this instance, warmed water (you can also use warmed milk or cream) helps to re-emulsify the ganache. Add the liquid a teaspoon at a time and stir, using a balloon whisk or spatula, mixing until the ganache becomes smooth and perfectly silky. The downside to this technique is that it may change the texture of the ganache to the extent that it may no longer be appropriate for its original use. For example, if you were planning to use it to make rolled truffles, the added liquid may mean that it now sets too softly.

Note: If ganache is an emulsion of chocolate and water, why do people think chocolate and water don't mix? Well, it's because if you add a couple of drops of water to a bowl of melted chocolate there actually isn't enough water. In a ganache, the fat is suspended in water, but when insufficient water is added there isn't enough for the fat to be suspended, so it overwhelms the water and seizes.

TEMPERING

When you buy chocolate, the manufacturer has tempered it. It will have a glossy shine and when broken into pieces will have a satisfying snap. Put simply, tempering is a process of heating and cooling to give chocolate its characteristic shine and snap. The fat crystals in cocoa butter, when melted in an uncontrolled manner, can form a variety of erratic patterns which can result in chocolate with an unpleasant grainy texture and a dull finish. By following the process of tempering you are left with just the 'beta-5 crystals', and this is what gives us the beautiful shine and snap of tempered chocolate. This is important when you are using the chocolate as a coating that you want to set and be stable at room temperature, such as coating truffles or dipping cookies. It is also important to use tempered chocolate when setting chocolate inside a mould, such as filled chocolates; when tempered chocolate sets it contracts slightly, meaning it will release from the mould easily. Do this with chocolate that hasn't been tempered and it will stick, very stubbornly, inside the mould. This process also raises the melting point of chocolate slightly, preventing it from melting when held.

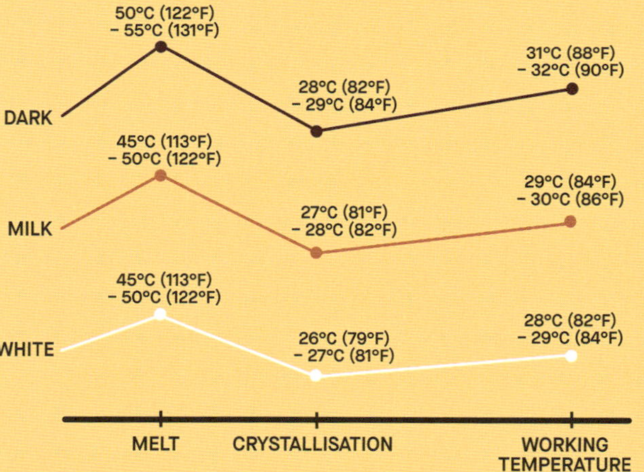

There are several ways to temper chocolate but not all of them are suitable for home bakers. Tabling, for example, involves spreading the melted chocolate over a large marble slab, not the most approachable technique for home kitchens. I prefer to use either the seeding method or the microwave method.

Tempering requires you to check the temperature of the chocolate, so an instant-read probe thermometer is an incredibly useful piece of kit. If you don't have one, the microwave method is a better option as technically it can be done without a thermometer.

SEEDING METHOD

The most reliable method for tempering at home, this uses a bain-marie to heat the chocolate.

Melt three-quarters of the chocolate you want to temper in a plastic or stainless-steel bowl set over a pan of simmering water. Heat until it reaches a temperature of 50–55°C (122–131°F) for dark chocolate and 45–50°C (113–122°F) for milk, white and caramelised white chocolate. Remove from the heat, add the remaining chocolate and stir vigorously until the temperature reduces to 28–29°C (82–84°F) for dark chocolate, 27–28°C (81–82°F) for milk chocolate and 26–27°C (79–81°F) for white and caramelised white chocolate, then very briefly place back on the heat, stirring constantly, until the chocolate reaches 31-32°C (88-90° F) for dark chocolate, 29-30°C (84-86° F) for milk and and 28-29ºC (82-84ºF) for white chocolate. The final temperature is known as the working temperature. This progression of temperatures is known as a 'tempering curve'.

Tips

- Finely chop the chocolate to ensure an even melt.
- Use a heatproof plastic or stainless-steel bowl, never a glass or ceramic one as they are very good at retaining heat, which can lead to you accidentally overheating the chocolate.

- Check the temperature of the chocolate regularly.
- Stir vigorously, to ensure even tempering.
- Use at least 300 g (10½ oz) chocolate, any less and temperature fluctuations are more likely. Any leftovers can be used another time.
- When buying good-quality chocolate in bulk, check the back of the packaging as it may include a specific tempering curve specific to that exact chocolate.

MICROWAVE METHOD

This is the method I use often, largely because it works extremely well with small amounts of chocolate. Having said that, you do need to keep a close eye on the chocolate. You don't strictly need a thermometer, although it's still advisable to use one.

Set the microwave to 50% power. Put the chocolate in a microwave-safe plastic bowl and heat in 20–25-second bursts. Between each burst give the chocolate a good stir, even if it looks as if nothing has happened. Repeat until about three-quarters of the chocolate has melted and the remaining quarter is still solid, reducing the bursts to around 10–15 seconds, as you near this target. Once this is reached, stir the chocolate vigorously until it is fully melted. Your chocolate should now be in temper. The chocolate should never go above 31–32°C (88–90°F) for dark chocolate, 30–31°C (86–88°F) for milk, white and caramelised white chocolate.

This method works because the chocolate is heated in very short bursts, meaning it never goes above the temperature at which it would become 'untempered'. If, when you remove the chocolate from the microwave, you've accidentally heated the chocolate above this temperature, add some extra 'seed' chocolate and continue, as per the instructions for seed tempering. Use incredibly short bursts of heat, no more than 5 seconds, to raise the temperature to its working temperature. Once the chocolate is melted and fully smooth it should be within the same range of 'working temperatures' found on the opposite page.

Tips

- Finely chop the chocolate to ensure even melting.
- Use a heatproof plastic bowl.
- Until you've gained confidence with this method, keep the time in the microwave to even shorter bursts; better to go slow than risk overheating the chocolate.
- Stir well between each burst of heat.

TESTING TEMPERED CHOCOLATE

To test that you have successfully tempered chocolate, dip a spatula or knife into the chocolate and allow any excess to drip back into the bowl. Set the spatula aside, at room temperature, for a couple of minutes. The chocolate should appear dry and if you rub your finger over the surface it shouldn't smudge.

A WORD ABOUT SHINE

Tempered chocolate is often described as shiny. When you buy a bar of chocolate this will be true, but the shine comes from the smooth mould in which it has been set. When you temper chocolate at home and use it to dip a cookie into or enrobe a truffle, it will have a soft sheen, but it won't be shiny. Don't worry about this, as long as it has a soft sheen and is streak free it will have been successfully tempered.

WHAT TO DO IF YOU MESS UP

I'm not going to lie, tempering chocolate can be tricky, and you may well mess it up occasionally. I still do, when I'm in a rush or get distracted. If you end up with un-tempered chocolate, let it set and then use it, as is, in any recipe where the chocolate is melted and mixed into other ingredients, such as brownies, cakes, even hot chocolate. You can also restart the process, using some extra tempered chocolate to act as the 'seed'. Never throw it away, it will always be usable in some way.

CARAMELISED WHITE CHOCOLATE

This style of chocolate was created by the French chocolate company Valrhona, supposedly after a chef left a bowl of white chocolate in a bain-marie unattended and it caramelised. Whilst you can now buy this chocolate, even from some supermarkets, it is also incredibly easy to make, all you need is good-quality white chocolate, something with at least 30% cocoa butter content.

OVEN METHOD

This method works well but is on the slow side. The most important part of the process is to make sure you thoroughly stir the chocolate as it cooks and to continue cooking it until it reaches a deep golden colour. I prefer to use a minimum of 300 g (10½ oz) white chocolate. You can use less, but this amount means it heats more evenly and is less prone to scorching.

Preheat the oven to 120°C (250°F). Roughly chop the chocolate and spread in oan even layer across a rimmed baking tray (sheet pan). Place the tray in the oven and leave for 10–15 minutes. Remove the tray from the oven and stir and spread it with a spatula. Continue cooking the chocolate for around an hour in total, stirring every 10 minutes until the white chocolate has become deep golden brown, almost the colour of dulce de leche. Once the chocolate is caramelised, I like to stir through a pinch of sea salt to elevate the caramelised flavour.

Pour the finished chocolate onto a separate baking tray lined with baking parchment and spread in an even layer. Place in the refrigerator until fully set, then break into shards and store in a dark cool place in a sealed container.

Note: When you remove the chocolate from the oven to give it a stir, you may find it has become stiff and grainy. Before you return it to the oven, make sure to stir it until the mixture becomes smooth again. If lumps remain, the finished chocolate can have an unpleasant texture.

MICROWAVE METHOD

This method is quicker, but it is also more hands-on and requires more frequent stirring. It is also my preferred method when only a small amount of the chocolate is required.

Put the chocolate in a heatproof bowl and place in the microwave. Heat in short, 45 second bursts, stirring very well between each blast of heat. Repeat this process until the chocolate looks a little crumbly and has started to take on some colour. At this point repeat this process, using shorter 20-second bursts of heat, until the chocolate has reached the desired level of caramelisation, finishing with a little salt. This entire process can take up to 15 minutes.

Pour the finished chocolate onto a baking tray (sheet pan) lined with baking parchment and spread in an even layer. Place in the refrigerator until fully set, then break into shards and store in a dark cool place in a sealed container.

Note: As with the oven method, the texture of the chocolate will change as it is heated, so make sure to stir vigorously, until smooth, after every blast of heat. Take care not to leave the chocolate in the microwave for too long as it can overheat and become scorched very easily.

USING YOUR CARAMELISED WHITE CHOCOLATE

Once it's caramelised, the white chocolate will no longer be in temper. Although you can retemper it at home, doing so can be tricky as the heating process can make it more viscous. If you want to use this form of chocolate in a recipe where tempered chocolate is called for, it's better to buy it, as it will be much easier to use.

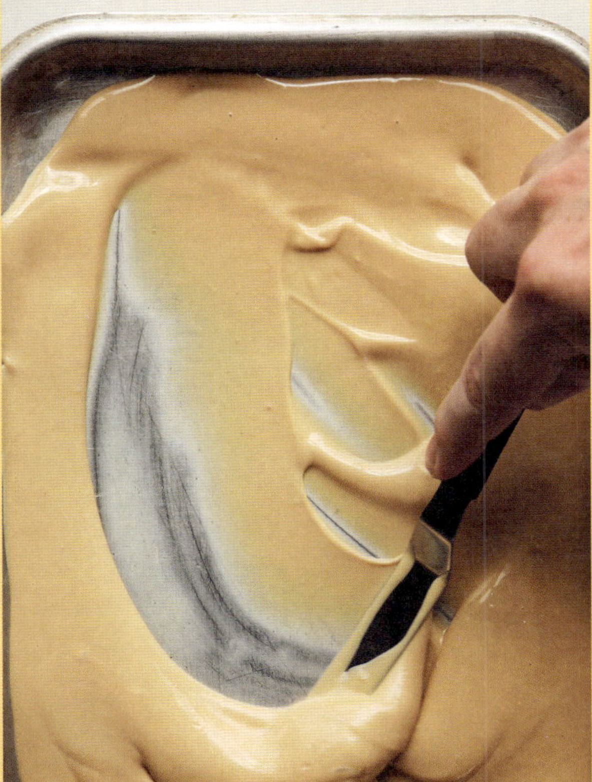

CAKES

CHOOSE YOUR ADVENTURE CHOCOLATE LAYER CAKE

Your ideal chocolate cake is likely different to mine. Your preference might be for frosting or buttercream, whereas I generally like a rich ganache. You might opt for milk chocolate whereas I prefer dark. Why then, one 'ultimate' chocolate cake recipe when I can provide a framework to make your own personal favourite? This base cake is a perfect starting point; fudgy and rich but balanced with a nice texture, which stops short of being more brownie than cake. When it comes to your choice of coating you have at hand a whole host of options, including the sour cream ganache here.

SERVES 12–16

Chocolate Cake

325 ml (1⅓ cups) strong black coffee
400 g (3½ sticks) unsalted butter, diced
375 g (1⅔ cups, packed) light brown sugar
100 g (1 cup + 2 tablespoon) cocoa powder (dutched)
125 g (4½ oz) dark chocolate (65–75% cocoa solids), finely chopped
5 large eggs
1 tablespoon vanilla extract
320 g (2½ cups + 1 tablespoons) plain (all-purpose) flour
1½ teaspoons baking powder
1½ teaspoons bicarbonate of soda (baking soda)
½ teaspoon fine sea salt

Sour Cream Ganache

400 g (14 oz) dark chocolate (65–70% cocoa solids), finely chopped
75 g (⅓ cup, packed) light brown sugar
400 ml (1⅔ cups) whipping (heavy) cream
150 ml (scant ⅔ cup) sour cream
large pinch flaked sea salt
50 g (3½ tablespoons) unsalted butter, diced

Alternative coatings

2 x Chocolate Swiss Meringue Buttercream (page 231)
1½ x Brown Butter Milk Chocolate Ganache (page 56)
2 x Whipped White Chocolate Ganache (page 234)

1 Preheat the oven to 170°C/150°C Fan (375°F) and lightly grease three 20 cm (8 in) round cake tins, lining the bases with baking parchment. To ensure the cakes come out level, use tins that are at least 5 cm (2 in) deep.

2 To make the cake batter, add the coffee, butter and sugar to a large saucepan and place over a low heat; cook until the butter is fully melted and the sugar has dissolved. Remove the pan from the heat and whilst hot add the cocoa and chocolate and whisk together until the chocolate is fully melted and there are no lumps of cocoa. Set aside for a couple minutes to cool.

3 Add the eggs and vanilla to the saucepan and whisk until the mixture is smooth. In a large mixing bowl, add the flour, baking powder, bicarbonate of soda and salt and whisk to combine. Pour the chocolate mixture into the bowl and stir with the whisk, just until a smooth batter is formed; overmixing at this stage can lead to a cake that domes too much.

4 Divide the batter equally between the cake tins and then give each tin a firm tap on the work surface, to eliminate any small air bubbles. Bake the cakes in the preheated oven for 30–35 minutes or until the cake springs back to a light touch and is just starting to pull away from the sides of the tins. Remove and cool, in the tins, on a wire rack for 10 minutes before carefully inverting the cakes onto a wire rack to cool completely.

5 To make the ganache, add the chocolate to a heatproof mixing bowl and melt (see page 24). Add the sugar, cream, sour cream and salt into a saucepan. Place over a medium heat and bring to a simmer. Pour a third over the chocolate and stir to combine. Add the remaining cream in two additions, stirring well to form a silky-smooth ganache. Add the butter and stir until the ganache is completely smooth. If you have a stick blender, use this to ensure a fully emulsified ganache (see page 26 for tips).

6 Set the ganache aside, at room temperature, until thick and spreadable, like the texture of buttercream.

Notes: Mixing the cocoa with a hot liquid, rather than mixing it with the flour, is referred to as 'blooming'; think of it like making a tea or a coffee, the heat of the liquid develops the flavour.

The cake uses dutched cocoa powder, but to achieve a dramatic contrast between the cake and ganache I sometimes use black cocoa powder, a variety of dutched cocoa powder that results in jet-black bakes.

7. To assemble, place the first layer of cake on a cake stand or serving plate and top with a small amount of ganache, spreading it in a thin layer that covers the entire surface of the cake. Repeat with the other two cake layers. Spread the remaining ganache over the top and sides of the cake, decorating as you prefer.
8. The cake (made with the sour cream ganache) will keep for 3–4 days, covered and at room temperature.

COCONUT AND CARDAMOM LAYER CAKE WITH CARAMEL GANACHE

This is a glorious cake for a very special occasion. I'm not going to sugarcoat it for you, though, it's a lot of work, so the person you're making it for needs to be worth it! Cardamom, coconut and caramel are three of my top flavours, making this one of my all-time favourite cakes. To prevent it becoming too sweet it is imperative to cook the caramel until it is a rich mahogany brown. If the caramel remains light, the frosting – and the cake as a whole – will taste too sweet.

SERVES 12–16

Coconut Cake

85 g (¾ stick) unsalted butter, room temperature
85 g (¼ cup + 2 tablespoons) unrefined coconut oil, room temperature
275 g (1⅓ cups) caster (superfine) sugar
2 teaspoons vanilla extract
4 large egg whites
335 g (2⅔ cups) plain (all-purpose) flour
2 teaspoons ground cardamom
3 teaspoons baking powder
1 teaspoon fine sea salt
275 ml (1 cup + 2 tablespoons) canned coconut milk
75 g (scant 1 cup) desiccated (dried shredded) coconut, lightly toasted

Coconut Pastry Cream

180 ml (¾ cup) whole milk
120 ml (½ cup) canned coconut milk
1 teaspoon vanilla bean paste
100 g (½ cup) caster (superfine) sugar
30 g (¼ cup) cornflour (cornstarch)
¼ teaspoon fine sea salt
3 large egg yolks
30 g (2 tablespoons) raw coconut oil

Caramel Ganache

250 g (9 oz) white chocolate, finely chopped
425 ml (1¾ cups) whipping (heavy) cream
150 g (¾ cup) caster (superfine) sugar
½ teaspoon flaked sea salt
50 g (3½ tablespoons) unsalted butter, diced
1 teaspoon vanilla bean paste

1 To make the pastry cream, add the milk, coconut milk, vanilla and half the sugar to a large saucepan, place over a medium heat and bring to a simmer. Meanwhile, add the remaining sugar, the cornflour and salt to a large bowl and whisk to combine. Add the egg yolks and whisk until smooth, about 30 seconds. Pour the hot milk mixture over the egg mixture, stirring as you pour to prevent the eggs from scrambling. Pour the custard back into the pan and cook, whisking constantly, until thick and bubbling. Cook for another minute or so before removing from the heat and scraping into a bowl. Add the coconut oil and stir until fully combined. Press a sheet of cling film (plastic wrap) onto the surface of the custard and refrigerate until needed.

2 To make the caramel ganache, add the chocolate to a large heatproof bowl and melt. Set aside. Add the cream to a small saucepan. Place the pan over a medium heat and bring to a simmer, then remove from the heat and set aside. Meanwhile, add the sugar to a medium saucepan and place over a medium heat. Cook the sugar, stirring occasionally, until it has melted and is the colour of an old penny, a deep copper brown. Add the salt and butter, swirling to combine, followed by half of the hot cream. Take care, as it will cause an eruption of steam when combined with the caramel. Once the bubbling has subsided, pour in the remaining cream. If the caramel has any lumps, place back over a low heat and stir until smooth.

3 Remove the pan from the heat and allow the caramel to cool for a minute before pouring a third of it over the chocolate. Stir vigorously to combine. Add the remaining caramel in two additions, stirring to form a smooth and silky ganache (see page 26 for tips). If you have a stick blender, use this to ensure a fully emulsified ganache. Pour in the vanilla and stir to combine. Cover and refrigerate until thoroughly chilled.

4 For the cake, preheat the oven to 180°C/160°C Fan (350°F). Lightly grease two 5 cm (2 in) deep 20 cm (8 in) round cake tins (pans) and line the bases with baking parchment.

5 To make the cake, add the butter, coconut oil and sugar to the bowl of a stand mixer, or use an electric hand mixer, and beat »»»

Note: Coconut oil comes in two varieties, refined and unrefined, sometimes referred to as virgin. For a natural coconut flavour, use the latter. Refined coconut oil has a more neutral flavour.

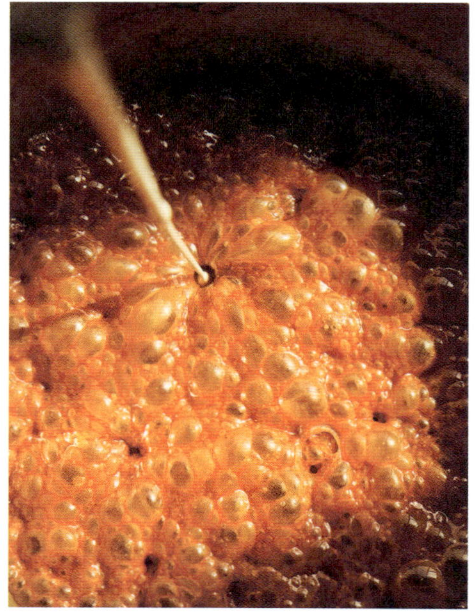

together for 5 minutes or until light and fluffy. Add the vanilla and beat briefly to combine. Add the egg whites one at a time, beating until fully combined before adding the next. In a separate bowl whisk together the flour, cardamom, baking powder and salt. Add the flour mixture to the butter mixture in three additions, alternating with the coconut milk, starting and finishing with the flour mixture. Finally, add the toasted coconut and stir into the batter.

6 Divide the batter between the two prepared tins, gently levelling out. Bake in the preheated oven for 30–35 minutes or until the cakes spring back to a light touch and are starting to come away from the sides of the tins. Remove and set aside to cool for 10 minutes before inverting onto a wire rack to cool completely.

7 When the cakes are ready to be assembled, remove the caramel ganache from the refrigerator and set on the counter as you work on the other elements.

8 Using a serrated knife slice each cake layer in two so you end up with a total of four layers. Remove the pastry cream from the refrigerator and beat until smooth and creamy. Place the first cake layer on a large plate or cake stand. Top with a third of the pastry cream and spread almost to the edges. Repeat this twice more and finish by placing the final cake layer on top.

9 Scrape the caramel ganache into the bowl of a stand mixer, with the whisk attachment attached, and whip it for 1–2 minutes or until it has lightened and is a thick but spreadable texture. Unlike whipped cream or some whipped ganache recipes, this whipping won't dramatically increase the caramel ganache in volume, it just makes it easier to use and gives a slightly creamier texture.

10 Spread the caramel ganache over the top and sides of the cake so that the entire cake is covered. Using your spatula, draw lines up the side of the cake to give an easy decorative style.

PEAR AND PECAN UPSIDE DOWN CAKE WITH COCOA CARAMEL

Upside down cakes meet at the intersection of cake and dessert, the topping turning the cake into something more substantial that only needs a scoop of ice cream or custard to transform it into the cosiest of puddings. In this recipe, the traditional caramel, made from butter and brown sugar, is made with the addition of cocoa powder, giving the cake both a dramatic look and a beautiful flavour that goes perfectly with the pear and pecan.

SERVES 8–10

Chocolate Chip Cake Batter

160 g (1¼ cups) plain (all-purpose) flour
1½ teaspoons baking powder
½ teaspoon fine sea salt
80 g (⅓ cup) unsalted butter, room temperature
200 g (¾ cup + 2 tablespoons, packed) light brown sugar
2 large eggs
½ teaspoon vanilla bean paste
100 ml (⅓ cup + 1 tablespoon) sour cream
75 g (2½ oz/roughly a scant ½ cup) chocolate chips

Cocoa Caramel

80 g (⅓ cup) unsalted butter, diced
150 g (⅔ cup, packed) light brown sugar
½ teaspoon vanilla bean paste
2 tablespoons cocoa powder (dutched or natural)
2 tablespoons boiling water
¼ teaspoon fine sea salt

Topping

3 ripe but firm pears, Bosc or Conference, peeled, cored and halved
60 g (½ cup) toasted pecans, roughly chopped

Note: Any form of cocoa can be used, though the brighter, fruiter flavours of the natural version work particularly well with the pear.

1 Preheat the oven to 180°C/160°C Fan (350°F) and lightly grease a deep 20 cm (8 in) round cake tin (pan), lining the base with baking parchment.

2 For the caramel, add all the ingredients to a small saucepan and cook, over a low heat, until everything is melted and smooth. Pour this caramel into the base of the prepared tin, swirling the pan so the caramel forms an even layer that coats the entire base. Place the pear halves, cut side down, into the caramel and scatter the pecans in the gaps around the pears.

3 To make the cake batter, add the flour, baking powder and salt to a large bowl and whisk together to combine. In a separate bowl, beat together the butter and sugar, for about 5 minutes or until light and fluffy. This can be done with a stand mixer, an electric hand mixer, or even a wooden spoon, if you prefer. Add the eggs, one at a time, beating until fully combined before adding the second. Add the vanilla and beat briefly until combined. Add half of the flour mixture, mixing on low speed just until smooth. Mix in the sour cream and once combined add the last of the flour mixture, mixing gently just until the odd speck of flour remains. Add the chocolate chips and mix briefly until you have a smooth batter and the chocolate is evenly distributed. Scrape into the tin and gently spread into an even layer.

4 Bake in the preheated oven for about 50 minutes or until the cake springs back to a light touch. Remove the cake from the oven and allow to cool for 10 minutes before turning out onto a serving plate.

5 The cake needs no other adornment, though I do like to serve it with a generous pour of cream or custard or a big scoop of crème fraîche.

TONKA BEAN MILK CHOCOLATE POUND CAKE

Tonka bean is not an ingredient you're going to find in any supermarket, and for that, I apologise. I do, though, encourage you to buy some online because the flavour is incredible, both fragrant and spicy, like a perfect blend of vanilla and bitter almond with a hint of clove and cinnamon. It's heady and intense and a little goes a very long way. Here, it gives this simple pound cake an incredible aroma and flavour, making it another of my favourite recipes. If you don't have access to tonka, you could make this using the seeds scraped from one vanilla pod or 2 teaspoons of vanilla bean paste. To serve, I like to top slices of the cake with a simple whipped milk chocolate ganache, a perfect partner to the tonka.

SERVES 8–10

Pound Cake

- 125 g (1 stick + ½ tablespoon) unsalted butter, room temperature
- 250 g (1¼ cups) caster (superfine) sugar
- 1 tonka bean, finely grated
- 120 g (generous ½ cup) full-fat cream cheese
- 250 g (2 cups) plain (all-purpose) flour
- 1¼ teaspoons baking powder
- ½ teaspoon fine sea salt
- 4 large eggs

Decoration

- 25 g (2 tablespoons) unsalted butter, melted
- Cocoa Nib Vanilla Powder (page 235), or granulated sugar
- 1 x Whipped Milk Chocolate Ganache (page 234)

Note: If you'd like the cake to have straight square sides, it can also be baked in a 23 × 10 × 10 cm (9 × 4 × 4 in) pullman loaf tin.

1. Preheat the oven to 180°C/160°C Fan (350°F). Lightly grease a 450 g (1 lb) loaf tin (pan) and line with a single sheet of baking parchment that overhangs the two long sides of the tin, securing it in place with a couple of metal binder clips.
2. Place the butter in the bowl of a stand mixer, or use an electric hand mixer, and beat for 1–2 minutes until creamy. Add the sugar and tonka bean and beat until light and fluffy, about 5 minutes. Add the cream cheese and beat until combined and lump free. In a separate bowl whisk together the flour, baking powder and salt. Beat the eggs into the batter one at a time, beating until fully combined before adding the next. Once all the egg has been combined, pour in the flour mixture and briefly combine. (Using a spatula to do this lowers the risk of over-mixing the batter, which leads to a tougher cake.)
3. Scrape the batter into the prepared tin and gently level out.
4. Tip: if you want the cake to look picture perfect, pipe a thin line of very soft butter along the length of the cake. This creates a weak point, forcing the cake to split neatly down the middle, instead of haphazardly. This is purely for aesthetic reasons, skip this if you wish.
5. Bake in the preheated oven for 55–60 minutes or until a skewer inserted into the cake comes out clean. Check the cake after 50 minutes and if it seems to be browning too much, lightly tent with foil. Remove and allow the cake to cool in the tin for 15 minutes before carefully lifting it out, using the overhanging parchment. Once the cake is cool enough to handle, brush all over with the melted butter and then coat entirely in the sugar.
6. To serve, use a serrated knife to slice into portions. Remove the ganache from the refrigerator and in a large bowl whisk until it holds soft peaks. Pipe or spoon atop the slices and garnish with any extra Cocoa Nib Vanilla Powder.
7. Before slicing it will keep for 3–4 days in a sealed container.

PEANUT BUTTER, MALTED CHOCOLATE AND BANANA LAYER CAKE

Banana bread has always played a linguistic game of make believe because, let's be honest, it's always been cake. This particular banana cake is one that owns its roots and proudly declares its cakey texture. It is light, fluffy and incredibly moist. Paired with a sweet and salty peanut butter frosting, it is tied together with a milk chocolate ganache flavoured with a hint of malt. Whilst the ganache can be made with any milk chocolate, I prefer the cake when it is made with a 'dark milk' chocolate (see page 19) as it has the strength of flavour that comes with a dark chocolate but the sweetness and creaminess of a classic milk chocolate, a perfect partner for the malt.

SERVES 12–16

Banana Cake

180 ml (¾ cup + 1 tablespoon) olive oil
250 g (1 cup + 2 tablespoons, packed) light brown sugar
3 large eggs
350 g (1½ cups) mashed banana, weighed without skins
250 g (2 cups) plain (all-purpose) flour
2¼ teaspoons baking powder
1 teaspoon bicarbonate of soda (baking soda)
½ teaspoon fine sea salt

Malted Ganache

100 g (3½ oz) milk chocolate (35–45% cocoa solids), finely chopped
100 ml (⅓ cup +1 tablespoon) whipping (heavy) cream
2 tablespoons malted milk powder
10 g (2 teaspoons) unsalted butter, room temperature

Peanut Butter Frosting

150 g (1⅓ sticks) unsalted butter, room temperature
150 g (generous ½ cup) smooth peanut butter
¼ teaspoon fine sea salt
250 g (2 cups) icing (confectioner's) sugar
1 teaspoon vanilla bean paste
2 tablespoons whipping (heavy) cream
a handful of chopped salted peanuts, to garnish

1. Preheat the oven to 180°C/160°C Fan (350°F). Lightly grease two 20 cm (8 in) round cake tins (pans) and line the bases with baking parchment.
2. In a large bowl, add the oil, sugar and eggs and whisk together until smooth. Add the banana and stir to combine. Add the flour, baking powder, bicarbonate of soda and salt and mix together with the whisk just until the flour is fully mixed into the batter. Don't worry if it seems a little lumpy, so long as there are no pockets of dry flour it's fine. Divide the batter evenly between the two tins and spread into even layers.
3. Bake in the preheated oven for 25–30 minutes or until the cakes are pulling away from the sides of the tins and they spring back to a light touch. Remove the tins from the oven and allow the cakes to cool for 10 minutes before inverting onto a wire rack to cool completely.
4. To make the ganache, add the chocolate to a small heatproof bowl or jug and melt in a bain-marie or the microwave (see page 24). Add the cream and malt powder to a small saucepan, place over a medium heat and bring to a simmer, whisking continually to help the malt powder to dissolve. Pour a third of the cream over the chocolate and stir vigorously together. Add the remaining cream in two additions, stirring together until a smooth and silky ganache is formed. Add the butter and stir until fully combined and the ganache is smooth. Set aside at room temperature until thick and spreadable.
5. For the frosting, add the butter and peanut butter to the bowl of a stand mixer, or use an electric hand mixer, and beat together, using the paddle attachment, for 2–3 minutes or until creamy and smooth. Add the salt and icing sugar and beat together for 6–8 minutes or until the frosting is very light and fluffy. To finish, add the vanilla and cream and beat briefly until fully combined.
6. To assemble, place one of the cake layers on a large plate or cake stand and spread the thickened ganache on top. Add a small

Note: You can use any flavourless oil in place of the olive oil. You can also substitute wholewheat flour for half of the plain flour, which will give the cake a nuttier flavour, at the slightest cost to the texture of the cake.

amount of the frosting and spread to cover the ganache. Top with the second cake layer and finish by spreading the remaining frosting over the top and then down the sides of the cake.

7 Garnish with a few chopped peanuts.

8 Kept covered, this cake will keep for up to 4–5 days.

RED VELVET CAKE WITH WHITE CHOCOLATE CREAM CHEESE FROSTING

Some people, I know, think red velvet a bit passé, dare I say basic, even. But I absolutely love it. The cake has a tang from the buttermilk and vinegar, and a light cocoa flavour. It is also, unashamedly, a perfect vessel for cream cheese frosting. I like to use a version of 'German Buttercream', which starts with a custard base. The resulting buttercream is incredibly smooth but also impossibly light, and for those who don't like traditional buttercreams, far less sweet, even with the white chocolate.

SERVES 12–15

Cake Layers

- 380 g (3 cups) plain (all-purpose) flour
- 75 g (¾ cup + 2 tablespoons) cocoa powder (natural)
- 1 teaspoon bicarbonate of soda (baking soda)
- ½ teaspoon fine sea salt
- 320 ml (1¼ cups) buttermilk
- 1 tablespoon vanilla extract
- 1 tablespoon apple cider vinegar
- 1 tablespoon red paste food colouring
- 225 g (2 sticks) unsalted butter, room temperature
- 350 g (1¾ cups) caster (superfine) sugar
- 3 large eggs

Buttercream

- 225 ml (¾ cup + 3 tablespoons) whole milk
- 150 g (¾ cup) caster (superfine) sugar
- 1 teaspoon vanilla bean paste
- 30 g (¼ cup) cornflour (cornstarch)
- 2 large eggs
- 100 g (3½ oz) white chocolate, finely chopped
- 1 tablespoon lemon juice
- 200 g (1¾ sticks) unsalted butter, room temperature
- 200 g (1 scant cup) full-fat cream cheese (see Notes overleaf)

1. To make the buttercream, add the milk, half the sugar and vanilla to a large saucepan. Place over a medium heat and bring to a simmer. Meanwhile, add the remaining sugar and cornflour (cornstarch) to a large heatproof bowl and whisk to combine. Add the eggs and whisk until smooth. Pour the hot milk mixture over the egg mixture, whisking as you pour to prevent the eggs from scrambling. Pour this custard mixture back into the saucepan and cook, whisking constantly, until it is bubbling and thick. Cook for a further minute before scraping into a large bowl. Add the chocolate and whisk until thoroughly melted and combined. Finally, add the lemon juice and mix briefly to combine. Press a sheet of cling film (plastic wrap) onto the surface and leave to cool to room temperature. You can make this ahead of time and refrigerate but, if doing so, make sure you allow it to come to room temperature before using, around 20°C (68°F) is ideal.
2. Preheat the oven to 180°C/160°C Fan (350°F). Lightly grease three 20 cm (8 in) round cake tins (pans) and line the bases with baking parchment.
3. Sift the flour, cocoa, bicarbonate of soda and salt into a large bowl, whisking to combine. Set aside. In a jug whisk together the buttermilk, vanilla, vinegar and food colouring, until the colouring is fully dissolved.
4. In the bowl of a stand mixer, or using an electric hand mixer, beat together the butter and the sugar for about 5 minutes, until light, fluffy and almost white. Add the eggs, one at a time, beating until fully combined before adding the next.
5. Once the eggs are fully combined, mix in the flour mixture in three additions, alternating with the buttermilk mixture, starting and finishing with the flour.
6. Divide the batter evenly between the three prepared cake tins and spread into even layers. Bake in the preheated oven for 25–30 minutes or until the cakes spring back to a light touch and are just starting to pull away from the sides of the tins. Remove and set aside to cool for 5–10 minutes before carefully inverting onto a wire rack to cool completely.

»»»

Notes: The method for the buttercream varies slightly depending on the type of cream cheese. If it comes in a tub, it is added at the end, straight from the refrigerator. If it comes in a 'block', as it often does in the US, it should be used at room temperature and added at the same time as the butter.

If you prefer an easier topping, you can use a double batch of the Whipped Cream Cheese Ganache (page 234).

The recipe calls for natural cocoa powder. If you use a Dutch processed cocoa the cake won't rise as much and will be less intensely red.

7 To finish the buttercream, add the butter, and cream cheese, if using the block style, and beat for about 5 minutes or until very pale and creamy. Briefly beat the custard with a spatula until it is smooth and free of lumps. Slowly add this to the mixer, while it's still running, a large spoonful at a time. When all the custard mixture has been added, you should be left with a buttercream-like texture. If using cream cheese from a tub, add this now, beating just until the buttercream is smooth.

8 Place one of the cake layers on a serving plate or cake stand and spread a thin layer of the buttercream on top. Repeat with the other cake layers. Spread the remaining frosting over the top and sides of the cake.

GUINNESS CHOCOLATE CAKE WITH WHIPPED CREAM CHEESE GANACHE

I've lost count of how many times I've been disappointed by Guinness cakes that have no identifiable flavour from the stout. However, I love this version, firstly because it is so unbelievably simple to make. Secondly, because it isn't overwhelmed by chocolate and actually delivers on the promise of a Guinness-flavoured cake. The topping is also very special because the typical sweet frosting is replaced by a silky, smooth, whipped cream cheese ganache that isn't too sweet.

SERVES 12

Guinness Chocolate Cake

120 ml (½ cup) neutral tasting oil
2 large eggs
200 g (¾ cup + 3 tablespoons, packed) light brown sugar
240 ml (1 cup) Guinness or other dark stout
125 g (1 cup) plain (all-purpose) flour
50 g (⅔ cup) cocoa powder (dutched)
1½ teaspoons baking powder
½ teaspoon bicarbonate of soda (baking soda)
½ teaspoon fine sea salt

Whipped Cream Cheese Ganache

100 g (3½ oz) white chocolate, finely chopped
150 ml (scant ⅔ cup) whipping (heavy) cream
150 g (⅔ cup) full-fat cream cheese, room temperature
1 teaspoon vanilla bean paste

1 To make the ganache, put the chocolate in a small heatproof bowl or jug and melt (see page 26). Pour the cream into a small saucepan, place over a medium heat and bring to a bare simmer. Pour a third of the cream over the chocolate and stir to combine. Mix in the remaining cream in two additions, stirring vigorously until the ganache is smooth and silky. Add the cream cheese and vanilla and stir to combine. Finish with a brief blend using a stick blender, to ensure the ganache is thoroughly emulsified. Cover and refrigerate for at least 4 hours, preferably overnight, until thoroughly chilled.

2 Preheat the oven to 180°C/160°C Fan (350°F) and lightly grease a deep 20 cm (8 in) round cake tin (pan), lining the base with baking parchment.

3 In a large bowl, mix together the oil, eggs, sugar and Guinness until smooth and lump free. Sift in the flour, cocoa, baking powder, bicarbonate of soda and salt. Whisk together briefly until a smooth cake batter is formed. Pour the batter into the prepared tin, then bake in the preheated oven for 40–45 minutes or until the cake is just starting to pull away from the sides of the tin. Remove and set aside for 10 minutes before carefully turning out onto a wire rack to cool completely.

4 To assemble, scrape the ganache into a large bowl and, using an electric mixer, whisk until it is thick and holds soft peaks. Scrape onto the top of the cake and spread in an even layer.

5 Once baked, the cake itself will keep for 3–4 days, in a sealed container at room temperature, but once the whipped ganache is added it will need refrigerating, if not serving on the same day. Kept refrigerated it will also keep for 3–4 days.

WHITE CHOCOLATE AND RASPBERRY PRINCESS CAKE

If you're bored of making classic layer cakes for your birthday, this is a fabulous alternative. It is delicious, of course, but also vibrant and incredibly joyous – just what you deserve! A take on the classic Swedish Princesstårta, or Princess Cake, it is modelled after the brilliant version made by pastry chef Hannah Ziskin, sold at Quarter Sheets in LA, which deviates from both the traditional flavour and design. I've also given it a chocolate twist. There are, admittedly, many elements to it, but they can all be prepared ahead to make things a little easier. Instead of the traditional pastry cream, I like to use a whipped crémeux, a custard-based ganache that makes for a really special cake.

SERVES 8

Olive Oil Genoise Cake

4 large eggs
135 g (⅔ cup) caster (superfine) sugar
1 teaspoon vanilla extract
¼ teaspoon fine sea salt
145 g (1 cup + 2 tablespoons) plain (all-purpose) flour
45 ml (3 tablespoons) olive oil

Milk Soak

75 ml (5 tablespoons) whole milk
1 teaspoon vanilla extract

White Chocolate Filling

1 x White Chocolate Crémeux (page 237), made with 175 g (6 oz) white chocolate, refrigerated

Raspberry Cream Filling

400 ml (1⅔ cups) whipping (heavy) cream
20 g (4 tablespoons) powdered freeze-dried raspberry powder
1 tablespoon caster (superfine) sugar

1 Preheat the oven to 180°C/160°C Fan (350°F). Lightly grease a 38 × 25 cm (15 × 10 in) Swiss (jelly) roll rimmed baking tray (pan) and line the base and sides with a single sheet of baking parchment.

2 Add the eggs, sugar, vanilla and salt to a large heatproof bowl and place over a pan of simmering water. Whisk gently until the mixture is hot to the touch and there are no grains of sugar remaining. Remove the pan from the heat and, using an electric mixer, whisk the mixture on high speed for 3 minutes, then reduce the speed to low and whisk for a further 2 minutes until it is thick and pale and holds a ribbon on the surface of the batter when the whisk is lifted from the bowl. The second period of mixing refines the foam, ensuring there are no large air bubbles, which produces a cake with a finer texture.

3 Sift over the flour in three additions, folding gently together, trying to keep the mixture as light as possible. You can do this with a spatula or metal spoon, but I prefer to use a balloon whisk as it is less prone to deflating the batter. Scoop a large spoonful of the batter into a second large bowl and pour in the olive oil. Mix vigorously with the whisk until a smooth shiny batter is formed. If the mixture remains separated, add a little more of the cake batter, mixing until emulsified.

4 Scrape the main batter on top of the oil mixture and fold together, until streak free. Scrape the finished batter into the prepared pan and gently spread into an even layer.

5 Bake in the preheated oven for 13–15 minutes or until the cake is a pale golden colour and feels firm to the touch. Remove from the oven and use the parchment to carefully slide the cake onto a wire rack to cool. Once cool, use a serrated bread knife to trim away the crisp edges, then slice into three 10 cm (4 in) wide rectangles. Using your fingers, gently rub away the top crust of the cake, leaving you with three pale cake layers. »»»

Decoration and Assembly

100 g (⅓ cup) raspberry jam
icing (confectioner's) sugar
350 g (12 oz) marzipan
½ teaspoon pink paste food colouring

6 For the soak, mix the ingredients together in a small bowl.

7 Remove the crémeux from the refrigerator, scrape into a large bowl and whisk until the cream holds medium peaks.

8 To assemble, place one of the cake layers on a serving plate and brush liberally with the milk soak. Spread or pipe with half the crémeux, in as even a layer as possible. Stir the jam to loosen slightly and then brush on the other two cake layers and place one, jam side down, on top, then brush this on its top with the milk soak. Repeat this layering process a second time.

9 For the raspberry cream, add everything to a large bowl and whisk until the cream holds stiff peaks. Spoon atop the cake and spread evenly, using a small spatula to form the cream so it has an arched shape that runs the length of the cake. Spread a very thin layer of the cream down the sides of the cake so that the layers are no longer exposed. Refrigerate until ready to cover.

10 Lightly dust a work surface with icing sugar and knead the marzipan until a little softer and more pliable. Add the colouring to the middle of the marzipan and fold over to seal in, then knead until the marzipan is a vibrant, evenly mixed, pink colour. The colouring can stain surfaces, so if you wish to avoid this you can put the marzipan in a glass bowl. Wearing gloves will also prevent the colouring staining your hands.

11 Lightly dust a work surface with a little icing sugar and roll out the marzipan until it is roughly 30 × 25 cm (12 × 10 in). Carefully lift the marzipan and drape over the cake. Use a sharp knife to trim away any excess.

12 Kept refrigerated the cake will keep for a couple days, but it's best on the day it is assembled.

BURNT HONEY AND CARAMELISED WHITE CHOCOLATE CAKE

Inspired by Medovik, an Eastern European layered honey cake, this takes its cue from a version sold at one of my favourite bakeries, Bristol's brilliant Farro Bakery, and is made with both panela sugar and einkorn flour, two ingredients that make for a particularly flavourful cake. Traditionally, the filling uses sour cream, but I like to double down on the caramelised flavours by making a whipped chocolate cream with burnt honey and caramelised white chocolate.

SERVES 10

Burnt Honey Cake

100 g (scant ⅓ cup) runny honey
120 g (½ cup) unsalted butter, diced
120 g (generous ½ cup, packed) panela or dark brown sugar
2 large eggs
1 teaspoon vanilla bean paste
400 g (3¼ cups) einkorn or plain (all-purpose) flour
1 teaspoon bicarbonate of soda (baking soda)
¼ teaspoon fine sea salt
½ teaspoon ground cinnamon

Honey Cream

400 ml (1⅔ cups) whipping (heavy) cream
100 g (scant ⅓ cup) runny honey
pinch fine sea salt
120 g (4¼ oz) caramelised white chocolate, melted
100 ml (⅓ cup + 1 tablespoon) sour cream

To assemble

150 ml (½ cup + 2 tablespoons) whole milk

Note: panela is a type of unrefined sugar from Latin America, it is available from some supermarkets and more widely in organic food stores and online. It has a rich and toasty molasses flavour. If you can't get your hands on any you can replace it with an equal amount of dark brown sugar.

1 To make the honey cream, pour the cream into a small saucepan and bring to a simmer. Remove from the heat and set aside.

2 Add the honey to a large saucepan, place over a medium heat and cook for 6–8 minutes or until it has darkened a couple shades and is starting to smell toasty, almost a touch bitter. Add the salt and a third of the hot cream. The mixture will bubble up aggressively and create a large amount of steam, so take care. Once the bubbling has subsided slightly, slowly pour in the remaining cream. Remove the pan from the heat and cool for a couple minutes. Add the chocolate to a large bowl and pour over a third of the honey cream mixture, stirring to combine. Add the remaining honey cream in two additions, stirring until smooth. Add the sour cream and stir to combine. Cover and refrigerate for at least 4 hours before using, preferably overnight.

3 To make the cake, place the honey into a large saucepan and cook over a medium heat for 6–8 minutes or until it has darkened and smells toasty, as for the filling. Add the butter and sugar and stir to combine, continuing to cook for a further 2 minutes. Remove from the heat and pour into a large bowl. Set aside to cool to room temperature. Once cool, whisk in the eggs and vanilla until fully combined. Finish by adding the flour, bicarbonate of soda, salt and cinnamon and stirring together to form a soft cookie-dough like batter. Cover the bowl and refrigerate the dough until firm, about 30 minutes.

4 Preheat the oven to 180°C/160°C Fan (350°F). Cut six pieces of baking parchment so that they fit the base of a 23 × 33cm (9 × 13 in) rimmed baking tray (quarter sheet pan), of which you'll need three. Line the bases of these three trays with the baking parchment.

5 Remove the dough from the refrigerator and divide into three equal portions. Roll out each piece of dough between two sheets of baking parchment, so that they fit your prepared baking trays. Remove the top piece of parchment and place on the trays.

6 Bake in the preheated oven for about 8 minutes or until the cakes are golden around the edges and spring back to a light touch. Remove the cakes from the trays and cool on wire racks. »»»

Once cooled, use a serrated knife to trim away about 5 mm (¼ in) from each side of the cake. Place the trimmings on a baking tray lined with baking parchment and bake for 6–8 minutes or until dry and crisp. Set aside to cool. Once cool, crumble into a powder.

7 To assemble, cut each rectangle of cake in half, so that you have 6 smaller rectangles. Remove the honey cream from the refrigerator and in a large bowl whisk until it holds soft peaks. Place one of the cake layers onto a serving plate and brush with a little of the milk. Top with a little less than a fifth of the cream and spread to cover the entire cake. Repeat this process until all the cake layers have been added. Spread the remaining cream across the outside of the cake, in what will be a very thin layer. Gently press the cake crumbs over the entirety of the cake and then refrigerate overnight. This may seem like a long time to wait but the cake needs time to absorb some of the moisture from the cream and milk to soften up so don't rush the process.

8 Kept in the refrigerator the cake will keep for 3–4 days.

S'MORES CAKE

A nostalgic classic of graham crackers (or digestives for my fellow Brits), marshmallow and chocolate, s'mores are pure campfire comfort and a toasty, almost smoky, treat. Getting that flavour into a cake isn't hard but it does involves fire, well, a blowtorch at least. The meringue used to make the buttercream is blowtorched multiple times before the butter is added, giving the finished buttercream that burnt marshmallow flavour, a technique I learned from Kassie Mendieta, a fellow baker in t he US. To give the cake the requisite flavour of graham crackers, half the white flour is replaced with wholemeal and the cake is made with brown butter to make it appropriately toasty. To finish, it is layered with a rich, brown butter milk chocolate ganache.

SERVES 12–16

Wholemeal Brown Butter Cake

225 g (2 sticks) unsalted butter, diced
265 g (1⅓ cups) caster (superfine) sugar
150 g (1 cup + 3 tablespoons) plain (all-purpose) flour
150 g (1 cup + 3 tablespoons) wholemeal (wholewheat) or plain (all-purpose) flour
2¼ teaspoons baking powder
½ teaspoon bicarbonate of soda (baking soda)
½ teaspoon fine sea salt
3 large eggs
120 ml (½ cup) buttermilk
1 teaspoon vanilla extract

Brown Butter Milk Chocolate Ganache

125 g (1 stick + 1 tablespoon) unsalted butter, diced
300 g (10½ oz) milk chocolate, finely chopped
300 ml (1¼ cups) whipping (heavy) cream
pinch flaked sea salt

Burnt Swiss Meringue Buttercream

2 large egg whites
150 g (¾ cup) caster (superfine) sugar
large pinch fine sea salt
240 g (2 sticks + 1 tablespoon) unsalted butter
1 teaspoon vanilla bean paste

1 For the ganache, add the butter to a small saucepan, place it over a medium heat and cook until browned. The butter will first bubble and splatter as the water cooks out. Once the noise reduces and the butter starts to foam, watch for the milk solids to become separated out, little brown flecks, as this is when the butter has browned. Pour into a small heatproof bowl and refrigerate until thick and spreadable but not fully solid, 30–60 minutes.

2 To make the ganache, put the chocolate in a heatproof bowl and melt (see page 26). Place the cream and salt in a small saucepan, bring to a simmer, then pour a third over the chocolate and stir to combine. Mix in the remaining cream, in two additions, stirring until a smooth and glossy ganache is formed, then add the browned butter and stir until thoroughly combined. Finish with a short blend using a stick blender, to ensure the ganache is thoroughly emulsified. Cover and set aside, at room temperature, for 2–3 hours or until thick and spreadable.

3 Preheat the oven to 180°C/160°C Fan (350°F). Lightly grease two 20 cm (8 in) round cake tins (pans) and line each base with a disc of baking parchment.

4 To make the cake, put the butter in a saucepan, place over a medium heat and cook until browned, following the instructions above, then pour into a large mixing bowl and add the sugar, whisking to combine. Set aside to cool for 10 minutes.

5 Sift the flours, baking powder, bicarbonate of soda and salt into a large bowl and whisk to combine.

6 Add the eggs, one at a time, to the butter mixture, whisking until fully combined before adding the next. Pour in the buttermilk and vanilla and whisk to combine. Add the dry ingredients and whisk briefly, just until a smooth batter is formed.

»»»

Tip: If the buttercream is too loose after adding the butter it will be because the meringue was too hot and needed to be whisked a little longer. If this happens, place the bowl in the refrigerator for 15 minutes, then re-whisk until thick and creamy. If the buttercream separates after the butter is added, the butter was likely too cold, but if you continue whisking it will eventually become smooth and creamy.

7 Divide the batter equally between the two tins, then bake in the preheated oven for about 25 minutes or until the cakes are pulling away from the sides of the tins and they spring back to a light touch. Allow them to cool in the tins for 10 minutes before turning out onto a wire rack to cool completely.

8 Use a serrated knife to slice each cake horizontally into two even layers. Place the first layer of cake onto a cake stand and top with a third of the ganache, spreading it in an even layer all the way to the edges. Repeat this layering twice more. Finish by placing the last layer of cake on top. Set aside whilst you make the buttercream.

9 Add the egg whites, sugar and salt to a large heatproof bowl and place over a pan of simmering water. Gently whisk just until the mixture is hot to the touch and you can no longer feel any grains of sugar. Remove the bowl from the heat and transfer to the bowl of a stand mixer. Whisk the meringue for 3–4 minutes until it begins to hold stiff peaks but is still very warm. Stop the mixer and lift the whisk from the bowl.

10 Use a blowtorch to caramelise the surface of the meringue, making it nice and toasty, as you would with a marshmallow over a fire. Make sure to blowtorch the meringue attached to the whisk as well. Whisk the meringue for a further 30 seconds before repeating the process. Do this blowtorching at least 7–8 times until the meringue has taken on a warm caramel tone. Whisk the meringue for a few minutes more until it is no longer hot. Turn the mixer to medium speed and slowly incorporate the butter, a few pieces at a time. Once all the butter has been added, add the vanilla and continue mixing until a buttercream texture is formed. Switch to the paddle attachment, turn the speed to low and mix until the buttercream is super silky and devoid of any air bubbles.

11 Spread the buttercream over the top and sides of the cake, decorating as you please.

12 Kept covered the cake will keep for up to three days.

TRIPLE CHOCOLATE MUFFINS

These very simple muffins are incredibly nostalgic, verging on retro, though I've updated them with a cocoa streusel for added texture. Whilst you can use any form of chocolate, if you want more defined chunks of chocolate dotted through your muffins, then this is a great time to pull out the chocolate chips. Because chips are made with less cocoa butter than other forms of chocolate, they hold their shape better when they melt, meaning they stay as defined pieces through the batter rather than blending into it.

MAKES 12

Triple Chocolate Muffins

100 g (¾ stick + 1 tablespoon) unsalted butter, diced
175 g (¾ cup + 1 tablespoon, packed) light brown sugar
40 g (½ cup) cocoa powder (natural)
240 ml (1 cup) sour cream
60 ml (¼ cup) whole milk
2 large eggs
250 g (2 cups) plain (all-purpose) flour
1 teaspoon bicarbonate of soda (baking soda)
½ teaspoon fine sea salt
50 g (1¾ oz/roughly a generous ¼ cup) dark chocolate chips
50 g (1¾ oz/roughly a generous ¼ cup) milk chocolate chips
50 g (1¾ oz/roughly a generous ¼ cup) white chocolate chips

Cocoa Streusel

120 g (1 cup) plain (all-purpose) flour
40 g (½ cup) cocoa powder (dutched or natural)
100 g (½ cup) caster (superfine) sugar
¼ teaspoon flaked sea salt
120 g (8½ tablespoons) unsalted butter, melted

1 To make the streusel, place the flour, cocoa, sugar and salt in a small bowl and whisk together to combine. Pour in the butter and stir with a knife to form a crumbly dough. Press into a ball, then refrigerate until needed, at least 30 minutes but up to three days.

2 Preheat the oven to 180°C/160°C Fan (350°F) and line a 12-hole muffin tin (pan) with paper liners.

3 To make the muffin batter, we are using, appropriately, the muffin method. Simply melt the butter, together with the sugar and cocoa, in a large heatproof bowl using a microwave, or in a saucepan over a low heat. Once fully melted, whisk in the sour cream, milk and eggs. In a separate bowl, whisk together all the dry ingredients and most of the chocolate chips, retaining a small amount for the tops of the muffins. Add this dry mixture to the wet mixture and stir together, with a spatula, just until a batter comes together. Don't worry about it being completely lump free, muffins actually have a slightly better texture when a little under-mixed. Divide the batter between the paper cases, trying to make them even so the muffins all bake at the same time and end up the same size. Remove the streusel from the refrigerator and crumble on top of the muffins, then finish by topping with the reserved chocolate chips.

4 Bake the muffins for 20 minutes or until they spring back to a light touch. Remove from the oven and allow to cool in the muffin tray for 5 minutes before carefully lifting out onto a wire rack to cool completely.

5 Kept covered, the muffins will keep for 2–3 days. They also freeze well for up to a month, although the streusel will soften when defrosted.

DOUBLE MARBLE LOAF CAKE

A marble cake with a bonus marble glaze, as beautiful in flavour as it is in appearance. The cake itself is very straightforward, a one-bowl batter that is then split in two so that cocoa powder can be added to half. Once baked, it needs nothing more than melted chocolate, mixed with a little oil, poured randomly over to create an almost zebra-like effect.

SERVES 10

Marble Loaf Cake

2 tablespoons cocoa powder (dutched or black)
2 tablespoons boiling water
170 g (1½ sticks) unsalted butter, room temperature
175 g (¾ cup + 2 tablespoons) caster (superfine) sugar
2 large eggs, lightly whisked
220 g (1¾ cups) plain (all-purpose) flour
1+ ½ teaspoons baking powder
¼ teaspoon bicarbonate of soda (baking soda)
½ teaspoon fine sea salt
100 ml (⅓ cup + 1 tablespoon) buttermilk
1 teaspoon vanilla extract

Marble Chocolate Glaze

125 g (4½ oz) dark chocolate (65–75% cocoa solids), roughly chopped
100 g (3½ oz) white chocolate, roughly chopped
30 ml (2 tablespoons) vegetable oil, divided equally

Note: I often bake this in a 23 × 10 × 10 cm (9 × 4 × 4 in) pullman loaf tin (pan), which has straight sides, which gives the cake an even more polished look.

1 Preheat the oven to 180°C/160°C Fan (350°F). Lightly grease a 450 g (1 lb) loaf tin (pan) and line with a single long strip of parchment so that the excess paper hangs over the long sides of the pan, securing in place with a couple of metal binder clips.

2 To make the cake, in a small bowl whisk together the cocoa powder and boiling water until a smooth paste is formed. Set aside. Place the butter and sugar in a large bowl and use an electric mixer to beat together until light and fluffy, about 5 minutes. Add the eggs to the butter mixture a little at a time, beating until fully combined before adding more. In a separate bowl whisk together the flour, baking powder, bicarbonate of soda and salt. With the mixer on low/medium speed, add the flour mixture to the butter mixture in three additions, alternating with the buttermilk and vanilla – starting and finishing with the flour mixture. Divide the batter evenly into two bowls and to one mixture, briefly beat in the cocoa paste.

3 Spoon both batters into the loaf tin, in a random pattern, then use a skewer to briefly swirl to create a marble effect. When swirling together, less is always more, too much swirling creates a less defined marbled pattern.

4 Bake in the preheated oven for about 45 minutes or until a skewer inserted into the cake comes out clean. Leave to cool in the tin for 15 minutes before using the parchment to lift the cake onto a wire rack to cool completely. Once the cake is at room temperature wrap in cling film (plastic wrap) and freeze for 30–60 minutes.

5 For the glaze, place the chocolates in separate small heatproof jugs and melt, using a microwave (see page 24), then stir half the vegetable oil into each chocolate. Remove the cake from the freezer, unwrap, and place on a cooling rack set over a baking tray (pan). Pour over about three-quarters of the dark chocolate glaze, covering as much of the cake as possible. Before it has a chance to set, drizzle over the white chocolate glaze, trying to create a marbled effect. Use the reserved dark chocolate glaze to create extra definition in the marbling and to fill in any uncoated spots on the cake. Lift the cake from the rack and set onto a platter. Allow the glaze to set and the cake to come to room temperature before serving.

6 Kept covered, the cake will keep for 3–4 days.

CHOCOLATE GÂTEAU BASQUE WITH SUMAC CHERRIES

A classic Gâteau Basque consists of a rich and buttery crust filled with pastry cream or a cherry jam, sometimes both. In this version, it has been given a cocoa makeover for a dramatic look and a rich, velvety chocolate flavour. The filling uses a chocolate pastry cream and, staying true to the classic, a layer of cherries. To ensure the fruit flavour isn't overwhelmed by the chocolate, I spike the compote with sumac, a bright and citrusy spice that is perfectly at home with both the chocolate and the cherry.

SERVES 8–10

Cocoa Crust

220 g (1¾ cups) plain (all-purpose) flour, plus extra for dusting
30 g (⅓ cup) cocoa powder (natural or dutched)
½ teaspoon fine sea salt
170 g (1½ sticks) unsalted butter, room temperature
150 g (¾ cup) caster (superfine) sugar
4 large egg yolks, plus 1 extra egg yolk for egg wash

Chocolate Filling

1 x Dark Chocolate Pastry Cream, made with a 60–70% dark chocolate (page 232)

Cherry Compote

300 g (10½ oz) sweet cherries, pitted and halved (fresh or frozen)
4 tablespoons caster (superfine) sugar
juice of ½ an orange
1 teaspoon sumac
¼ teaspoon vanilla bean paste
pinch fine sea salt
2 teaspoons cornflour (cornstarch)

1 To make the compote, add the cherries, sugar, orange juice, sumac, vanilla and salt to a saucepan, place over a medium heat and bring to the boil. Reduce the heat and cook at a simmer for about 10 minutes or until the liquid has reduced to a syrupy consistency. Pour a little of this liquid into a small bowl and whisk in the cornflour to make a slurry. Scrape this mixture back into the pan and cook for about a minute until the compote has thickened significantly. Scrape into a bowl, cover and refrigerate until needed.

2 Lightly grease a 23 cm (9 in) cake or tart tin (pan), preferably one that is about 3.5 cm (1½ in) deep. Line the base with parchment paper.

3 To make the crust, mix together the flour, cocoa and salt. In the bowl of a stand mixer, or using an electric hand mixer, beat together the butter and sugar for about 5 minutes or until light and fluffy. Add the yolks one at a time, beating until fully combined before adding the next. Add the flour mixture and mix together until a soft dough is formed. Divide the dough into two pieces, one slightly larger than the other. Place each ball of dough between two sheets of cling film (plastic wrap) or baking parchment and use the base of your tin to press into a flat disc almost the same size as the base. This will make rolling out the dough a lot easier later on. Refrigerate both rounds of dough until firm, about 4 hours.

4 To assemble the gâteau, remove the slightly bigger of the two pieces of dough from the refrigerator and, on a lightly floured work surface, roll out into a circle about 32 cm (12½ in) in diameter. If the dough feels soft or warm once you've finished rolling it out, put it back in the refrigerator to chill before using. Gently drape the dough into your tin, pressing into the sides of the tin. Leave the excess dough hanging over the sides. Spoon the cherry filling onto the base of the crust and spread in an even layer. Remove the pastry cream from the refrigerator and beat until smooth. Spoon or pipe atop the cherry filling, spreading in an even layer.

5 Roll out the second piece of dough until it is a little over 23 cm (9 in) in diameter. Brush the bottom crust, where it sits on the rim of the tin, with a little beaten egg yolk, then drape the second piece of dough on top, pressing the edges of the pastry together to seal. Trim away the excess dough. Brush the top of the gâteau with beaten egg yolk, then refrigerate for 30 minutes while you preheat the oven to 180°C/160°C Fan (350°F).

6 Use the tines of a fork to draw a pattern atop the gâteau. Traditionally, this would have been some sort of simple cross-hatch pattern but you can use whatever design you like, or you can skip this step entirely. Doing it after the gâteau has been refrigerated, though, will give it more definition.

7 Bake for 50–60 minutes or until the crust is a deep golden brown. Remove from the oven and set aside until fully cooled, at least 2 hours. Stored in the refrigerator, the gâteau will keep for up to three days.

RHUBARB AND WHITE CHOCOLATE SNACK CAKE

I grew up in the 'Rhubarb Triangle', a part of Yorkshire renowned for its many forced rhubarb farms. This type of rhubarb is grown in dark sheds, which speeds up its growth, as the stems stretch to find a source of light. This results in both an early harvest, in the depths of winter, and a particularly slender form with a bright pink hue and a less-fibrous texture. This simple snack cake, which pairs it with a little lemon zest, but also white chocolate to balance the acidity, is a great way to celebrate it. This is the sort of cake that demands to be served alongside a cup of tea or a steaming mug of coffee but, should you wish to take it from afternoon treat to evening dessert, it is wonderful served with a generous pour of vanilla custard.

SERVES 8

170 g (1½ sticks) unsalted butter, room temperature
150 g (¾ cup) caster (superfine) sugar
zest 1 lemon
3 large eggs
½ teaspoon vanilla bean paste
150 g (1½ cups) ground almonds (almond flour)
50 g (⅓ cup + 1 tablespoon) plain (all-purpose) flour
¾ teaspoon baking powder
½ teaspoon fine sea salt
150 g (5½ oz) forced rhubarb (trimmed weight), cut into 1 cm (½ in) lengths
75 g (2½ oz/roughly a scant ½ cup) white chocolate, roughly chopped
2 tablespoons flaked almonds

Note: The cake can be made with any variety of rhubarb, but if the stems are particularly thick you may want to dice them into smaller chunks.

1. Preheat the oven to 180°C/160°C Fan (350°F). Lightly grease a 20 cm (8 in) round, 5 cm (2 in) deep, cake tin (pan) and line the base with baking parchment.
2. Using either a stand mixer or an electric hand mixer and a large mixing bowl, beat together the butter, sugar and zest until the mixture is light and fluffy, about 5 minutes. Add the eggs, one at a time, beating until fully combined before adding the next. Add the vanilla and beat briefly to combine. Add the ground almonds, flour, baking powder and salt, mixing briefly just until evenly combined and a smooth batter has been formed. Add about two-thirds of the chocolate and half the rhubarb and mix briefly to distribute throughout the batter.
3. Scrape the batter into the prepared cake pan and spread into an even layer. Scatter over the remaining rhubarb and the chocolate and flaked almonds.
4. Bake in the preheated oven for 30–35 minutes or until the cake starts to pull away from the sides of the tin. Remove from the oven and set aside for 15 minutes before carefully turning out onto a serving plate.
5. Kept covered, the cake will keep for up to three days.

FLOURLESS GRASSHOPPER CAKE

Named after the classic cocktail, this cake is topped with a peppermint white chocolate ganache and a layer of whipped cream to replicate the look and feel of the drink. Flourless chocolate cakes are typically made like a chocolate mousse and then baked. In this version, I've added ground almonds (almond flour) to give the cake a little more substance. To give it the look of the cocktail, there is a little food colouring in the ganache, but feel free to leave it out if you prefer.

SERVES 10–12

Flourless Chocolate Cake

170 g (1½ sticks) unsalted butter, diced
170 g (6 oz) dark chocolate (65–75% cocoa solids), roughly chopped
5 large eggs
150 g (⅔ cup, packed) light brown sugar
75 g (¾ cup) ground almonds (almond flour)
2 tablespoons cocoa powder (dutched or natural)
¼ teaspoon fine sea salt

Peppermint Ganache

250 g (9 oz) white chocolate, finely chopped
120 ml (½ cup) whipping (heavy) cream
green food colouring (optional)
30 g (2 tablespoons) unsalted butter, diced and at room temperature
½ teaspoon peppermint extract

Topping

300 ml (1¼ cups) whipping (heavy) cream, whipped to stiff peaks
25 g (1 oz) milk, dark or white chocolate, grated

1 Lightly grease a 20 cm (8 in) springform tin (pan), or a loose-bottomed cake tin of the same size, and line the base and sides with baking parchment.

2 Preheat the oven to 180°C/160°C Fan (350°F).

3 Put the butter and chocolate in a large heatproof bowl, place over a pan of simmering water and heat, stirring occasionally, until fully melted. You can also melt this mixture using a microwave, using short bursts to prevent the chocolate from burning. Remove the bowl from the heat and set aside. In a separate bowl, add the eggs and sugar and use an electric mixer to whisk together until thick and pale, about 3–5 minutes. Add the almonds, cocoa and salt and gently fold them into the egg mixture until just combined, keeping the mixture as light as possible. Pour it into the bowl of chocolate and fold together, just until combined and streak free. Pour this mixture into the prepared cake tin and gently level out with the back of a spoon.

4 Bake the cake for 30 minutes or until the edges are firm but the centre feels a little delicate when pressed, as if it's not yet fully cooked. Remove from the oven and allow to cool. As it cools the centre of the cake should collapse slightly, but if it is resistant lightly press on it with the back of a spoon to create a crater that can be filled with the ganache once the cake is cooled.

5 To make the ganache, melt the chocolate using either a microwave or bain-marie, then pour into a jug. Add the cream and colouring, if using, to a saucepan, bring to a simmer, then pour a third over the ganache and stir to combine. Add the remaining cream in two additions, stirring well until the ganache is smooth and silky. Add the butter, peppermint extract and food colouring, if using, and stir until fully combined. Pour the ganache atop the cake and spread into an even layer, leaving the raised edge of the cake clear. Set the cake aside for around an hour to allow the ganache to set, then top with the whipped cream and a little grated chocolate.

6 The cake can be refrigerated for up to 3 days but add the ganache and cream to the cake on the day you want to serve it. Once refrigerated, the texture will become fudgier.

CHOCOLATE AND WHIPPED CARAMEL CAKE

This cake was originally created for my friend Jessica, who has very generously declared it to be the best cake she has ever eaten. Multiple thin layers of chocolate cake are layered with a silky ganache and one of my all-time favourite creations, whipped caramel. Although it is a small cake, it is relatively rich, so it is still more than enough to serve eight.

SERVES 8

Chocolate Cake

45 g (3 tablespoons) unsalted butter, diced
50 g (1¾ oz) dark chocolate (65–75% cocoa solids)
80 g (⅔ cup) plain (all-purpose) flour
50 g (scant ½ cup) wholemeal (wholewheat) rye flour, or plain (all-purpose) flour
½ teaspoon baking powder
1 teaspoon bicarbonate of soda (baking soda)
¼ teaspoon fine sea salt
125 g (½ cup + 1 tablespoon, packed) light brown sugar
25 g (⅓ cup) cocoa powder (dutched)
100 ml (⅓ cup + 1 tablespoon) hot black coffee
100 ml (⅓ cup + 1 tablespoon) buttermilk
1 large egg

Whipped Salted Caramel

150 g (¾ cup) caster (superfine) sugar
200 ml (¾ cup + 1 tablespoon) whipping (heavy) cream
15 g (1 tablespoon) unsalted butter
pinch flaked sea salt

Ganache

230 g (8 oz) dark chocolate, 60–70% cocoa solids, finely chopped
180 ml (¾ cup) whipping (heavy) cream
2 tablespoons golden syrup or honey
185 g (1⅔ sticks) unsalted butter, diced and at room temperature

1 For the caramel, add the sugar to a medium-sized saucepan and place over a medium heat. Pour the cream into a separate small saucepan, place over a medium heat, bring to a simmer, then remove from the heat. Cook the sugar until it is fully melted and caramelised to a dark coppery brown colour. Add the butter and salt and swirl to combine. Carefully pour in half the cream; it will bubble up aggressively, so take care and allow the bubbling to subside before pouring in the rest. Because you warmed the cream prior to adding it to the melted sugar you should have a smooth sauce, if not, turn the heat to low and stir until smooth. Pour the smooth caramel into a large bowl and set aside for 30 minutes before transferring to the refrigerator to chill for 3–4 hours. To whip the caramel, it needs to be cold but still spreadable, so keep an eye on it and take out when at the desired texture. If chilled for too long it will become too firm, so you'll need to gently reheat it very slightly to enable you to whisk it.

2 To make the ganache, put the chocolate in a large heatproof jug and melt (see page 24). Pour the cream and golden syrup into a small saucepan, place over a medium heat and bring to a simmer. Remove from the heat and pour a third over the chocolate and stir to combine. Add the remaining cream in two additions, stirring well until a silky-smooth ganache is formed. Add the butter and stir into the ganache until it is smooth. If you have one, finish with a brief blend using a stick blender, to ensure the ganache is thoroughly emulsified. Set aside until it is thick but spreadable.

3 Preheat the oven to 180°C/160°C Fan (350°F). Lightly grease two 15 cm (6 in) round cake tins (pans) and line the bases with baking parchment.

4 To make the cake, put the butter and chocolate in a bowl set over a pan of simmering water and heat, stirring occasionally, until the butter and chocolate are both fully melted. Meanwhile, mix together the flours, baking powder, bicarbonate of soda, salt, brown sugar and cocoa. If you use good-quality brown sugar and cocoa they may be prone to forming lumps (due to the amount of molasses in the sugar and the fat in the cocoa powder). If this happens pass them through a fine-mesh sieve to ensure a lump-free mixture.

»»»

Notes: Because the cake elements are not particularly stable in warm situations I refrigerate them if not serving close to assembly, but remove them a couple hours before serving to ensure the cake is not refrigerator cold.

The cake is moist enough, and made with enough fat, that you can happily substitute black cocoa for the regular dutched cocoa, should you want a more dramatic colour.

5 Remove the bowl of chocolate from the heat and stir in the coffee, then the buttermilk. Once smooth, add the egg and whisk until smooth and combined. Pour the liquid ingredients into the flour mixture and briefly whisk until a smooth batter is formed. Don't over whisk as you can end up developing the gluten in the batter, leading to a less tender cake. This is doubly important if using rye flour as it can lead to an unpleasant gummy texture. Divide the batter equally between the prepared tins.

6 Bake in the preheated oven for 20–25 minutes or until the cakes spring back to a light touch and have started to pull away from the sides of the tins. Allow the cakes to cool for 10 minutes before turning out onto a wire rack to cool completely.

7 Remove the caramel from the refrigerator and, using an electric hand mixer, whisk on medium/high speed until the caramel turns light and pale and is holding soft peaks. It won't be as light as whipped cream or meringue, but it should be thick enough that it can hold its own shape. If the whipped caramel feels loose, it likely needed a little longer in the refrigerator. To rectify this, pop the bowl back in the refrigerator for 30 minutes before whisking again briefly, but then use it immediately.

8 To assemble, use a serrated knife to slice each cake layer into two thinner layers. Place the first cake layer onto a serving plate and spread with a little of the ganache, leaving a small border around the outside edge. Add a third of the caramel and spread so it covers the ganache layer. Repeat this layering process twice more before adding the final layer of cake. Spread the remaining ganache over the top and sides of the cake, then set aside until the ganache has set.

9 Kept refrigerated, this cake will keep for up to 5 days.

TIRAMISU CHIFFON CAKE

This may not be a tiramisu that any Italian would recognise but all the prerequisite elements are included. Coffee-soaked sponge, check, mascarpone cream, check, cocoa powder, check! It also tastes like a classic tiramisu, it's just that the dessert has been turned into a beautiful cake. Made with a chiffon sponge, this vertical roll cake is soaked with coffee and rum and then rolled up with a whipped mascarpone ganache.

SERVES 8

Chiffon Cake

80 g (⅓ cup + 1 tablespoon) caster (superfine) sugar
30 g (¼ cup) plain (all-purpose) flour
30 g (¼ cup) cornflour (cornstarch)
½ teaspoon baking powder
¼ teaspoon fine sea salt
45 ml (2 tablespoons + 2 teaspoons) neutral tasting oil
4 large eggs, separated
45 ml (2 tablespoons + 2 teaspoons) whole milk
½ teaspoon cream of tartar
a little icing (confectioner's) sugar

Coffee Soak

80 ml (⅓ cup) espresso or strong black coffee
25 ml (1½ tablespoons) dark rum

Mascarpone Ganache

150 g (5½ oz) white chocolate, finely chopped
225 ml (scant 1 cup) whipping (heavy) cream
225 g (1 cup) mascarpone
1 teaspoon vanilla bean paste

cocoa powder (dutched or natural), for decoration

1 For the ganache, place the chocolate in a heatproof bowl or large jug and melt, using a microwave or bain-marie (see page 24). Pour the cream into a saucepan, bring to a bare simmer, then pour a third over the chocolate and stir with a spatula to combine. Pour in the remaining cream, in two additions, stirring well until smooth and glossy. Add the mascarpone and vanilla and stir until smooth and lump free. If you have one, finish with a brief blend using a stick blender, to ensure the ganache is thoroughly emulsified. Cover and refrigerate for at least 4 hours before using.

2 Preheat the oven to 180°C/160°C Fan (350°F). Lightly grease the base of a 38 × 25 cm (15 × 10 in) Swiss (jelly) roll rimmed baking tray (pan) and line the base with baking parchment. If the chiffon cake is to rise properly it is essential the sides of the baking tray remain clean with no fat on them at all.

3 For the cake, place half of the sugar, the flour, cornflour, baking powder and salt in a large bowl and whisk together to combine. Add the oil, egg yolks and milk and whisk until smooth. In a separate bowl whisk together the egg whites and cream of tartar, preferably using an electric mixer, until the meringue is foamy. Slowly rain in the remaining sugar and continue whisking until the meringue holds soft peaks. Add the meringue to the yolk mixture in three additions, folding gently until combined and streak free. Scrape into the prepared baking tray and gently level out. Lift the tray about 15 cm (6 in) from the work surface, then drop it back down. This will help eliminate any large air pockets in the batter.

4 Bake in the preheated oven for 20 minutes or until the cake is lightly browned and springs back to a light touch. Remove from the oven and drop the tray onto the work surface as you did before. This prevents the cake shrinking too much as it cools. Set aside for 5 minutes before using a rounded-edge knife or spatula to cut the sides of the cake away from the sides of the tray, turn it out onto a large sheet of baking parchment, peel away the original baking parchment, then leave it until fully cooled. The edges of the cake will be crisp, so to ensure the cake rolls up easily, use a serrated knife to trim these off. Unlike some other rolled cakes this chiffon sponge remains flexible even after it is fully cooled, so it doesn't need rolling up whilst still warm. »»»

5. For the coffee soak, mix together the coffee and rum.
6. To assemble, brush the entire cake with the coffee soak. Scrape the ganache into a large bowl and whisk until it holds soft peaks. This ganache is easy to over-whip, so keep a close eye on the final texture, and preferably whisk by hand. Spread most of the ganache over the cake in a thin, even layer, retaining about a fifth for decoration. Cut the cake into four long strips. Working with one strip at a time, roll up like a Swiss roll. When one roll is finished line it up with the next strip and continue to roll up until all the strips of cake have been added. Place the cake, swirl side facing up, onto a large plate or cake stand.
7. Scrape the remaining ganache into a piping bag fitted with a small round piping tip. Use half to pipe random mounds on top of the cake, then dust the top with a little cocoa powder before doing the same with the rest of the ganache.
8. The cake is best eaten the day it is assembled but can be stored in the refrigerator for 2–3 days.

SUPER SPEEDY CHOCOLATE SNACK CAKE

This is your 'in case of emergency' chocolate cake, the recipe you pull out when you have last-minute guests or simply need a quick, easy dessert. It also happens to be an incredibly good vegan chocolate cake, dense and fudgy like all good chocolate cakes should be. A simple one-layer affair, it can be dressed up or down depending on the occasion. I like to keep things straightforward, with a glaze made with a 'water ganache'. Alternatively, it makes a great dessert, served with a hot fudge sauce and a scoop of vanilla ice cream.

SERVES 8

Chocolate Cake

240 ml (1 cup) soya (soy) milk
175 g (generous ¾ cup, packed) light brown sugar
100 ml (⅓ cup + 1 tablespoon) vegetable oil
1 teaspoon apple cider vinegar
75 g (scant ⅔ cup) plain (all-purpose) flour
75 g (scant ⅔ cup) wholemeal (wholewheat) rye flour
50 g (⅔ cup) cocoa powder (dutched)
1 teaspoon instant espresso powder
½ teaspoon baking powder
1 teaspoon bicarbonate of soda (baking soda)
½ teaspoon fine sea salt

Water Ganache Glaze

100 g (3½ oz) dark chocolate (70% cocoa solids)
2 tablespoons, packed, light brown sugar
75 ml (5 tablespoons) water
15 g (1 tablespoon) refined coconut oil

Notes: If you don't have rye flour, you can substitute it with an equal amount of plain (all-purpose) flour.

Coconut oil comes in two varieties, virgin and processed. If labelled as virgin (or something similar) it will taste of coconut; processed oil is odourless and has a neutral taste. Either can be used for this cake, but I prefer to use an odourless version so the flavour is purely about the chocolate.

1 Preheat the oven to 180°C/160°C Fan (350°F). Lightly grease a deep 20 cm (8 in) round cake tin (pan) and line the base with baking parchment.

2 To make the cake, put the milk, sugar, oil and vinegar in a large jug and whisk until smooth. Brown sugar, especially unrefined versions which contain higher levels of molasses, can be lumpy, so sift it before using if needed.

3 Place the remaining ingredients in a large bowl and whisk together to combine. Pour the liquid ingredients into the dry ingredients and stir with a whisk just until a smooth cake batter is formed. If using rye flour, it is doubly important not to over whisk the batter; rye flour can become gummy if mixed for too long. Pour into the prepared tin and bake for 35–40 minutes or until the cake springs back to a light touch and is coming away from the sides of the tin. Remove from the oven and allow to cool for 10 minutes before turning out onto a wire rack to cool completely.

4 To make the ganache, put the chocolate in a small heatproof jug and melt (see page 24). Put the sugar and water in a small saucepan, place over a medium heat and cook, covered with a lid, until the sugar has dissolved and the water has just come to a simmer. Pour a third of the syrup over the chocolate and stir to combine. Pour in the remaining syrup, in two additions, stirring until the mixture forms a silky-smooth ganache. Add the coconut oil and stir to combine. Once made, the ganache should have a thick but pourable consistency. If the ganache seems thin, leave for about 15 minutes, until thickened slightly. Pour the ganache over the cake, allowing the excess to drip down the sides.

5 Kept covered, this cake will keep for 4–5 days.

COOKIES & BARS

MISO AND WHITE CHOCOLATE COOKIES

If the idea of white chocolate cookies makes you yawn with boredom, then allow this recipe to shift your opinion. Here, the white chocolate and all its supposedly problematic features (too sweet + one note) are balanced by the addition of miso. This tangy fermented bean paste adds depth and rich savoury notes that round out the sweetness of the white chocolate, helping to make these cookies a sweet and salty joy.

MAKES 12

225 g (1 cup) unsalted butter, room temperature
200 g (¾ cup + 2 tablespoons, packed) light brown sugar
150 g (¾ cup) caster (superfine) sugar
2 large eggs
65 g (4 tablespoons) white miso paste
1 teaspoon vanilla extract
300 g (scant 2½ cups) plain (all-purpose) flour
100 g (generous ¾ cup) wholemeal plain (all-purpose) flour
½ teaspoon fine sea salt
¾ teaspoon bicarbonate of soda (baking soda)
¾ teaspoon baking powder
350 g (12 oz/roughly 2 cups) white chocolate discs, feves or roughly chopped bar
flaked sea salt, for garnish (optional)

Note: If you don't want to bake the cookies all at once you can freeze the balls of dough. They can be baked from frozen, but will need an additional 1–2 minutes cooking time.

1 Add the butter and sugars to the bowl of a stand mixer, or use an electric hand mixer and large bowl, and beat until light and fluffy, about 5 minutes. Add the eggs, one at a time, beating until fully combined before adding the second. Add the miso and vanilla and mix until evenly combined. In a separate bowl, whisk together the flours, salt, bicarbonate of soda and baking powder. Add the flour mixture to the butter mixture and mix on low speed just until an evenly mixed cookie dough is formed. Add the chocolate and mix briefly, just until evenly distributed.

2 Cover the bowl and refrigerate the dough for 4 hours until firm.

3 Preheat the oven to 180°C/160°C Fan (350°F) and line two large baking trays (half sheet pans) with baking parchment. Roll into balls weighing roughly 70 g (2½ oz) each, and place six balls onto each of the prepared trays, spacing them out evenly. Sprinkle each cookie with a little flaked sea salt and bake for 13–15 minutes or until golden around the edges but still a little pale in the centre. Leave to cool on the trays for 5 minutes before transferring to a wire rack to cool completely. Repeat with the second batch of dough balls.

4 Kept covered, these cookies will keep for 3–4 days.

DOUBLE CHOCOLATE OLIVE OIL COOKIES

If you are partial to a brownie, you'll love these intensely chocolatey, fudgy cookies. They may look nostalgic, but the olive oil, nutty rye flour and generous sprinkling of salt give them a sophisticated flavour.

MAKES 8

5½ tablespoons soya (soy) milk, or other non-dairy option, or cow's milk if you don't need them to be vegan
40 g (⅓ cup) cocoa powder (dutched)
100 ml (⅓ cup + 1 tablespoon) olive oil
185 g (¾ cup + 1 tablespoon, packed) light brown sugar
140 g (1 cup + 2 tablespoons) plain (all-purpose) flour
75 g (¾ cup) wholemeal (wholewheat) rye flour
½ teaspoon bicarbonate of soda (baking soda)
½ tsp fine sea salt
150 g (5½ oz/roughly a scant 1 cup) dark chocolate, roughly chopped
flaked sea salt, for sprinkling (optional)

Note: Your choice of oil will determine the end flavour of the cookies. If you use a lightly flavoured olive oil, the flavour will be very subtle, dominated by the cocoa and chocolate. For a more prominent flavour, use an olive oil with a pronounced fruity flavour that will pair well with the chocolate.

1 Preheat the oven to 180°C/160°C Fan (350°F) and line a large baking tray (half sheet pan) with baking parchment.

2 Pour the milk into a saucepan and bring to a simmer. Meanwhile, place the cocoa in a mixing bowl. Pour the hot milk into the cocoa and whisk to form a paste. Pour in the oil and whisk to combine. Sift in the light brown sugar and whisk to combine. Add the remaining dry ingredients and, using a spatula, mix to form a thick cookie dough. Add the chocolate and stir to evenly distribute.

3 Divide the dough into eight equal portions and roll each piece into a ball. The dough can feel a little oily but don't worry, that's how it should be at this stage. Place the balls on the prepared tray and sprinkle each with a little flaked sea salt, if using.

4 Bake in the preheated oven for about 16 minutes. When the cookies are baked they'll remain incredibly soft in the centre, with just a little firmness at the edges, but as they cool they'll firm up beautifully to give a dense fudgy texture.

5 Once fully cooled the cookies can be stored in a sealed container for 3–4 days.

Pictured on page 79.

COCOA NIB RUM RAISIN COOKIES

I have often said that the oatmeal raisin is the unfairly maligned member of the cookie family. It's not given the fanfare of a chocolate chip nor the respect of a classic shortbread. I think this needs to change. Whilst from the outside these cookies may look rather simple, the addition of cocoa nibs really elevates the flavour, enhancing the fruitiness of the raisins and giving the cookies a little extra texture.

MAKES 16

4 tablespoons dark rum
150 g (generous 1 cup) raisins
150 g (1⅓ sticks) unsalted butter, room temperature
150 g (⅔ cup, packed) light brown sugar
100 g (½ cup) caster (superfine) sugar
1 teaspoon vanilla extract
2 large eggs
225 g (1¾ cups) plain (all-purpose) flour
2 tablespoons skimmed (non-fat) milk powder
1½ teaspoons baking powder
1 teaspoon bicarbonate of soda (baking soda)
1 teaspoon fine sea salt
200 g (2½ cups) rolled oats
35 g (¼ cup) cocoa nibs, plus extra for garnish

Note: You can turn these into fully-fledged chocolate chip oatmeal raisin cookies by adding chunks of dark or milk chocolate to the dough, roughly 300 g (10½ oz). If you do this, I advise dividing the dough into at least 20–22 cookies.

1 The day before you want to make these cookies, pour the rum over the raisins and cover, setting aside to soak. When ready to use, drain off any rum that hasn't been absorbed. If you want to avoid this step, put the raisins, rum and 4 tablespoons of water in a small saucepan, place over a low heat and cook until the raisins are plump and have absorbed the liquid. Set aside to cool before using.

2 Next, add the butter and sugars to the bowl of a stand mixer, or use a large bowl and electric hand mixer, and beat together with the paddle attachment until light and fluffy, about 5 minutes. Add the vanilla and mix briefly until distributed. Add the eggs, one at a time, beating until fully combined before adding the second. In a separate bowl, whisk together the flour, milk powder, baking powder, bicarbonate of soda, salt and oats. Add the dry ingredients to the butter mixture and mix on low speed until a soft cookie dough is formed. Tip in the cocoa nibs and the raisins and mix briefly, just until evenly distributed. Cover the bowl and refrigerate the dough for about 4 hours or until firm.

3 Preheat the oven to 180°C/160°C Fan (350°F) and line two large baking trays (half sheet pans) with baking parchment.

4 Remove the dough from the refrigerator and divide into 16 equal-sized portions, preferably by weight or eyeballing it if you prefer. Roll each piece of dough into a ball, place onto the prepared trays and bake for about 12 minutes or until golden around the edges but still a little pale in the centre. Remove and set aside for 5 minutes before carefully transferring to a wire rack to cool completely.

5 Stored in a sealed container, the cookies will keep for 3–4 days.

CHOCOLATE ORANGE JAFFA CAKES

Inspired by the British supermarket favourite, these little cakes are topped with orange jelly and coated in dark chocolate. In my version, the plain sponge is replaced with an almond financier cake, making the whole thing a little more luxurious.

MAKES 12

Financier Cake

80 g (¾ stick) unsalted butter, diced
zest of 2 oranges
2 large egg whites
60 g (scant ⅔ cup) ground almonds (almond flour)
20 g (2½ tablespoons) plain (all-purpose) flour
80 g (⅔ cup) icing (confectioner's) sugar
pinch fine sea salt

Orange Jelly

3 sheets gelatine
200 ml (¾ cup + 1 tablespoon) orange juice (3–4 navel oranges)
½ tablespoon caster (superfine) sugar
a few drops orange extract (optional)

Chocolate Coating

125 g (4½ oz) dark or milk chocolate, tempered (see page 30)

1 To make the jelly, line a 20 cm (8 in) round cake tin (pan) with a couple of layers of cling film (plastic wrap). Add the gelatine to a small bowl, cover with ice-cold water and set aside for 5 minutes or until soft. Put the orange juice, sugar and orange extract, if using, in a small saucepan, place over a medium heat and bring to a simmer. Remove the pan from the heat. Remove the gelatine from the water and squeeze out any excess. Add the gelatine to the orange mixture and stir to combine. Once the gelatine has dissolved, pour the jelly into the prepared tin. Transfer to the refrigerator and leave until set, a couple hours.

2 For the cake bases, lightly grease a 12-hole muffin tin (pan) and preheat the oven to 180°C/160°C Fan (350°F). Most muffin tins are made with a non-stick coating but if yours isn't, dust the holes with a thin coating of flour, tapping out any excess, to ensure the cakes release once baked. Put the butter and orange zest in a small saucepan and place over a medium heat to brown. At first, the butter will splatter, as the water cooks out, but it will then start to foam. It is at this stage you need to watch for the appearance of brown flecks as this is the sign the butter is browned. Whilst the butter cooks, place the remaining cake ingredients in a bowl and stir to form a thick batter. As soon as the butter browns, pour it into the batter and stir until fully combined. The batter can then be used immediately or, if you prefer, it can be refrigerated for up to two days.

3 Spoon the batter evenly into the muffin tin holes, then bake in the preheated oven for 8–9 minutes or until the cakes have a golden ring around the edges. Remove from the oven and set aside for 1–2 minutes before turning out onto a wire rack to cool completely.

4 To assemble, remove the jelly from the refrigerator and, using a 3.5–4cm (around 1½ in) round cookie cutter, cut out 12 discs of jelly, setting one atop each cake round. Leave for 10 minutes before adding the chocolate. If the jelly is cold the chocolate will set too quickly and it will be hard to get an even coating, so do not skip this 10-minute pause.

5 Spoon a little of the tempered chocolate on top of the jelly, using the spoon to spread it evenly and tease it over the sides and onto the cake. Set aside until the chocolate has set.

6 Kept in a sealed container, the cakes will keep for around 4 days.

MATCHA MARBLE COOKIES

If matcha and white chocolate are a match made in heaven, then surely using caramelised white chocolate would amp up the flavour even more? The toasty flavour of the roasted chocolate adds a hint of caramel and a little more depth than a classic white chocolate and matcha combination. To make these cookies a bit more fun, and give them an exciting visual appeal, the dough is split in half and the matcha added to just one of the halves. The two doughs are then rolled together, giving the cookies a marbled effect.

MAKES 16

200 g (1¾ sticks) unsalted butter, room temperature
125 g (½ cup + 1 tablespoon, packed) light brown sugar
125 g (½ cup + 2 tablespoons) caster (superfine) sugar
2 large eggs
1 teaspoon vanilla extract
375 g (3 cups) plain (all-purpose) flour
1 teaspoon baking powder
1 teaspoon bicarbonate of soda (baking soda)
1 teaspoon fine sea salt
2 tablespoons matcha powder
2 tablespoons whole milk
185 g (6½ oz/roughly 1 generous cup) caramelised white chocolate discs/fèves, or a roughly chopped bar

Note: If you don't want to bake the cookies all at once you can freeze the balls of dough. They can be baked from frozen, but will need an additional 1–2 minutes cooking time.

1. Put the butter and sugars in the bowl of a stand mixer and beat with the paddle attachment until light and fluffy, about 5 minutes. Add the eggs, one at a time, beating until fully combined before adding the second. Add the vanilla and beat briefly until combined. In a separate bowl whisk together the flour, baking powder, bicarbonate of soda and salt. Add the flour mixture to the butter mixture and combine on low speed, just until a uniform cookie dough is formed.
2. Divide the dough into two equal portions. In a small bowl whisk together the matcha and milk to make a paste. Add this to one of the cookie dough portions, mixing until thoroughly combined. Divide the chocolate between the two portions of dough and mix until evenly distributed. Cover each portion of dough and refrigerate for 4 hours or until firm.
3. Preheat the oven to 180°C/160°C Fan (350°F) and line two large baking trays (pans) with baking parchment.
4. To form the cookies, roll each portion of dough into 16 equal-sized balls. Take one ball of matcha dough and one ball of the plain dough and squash them together, rolling into a ball. Place eight balls of dough on each of the prepared trays. Bake for 15–16 minutes or until the edges are lightly browned but the centres still a little pale. Remove from the oven and allow to cool on the trays for 5 minutes before carefully transferring to a wire rack to cool completely.
5. Kept in a sealed container, these cookies will keep for up to 4 days.

PASSION FRUIT MILK CHOCOLATE BARS

Whenever I'm asked for my favourite flavour combinations, I'm guaranteed to mention the pairing of sweet and rich milk chocolate and citrus-like passion fruit. Taking inspiration from the classic American lemon bar, these start with a crumbly cocoa base which is topped with a layer of passion fruit and finished with a dollop of whipped milk chocolate ganache. Sweet and sharp, rich and fruity.

MAKES 12–16

Crisp Cocoa Base

200 g (1⅔ cups) plain (all-purpose) flour
35 g (⅓ cup + 2 tablespooons) cocoa powder (dutched)
65 g (⅓ cup) caster (superfine) sugar
65 g (scant ⅓ cup, packed) light brown sugar
¼ teaspoon fine sea salt
150 g (1⅓ sticks) unsalted butter, melted

Passion Fruit Custard

zest of 3 lemons
325 g (1⅔ cups) caster (superfine) sugar
1½ tablespoons cornflour (cornstarch)
4 large eggs
2 large egg yolks
120 ml (½ cup) lemon juice (roughly 3 lemons)
160 ml (⅔ cup) passion fruit juice
¼ teaspoon fine sea salt
75 g (⅔ stick) unsalted butter, diced
1 teaspoon vanilla bean paste

1 x batch Milk Chocolate Whipped Ganache (page 234)

Note: The custard layer can be made with any citrus, though the flavour pairing will be different. You could make an orange custard layer (reducing the sugar content slightly) and pair it with a dark-milk or dark chocolate, or a lime custard and pair it with a white chocolate cream.

1 Preheat the oven to 180°C/160°C Fan (350°F). Lightly grease a 23 × 33 cm (9 × 13 in) brownie tin (pan) and line with a single sheet of baking parchment, so that the paper overhangs the two long sides of the tin, securing the parchment in place with a couple metal binder clips.

2 To make the base, sift all the ingredients, except the butter, into a large mixing bowl. Cocoa powder and brown sugar both have a tendency to form lumps, so sifting helps prevent this. Pour in the melted butter and stir with a knife until a crumbly mixture is formed. Scrape this into the prepared tin and use your hands to press and distribute it evenly across the entire base. Pop the tin in the freezer for 10 minutes, then remove it and dock the base with a fork, to ensure it doesn't puff up during baking.

3 Bake for 30–35 minutes or until set and firm to the touch. Remove and set aside while you prepare the passion fruit custard.

4 Place the zest and sugar in a large saucepan and use your hands to rub the zest into the sugar, doing so until the sugar feels damp and the mixture is fragrant. Add the cornflour, eggs and yolks and whisk together until smooth. Pour in the two fruit juices and salt and whisk to combine. Place the pan over a medium heat and cook, stirring constantly, until the mixture starts to bubble and thicken. Remove the pan from the heat and whisk in the butter and vanilla. Immediately pour this mixture over the cocoa base, through a fine-mesh sieve if you want to remove the zest, spreading out into an even layer.

5 Place the bars back into the oven for about 15 minutes, just until the edges of the custard are set and the centre has a gelatinous wobble. Remove and set aside until cool before transferring to the refrigerator for a few hours.

6 To serve, use the overhanging parchment to carefully lift the bars from the tin. Use a sharp knife to cut into small squares. Remove the ganache from the refrigerator and scrape into a large bowl. Using an electric hand mixer, whisk briefly, until soft peaks form, stopping before the ganache has a chance to turn grainy. Spoon or dollop a little whipped ganache onto each of the passion fruit bars and, if you like, decorate with a little grated milk chocolate.

7 Kept in the refrigerator, these bars will keep for 2–3 days.

CHOCOLATE AND ABSINTHE CANELÉS

The town of Saint-Émilion is one of my favourite places in France. Small and perfectly picturesque, it is probably most famous for its wine. For me, though, its significance lies in the fact that it was the place I first tried another of the region's specialities, the canelé. These little baked custards are traditionally made using copper moulds that are coated with beeswax and have the most enchanting texture, being incredibly crisp on the outside and soft and custardy in the centre. Usually, they are flavoured with rum and vanilla but I have given them a chocolate makeover and also switched out the rum for another French creation, absinthe.

MAKES 12

Canelé Batter

500 ml (2 cups + 1 tablespoon) whole milk
1 vanilla pod
50 g (1¾ oz) dark chocolate (85% cocoa solids), finely chopped
5 large egg yolks
65 g (½ cup) plain (all-purpose) flour
20 g (¼ cup) cocoa powder (dutched or natural)
¼ teaspoon fine sea salt
50 g (3½ tablespoons) cold unsalted butter
75 g (generous ⅓ cup) caster (superfine) sugar
75 g (⅓ cup, packed) light brown sugar
3 tablespoons absinthe (or dark rum if you prefer)

Coating

100 g (scant ½ cup) beeswax (or for simplicity use spray cake release)

Note: The traditional tin-lined copper moulds are an expensive piece of kit. Stainless-steel moulds are now available and are a more cost-effective but still effective alternative. If you don't have individual moulds, you can use a muffin tin (pan), but avoid silicone moulds as I have yet to make a version with this material that has the correct texture. If you can't get your hands on beeswax, I have also had success with spray cake release; if using this, the moulds can be sprayed at room temperature just before filling with custard.

1 Pour the milk into a saucepan. Cut the vanilla pod in half along its length and scrape out the seeds, adding both the pod and the seeds to the pan. Heat the milk until it comes to a simmer, then remove from the heat, cover, and set aside for an hour to infuse. Place the pan back on the heat and bring the milk to a bare simmer. Remove the pan from the heat and add the chocolate. Set aside for a couple of minutes before stirring together until the chocolate is fully melted and combined. Remove the vanilla pod and set aside for another use (see page 22). Add the yolks to a large jug and pour over the hot milk mixture, whisking gently as you combine. Set aside.

2 Into the bowl of a food processor add the flour, cocoa, salt and butter and pulse until the mixture resembles fine breadcrumbs. Alternatively, you can do this by hand, adding the ingredients to a large bowl and rubbing them together to get the same texture. Add the sugars to the flour mixture and pulse/stir together to combine. Pour the milk mixture into the processor/bowl and pulse/whisk until smooth and lump free. If using a food processor pour the milk through the funnel tube in a steady stream whilst the processor is running to ensure a lump-free batter.

3 Pass the custard through a fine-mesh sieve, into a large jug, to remove any lumps. Stir in the absinthe, then cover with a sheet of cling film (plastic wrap), pressing it onto the surface of the custard to prevent a skin forming. Refrigerate for 24–36 hours before using.

4 Preheat the oven to 200°C/180°C Fan (400°F).

5 If using individual moulds and beeswax you need to prepare them at least an hour before using. Place the moulds on a baking tray (pan) and bake for 5–10 minutes until nice and hot. Meanwhile, place the beeswax in a small heatproof jar and melt either in a microwave or by placing the jar in a pan of simmering water. Remove the moulds from the oven but don't turn if off (see opposite). Pour the beeswax into one of the moulds so that it is full to the brim, then pour the beeswax from one mould to another, coating each of them with a thin layer of beeswax,

Note: Beeswax is very sticky and annoying to clean, so melting the wax in a jar prevents any tricky washing up as the leftovers can be stored in the jar for another time. You can buy beeswax easily online or from honey- and soap- making supply shops.

turning the coated moulds upside down onto a piece of baking parchment as you go. Set aside until cooled to room temperature. Once cooled, the layer of beeswax will be very thin and it may even look as if there is nothing there. Any excess beeswax can be left in the jar and used again for your next batch.

6 To ensure the canelés bake properly, without expanding out of their moulds, leaving you with a pale white top, you need to ensure the oven is thoroughly hot, so I like to preheat it for a full hour.

7 Remove the custard from the refrigerator and stir to dissipate any last bubbles on the surface. Divide the custard between the moulds, filling them to within about 1 cm (½ in) from the lip. Place the moulds on a baking tray (quarter sheet pan) and bake for 60 minutes or until the custards are very dark but not quite burnt. Remove from the oven and immediately turn out onto a wire rack, leaving for an hour before enjoying.

8 Canelés are best on the day they are baked and, truthfully, their texture is best within 5 hours of baking. They can, however, be enjoyed for up to three days after baking and can be refreshed by baking for 5 minutes at 200°C/180°C Fan (400°F) to restore some of the crisp texture.

Image overleaf »

CARAMEL TIM TAMS

The supermarket aisle is a treasure trove of delicious cookies, from Oreos and mint Milanos in the US to Custard Creams and Chocolate Hob Nobs in the UK. On the other side of the world, in Australia, the Tim Tam is my cookie of choice, but this could be because it's one of the only ones I've been able to try. This homemade version sandwiches two chocolate cookies with a simple chocolate cream and salted caramel, then dips the whole thing in chocolate.

MAKES 12

Chocolate Cookies

135 g (generous 1 cup) plain (all-purpose) flour
20 g (¼ cup) cocoa powder (dutched or natural)
¼ teaspoon bicarbonate of soda (baking soda)
¼ teaspoon fine sea salt
115 g (1 stick) unsalted butter, room temperature
60 g (¼ cup + 1 tablespoon) caster (superfine) sugar
60 g (generous ¼ cup, packed) light brown sugar

Caramel Filling

115 g (½ cup + 1 tablespoon) caster (superfine) sugar
100 ml (⅓ cup + 1 tablespoon) whipping (heavy) cream
10 g (2 teaspoons) unsalted butter
¼ teaspoon flaked sea salt

Chocolate Cream Filling

30 g (2 tablespoons) unsalted butter, room temperature
60 g (½ cup) icing (confectioner's) sugar
1 tablespoon cocoa powder (dutched or natural)
1 tablespoon whipping (heavy) cream
pinch fine sea salt

Coating

350 g (12 oz) dark or milk chocolate, tempered (see page 30)

1 To make the cookies, place the flour, cocoa, bicarbonate of soda and salt in a bowl and combine. Put the butter and sugars in a large bowl and, using an electric mixer, beat together for 2–3 minutes until the mixture is smooth and creamy. Add the flour mixture and, on low speed, mix just until it is incorporated into the butter, stopping when the dough is still a little crumbly but you can no longer see any flour. The mixture will go from grey and powdery to dark and crumbly; it is at this stage you can stop mixing. Tip out onto the work surface and, using your hands, carefully bring together into a uniform dough. Roll out the dough between two pieces of baking parchment, into a rectangle just slightly larger than 20 × 26 cm (8 × 10 in), to a thickness of about 3–4 mm (¼ in). Place the dough on a large baking tray (half sheet pan) and refrigerate for an hour until firm.

2 When the dough is firm, trim to size and cut the rectangle into three strips, 26 cm (10 in) in length. Then cut each strip into eight small rectangles. Transfer the cookies back to the baking tray and use a fork to dock each one a couple of times. Transfer to the refrigerator whilst you preheat the oven.

3 Preheat the oven to 180°C/160°C Fan (350°F), then bake the cookies for 12–14 minutes or until dry and firm. Remove and set aside to cool.

4 For the caramel filling, put the sugar in a small saucepan, place over a medium heat and cook until it has melted and caramelised to a deep copper colour. Meanwhile, pour the cream into a separate saucepan, bring to a simmer, then remove from the heat and set aside. Add the butter and salt to the caramelised sugar and, once it has fully melted, pour in the cream. Stir until smooth, then pour into a bowl and set aside to cool slightly before covering and transferring to the refrigerator to cool.

5 For the chocolate cream filling, beat the butter in a mixing bowl until light and creamy, about 2 minutes. Add the icing sugar and beat for 5 minutes or until light and fluffy. Add the cocoa, cream and salt and beat until evenly combined.

6 To assemble, transfer the fillings to separate piping bags, both fitted with small round piping tips. Onto the base of half the

cookies, pipe a chocolate border around the edge, then pipe caramel into the centre. Sandwich together with a second cookie, pressing gently to ensure they're fully stuck together.

7 To coat, drop the cookies, one at a time, into the tempered chocolate. Flip over the cookie to ensure it is completely coated, then carefully lift out using a fork. Tap the fork on the side of the bowl to allow any excess chocolate to drip back in. Transfer the cookie back onto the baking tray and set aside at room temperature until the chocolate has fully set. If you want to make this a little easier you can simply dip the cookies halfway into the chocolate.

8 Kept in a sealed container, these will keep for 3–4 days.

Image on page 91.

CHILLI LIME CHOCOLATE CRINKLES

I am always a little sceptical when chocolate is combined with chilli, as too often the balance is off and the chocolate is entirely overpowered. My favourite way to pair the two is to add a bright fruity element, which harmonises everything and makes a truly delicious combo. In this recipe lime plays the role of peacekeeper, partnering perfectly with the chocolate and chilli.

MAKES 8

Chocolate Crinkle Cookies

60 ml (¼ cup) neutral tasting oil
50 g (¼ cup) caster (superfine) sugar
100 g (scant ½ cup, packed) light brown sugar
1 large egg
100 g (generous ¾ cup) plain (all-purpose) flour
40 g (½ cup) cocoa powder (dutched)
¼ teaspoon bicarbonate of soda (baking soda)
¼ teaspoon fine sea salt

Chilli Lime Curd

1 large egg
50 g (¼ cup) caster (superfine) sugar
zest 1 lime
¼ teaspoon chilli (red pepper) flakes
65 ml (5 tablespoons) lime juice, roughly 2 limes
30 g (2 tablespoons) unsalted butter, diced

Coating

icing (confectioner's) sugar

Finishing

zest 1 lime
chilli (red pepper) flakes

Note: Usually, a curd is cooked gently in a bain-marie but here it is cooked directly in the pan. To do this successfully, without overcooking the egg, keep the heat very low and stir the mixture constantly.

1. To make the curd, put everything except the butter into a small saucepan, place over a low heat and cook, stirring constantly, until the mixture thickens and reaches 75–80°C (167–176°F) or thickens enough to coat the back of a spoon. Pour into a small bowl, passing through a sieve to remove any lumps. Add the butter and stir until fully combined. Cover and refrigerate until needed.
2. To make the cookie dough, place the oil, sugars and egg in a large bowl and whisk until well combined, 1–2 minutes. Add the flour, cocoa, bicarbonate of soda and salt and mix with a spatula to form a thick, brownie-like dough. Cover and refrigerate for 30 minutes until slightly thickened. After this the finished dough will still be relatively soft but the short rest allows the flour to hydrate and stops the cookies from spreading too much.
3. Preheat the oven to 180°C/160°C Fan (350°F) and line a large baking tray (half sheet pan) with baking parchment.
4. Use a small mechanical ice cream scoop to form the dough into balls, drop them, one at a time, into a small bowl of icing sugar and roll into neat balls, ensuring they are thoroughly coated in a generous layer of the sugar. Place on the prepared tray, setting them well apart to allow for spreading.
5. Bake for 10–12 minutes or until cracked and puffed up. The edges of the cookies will be set and a little firm. When the cookies are fresh from the oven and still a little warm, use a tablespoon measure to press down on the centre of each to form a small well. Spoon a little curd onto each cookie and sprinkle with a few chilli flakes and a little extra lime zest. Allow to cool fully before enjoying.
6. Kept in a sealed container, these cookies will keep for around 4 days.

RASPBERRY AND PISTACHIO WHITE CHOCOLATE CHIP COOKIES

These raspberry swirled cookies are absolutely jam packed with flavour, and with actual jam! The combination of white chocolate, pistachios and raspberry jam makes for a delicious, texture-filled treat.

MAKES 12

165g (1½ sticks) unsalted butter, diced
165 g (¾ cup + 1 tablespoon) caster (superfine) sugar
1 large egg
½ teaspoon vanilla extract
225 g (generous 1¾ cups) plain (all-purpose) flour
1 teaspoon baking powder
½ teaspoon fine sea salt
50 g (generous ⅓ cup) pistachios, roughly chopped
100 g (3½ oz/roughly a generous ½ cup) white chocolate, discs, feves or roughly chopped bar
60 g (3 tablespoons) raspberry jam

1 Line two large baking trays (half sheet pans) with baking parchment.

2 Place the butter in a small saucepan and heat just until melted. Pour into a large bowl and add the sugar. Stir together with a whisk, then set aside for 5 minutes to cool slightly. Add the egg and vanilla and whisk until a smooth, shiny batter is formed. In a separate bowl, whisk together the flour, baking powder and salt. Add the flour mixture to the butter mixture and stir to form a soft dough. Add the pistachios and chocolate and stir to combine. The dough should feel soft but scoop-able. If it feels too loose, cover and leave for 10 minutes, during which time it should thicken slightly.

3 Dollop the jam randomly over the surface of the dough and use a knife to very gently swirl and fold it in. The aim is to end up with a dough that has a mix of swirls and pockets of jam, stir too much and the jam will lose definition. Use a 60 ml (¼ cup) mechanical ice cream scoop to form the cookies, placing the rounds onto the prepared trays. Refrigerate for 2 hours before baking. If you want the cookies to look extra special, gently roll the chilled balls of dough in a few extra chopped pistachios

4 Preheat the oven to 180°C/160°C Fan (350°F).

5 Bake the cookies for about 16 minutes or until the edges are golden but the centres are still a touch pale. Remove and cool on the trays for 5 minutes before carefully transferring to a wire rack to cool completely.

6 Kept in a sealed container, these cookies will keep for up to 5 days.

S'MORES BROWNIES

Whoever came up with the idea for s'mores is a certified genius! A caramelised and melty marshmallow, warm gooey chocolate and a crisp cookie. It's like they were designed for maximum pleasure. In this recipe I have taken the flavours of a classic s'mores and transferred them onto a thin brownie layer, making a perfect little parcel.

MAKES 12–16

Biscuit Base

155 g (scant 1¼ cups) finely crushed digestives (graham crackers)
¼ teaspoon flaked sea salt
1¼ tablespoons, packed, light brown sugar
65 g (4½ tablespoons) unsalted butter, melted

Brownie

130 g (generous 1 cup) plain (all-purpose) flour
35 g (⅓ cup + 2 tablespoons) cocoa powder (dutched)
¼ teaspoon fine sea salt
¼ teaspoon baking powder
225 g (8 oz) dark chocolate (65–75% cocoa solids), roughly chopped
150 g (1⅓ sticks) unsalted butter, diced
3 large eggs
110 g (½ cup + 1 tablespoon) caster (superfine) sugar
165 g (¾ cup, packed) light brown sugar
1 teaspoon vanilla extract

Meringue Topping

4 sheets gelatine
2 large egg whites
125 g (½ cup + 2 tablespoons) caster (superfine) sugar
pinch fine sea salt
pinch cream of tartar
½ teaspoon vanilla bean paste

1 Preheat the oven to 180°C/160°C Fan (350°F). Lightly grease a 23 × 33 cm (9 × 13 in) brownie tin (pan) and line with a single sheet of baking parchment so the excess hangs over the two long sides, securing the parchment with a couple of metal binder clips.

2 For the base, pour the biscuit crumbs into a bowl and stir through the salt and sugar. Drizzle in the butter and stir together until evenly combined. Tip this mixture into the prepared tin and compact into an even layer. Set aside.

3 Sift the flour, cocoa, salt and baking powder into a large bowl. Place the chocolate and butter in a separate heatproof bowl, set over a pan of simmering water, and heat, stirring occasionally, until fully melted. Remove and set aside.

4 Meanwhile, place the eggs, sugars and vanilla in a large bowl and, using an electric mixer, whisk together for 3–4 minutes or until the eggs have at least doubled in volume and the mixture is pale and fluffy. This whisking action helps to give the finished brownie both a shiny crust and the ideal dense and fudgy texture. With the mixer still running, pour in the slightly cooled chocolate mixture, whisking until fully combined. Switching to a spatula, pour in the flour mixture and fold together just until everything is combined, the odd speck of flour is fine. Scrape the batter into the prepared tin and spread into an even layer.

5 Bake in the preheated oven for 20–25 minutes until puffed up a little but still gooey inside. Allow to cool at room temperature whilst you make the marshmallow topping.

6 Add the gelatine to a small bowl and cover with ice-cold water. Set aside for 5 minutes or until softened. Put the remaining ingredients in a heatproof bowl and place over a pan of simmering water. Whisk gently until the mixture is hot to the touch and you can no longer feel any grains of sugar. Remove from the heat. Remove the gelatine from the water and squeeze out any excess water. Add the gelatine to the hot egg white mixture and then, using an electric mixer, whisk on high speed until the mixture holds stiff peaks but is still warm. It is essential to heat the egg white and sugar mixture until hot to ensure the gelatine fully melts.

7 Scrape the glossy marshmallow onto the brownie and spread into an even layer. Transfer to the refrigerator until the marshmallow has set.

»»»

8 Lift the brownies from the pan and use a sharp knife to cut into squares. The marshmallow can make it tricky to get clean slices so dip the knife into very hot water before you make each cut. Then use a kitchen blowtorch to caramelise the top layer of marshmallow. If not eating them straightaway, I prefer to blowtorch them just prior to serving.

9 Kept in a sealed container, in the refrigerator, the brownies will keep for at least 4–5 days.

MILK CHOCOLATE SPECULOOS COOKIES

A classic shortbread is made with a 1:2:3 ratio: 1 part sugar, 2 parts butter and 3 parts flour. In this recipe I've used a similar ratio but changing it a little results in an entirely different texture. Instead of 1:2:3, this recipe uses 1:3:3: 1 part butter, 3 parts sugar and 3 parts flour. This ratio, along with the addition of egg yolks and bicarbonate of soda (baking soda), makes for a light and crisp cookie, very similar to commercial versions of speculoos. To make something as warm and as toasty as those beautiful Belgian biscuits, I have used a light hand with the spicing, so that the caramel notes in the brown sugar still shine through. And to give them a little added flair, they are sandwiched together with a milk chocolate filling.

MAKES 12

Speculoos Cookies

- 50 g (3½ tablespoons) unsalted butter, room temperature
- 150 g (⅔ cup, packed) light brown sugar
- 2 large egg yolks
- 2 teaspoons vanilla extract
- 150 g (scant 1¼ cups) plain (all-purpose) flour
- ½ teaspoon bicarbonate of soda (baking soda)
- ½ teaspoon fine sea salt
- ½ teaspoon ground cinnamon
- ¼ freshly ground nutmeg
- ¼ teaspoon ground cardamom
- ⅛ teaspoon ground clove
- 2 tablespoons flaked (slivered) almonds (optional)

Milk Chocolate Filling

- 100 g (3½ oz) milk chocolate (40–50% cocoa solids)
- 25 g (2 tablespoons) unsalted butter, diced

1. Put the butter and sugar in a large bowl and, using an electric mixer, beat together for 8–10 minutes. The ratio of sugar to butter means it will take longer than normal to get lightness into the butter. Once the butter mixture is light and pale, add the egg yolks and vanilla and beat for a minute or until fully mixed into the butter.
2. Place all the dry ingredients, except the almonds, in a separate bowl, and whisk to combine. Add the flour mixture to the butter mixture and, on a low speed, mix together to form a smooth uniform dough. Cut a large sheet of baking parchment to the size of a large baking tray (half sheet pan). Place the dough on the baking parchment and cover with a second sheet the same size. Roll out the dough to a thickness of about 3 mm (⅛ in). Slide the dough onto the baking tray and transfer to the refrigerator for at least an hour or until firm.
3. Preheat the oven to 180°C/160°C Fan (350°F) and line two large baking trays with baking parchment.
4. Remove the dough from the refrigerator and peel back the top sheet of baking parchment. Scatter over the almonds and lightly pass over them with a rolling pin so they adhere to the top of the dough. Use a 6 cm (2½ in) round cookie cutter to cut out as many cookies as possible, cutting them close together to keep the re-rolling of the dough to a minimum. Gather the scraps and knead briefly to bring together as a uniform dough, then re-roll as before, cutting out the final batch of cookies.
5. Place the cookies on the prepared trays and bake for 15–16 minutes or until the cookies are lightly browned. Remove and set aside to cool for 5 minutes before transferring to a wire rack to cool completely.
6. For the filling, melt the chocolate and butter using the microwave or a bain-marie (see page 24), then set aside until the chocolate is thick but spreadable. Spoon a little chocolate onto the back of half of the cookies, sandwiching together with a second cookie. Store at room temperature for up to 3 days.

BROWN BUTTER CARAMELISED WHITE CHOCOLATE COOKIES

Despite my love for white chocolate, it is impossible to argue with the idea that some recipes made with it are simply too sweet. To make a delicious white chocolate cookie that doesn't fall into the 'too sweet' camp, I like to use the combination of caramelised white chocolate and brown butter, which adds a deliciously nutty roasted flavour. A final sprinkling of flaked sea salt turns these into a delightfully sweet and salty treat that is guaranteed to win over any hater of white chocolate.

MAKES 6

50 g (scant ¼ cup, packed) light brown sugar
50 g (¼ cup) caster (superfine) sugar
50 g (3½ tablespoons) unsalted butter
1 tablespoon skimmed milk powder (non-fat dry milk)
1 large egg yolk
2 tablespoons whole milk
¼ teaspoon vanilla bean paste
125 g (1 cup) plain (all-purpose) flour
¼ teaspoon fine sea salt
¼ teaspoon baking powder
¼ teaspoon bicarbonate of soda (baking soda)
50 g (1¾ oz/roughly, a generous ¼ cup) caramelised white chocolate, roughly chopped
flaked sea salt, for sprinkling

To decorate

75 g (2½ oz/roughly, a scant ½ cup) caramelised white chocolate, melted

1. Put the two sugars in a large mixing bowl and set aside. Add the butter and milk powder to a small saucepan, place over a medium heat and cook until browned, stirring constantly to prevent the milk powder from catching on the bottom of the pan. Once you can see brown flecks in the butter and it has a nutty aroma, pour over the sugars and stir together with a whisk. Leave to cool for a couple minutes, then add the egg yolk, milk and vanilla and whisk until smooth. Add the flour, salt, baking powder and bicarbonate of soda and stir together with a spatula to form a dough. Add the chocolate and stir to distribute. Cover and refrigerate the dough for an hour before baking.
2. Preheat the oven to 180°C/160°C Fan (350°F) and line a large baking tray (pan) with baking parchment.
3. Divide the dough into six equally sized pieces and roll into balls. Place on the prepared tray and sprinkle with a little flaked sea salt. Bake for 12–13 minutes until lightly browned around the edges. Remove and set aside to cool on the tray for 5 minutes before carefully transferring to a wire rack to cool completely.
4. To decorate, dip the cookies halfway into the melted chocolate, allowing any excess to drip back into the bowl. Place the cookies back on the parchment-lined tray and refrigerate just until the chocolate has set.
5. Stored in a sealed container, the cookies will keep for 3–4 days.

COSY COCOA SPICE COOKIES WITH CREAM CHEESE FILLING

Chocolate is most often used as the dominant central flavour in baking, but sometimes you can use it as a secondary flavour. Here, in the form of cocoa, it is used to add a warmth and depth that plays really well against the flavour of molasses and the warm spices. If you want a stronger chocolate flavour, you could add a thin layer of ganache to the filling.

MAKES 15

Cookies

125 g (1 stick + 1 tablespoon) unsalted butter
175 g (generous ¾ cup, packed) light brown sugar
75 g (scant ¼ cup) black treacle (molasses)
1 large egg
1 large egg yolk
275 g (2¼ cups) plain (all-purpose) flour
15 g (2½ tablespoons) cocoa powder (dutched or natural)
1 tablespoon ground ginger
½ teaspoon freshly grated nutmeg
¼ teaspoon black pepper
1 teaspoon bicarbonate of soda (baking soda)
½ teaspoon salt

Coating

demerara sugar

Filling

50 g (3½ tablespoons) unsalted butter, room temperature
125 g (1 cup) icing (confectioner's) sugar
½ teaspoon vanilla bean paste
50 g (scant ¼ cup) full-fat cream cheese, room temperature
pinch fine sea salt

1 To make the cookie dough, melt the butter, in a saucepan or in the microwave, then pour into a large mixing bowl along with the sugar and treacle, stirring to combine. Leave to cool for a few minutes before adding the egg and egg yolk. Using an electric mixer, on medium/high speed, mix for 2 minutes until fully combined and slightly paler in colour. In a separate bowl, whisk together the flour, cocoa, spices, bicarbonate of soda and salt. Add the flour mixture to the butter mixture and mix just until a uniform dough is formed. Cover and refrigerate until firm, about 2 hours.

2 Preheat the oven to 180°C/160°C Fan (350°F) and line two large baking trays (pans) with baking parchment.

3 Roll the dough into 30 small balls. If you have a small mechanical ice cream scoop this is perfect for the job. Roll the balls in demerara sugar, then place on the prepared trays.

4 Bake the cookies for 10 minutes or until the surfaces are lightly cracked and the edges are set. Remove the cookies from the oven and allow them to cool for 5 minutes before transferring to a wire rack to cool completely.

5 To make the filling, add the butter to a large bowl and beat, preferably with an electric mixer, until very soft and pale, 2–3 minutes. Add the icing sugar and vanilla and beat until smooth. The mixture will seem a little thick at this stage. Add the cream cheese and salt and mix just until smooth and lump free.

6 Spoon or pipe filling on half the cookies, then sandwich with a second cookie.

7 Kept in a sealed container, the cookies will keep in the refrigerator for 3–4 days.

BROWN BUTTER RYE CHOCOLATE CHIP COOKIES

Chocolate chip cookies might include the word chip but, in my opinion, the easiest thing you can do to elevate your cookie game is to skip the chips and use a better form of chocolate. A chopped bar, bag of wafers, callets or feves will automatically up the quality, as these forms of chocolate will melt and meld into the dough as the cookies bake, resulting in a cookie with significantly better texture and flavour.

MAKES 12

115 g (1 stick) unsalted butter, diced
165 g (¾ cup, packed) light brown sugar
50 g (¼ cup) caster (superfine) sugar
1 large egg yolk
1 large egg
1 teaspoon vanilla bean paste
175 g (scant 1½ cups) plain (all-purpose) flour
60 g (generous ½ cup) wholemeal (wholewheat) rye flour
½ teaspoon baking powder
½ teaspoon bicarbonate of soda (baking soda)
½ teaspoon fine sea salt
250 g (9 oz/roughly 1½ cups) dark chocolate (60–70% cocoa solids), roughly chopped
a little flaked sea salt

Tip: If using a bar of chocolate, roughly chop to create a variety of different-sized pieces. Wafers, callets and fèves can be added without chopping, though I like to give them a very rough chop to create some variation.

Note: Chilling the dough for longer than an hour is optional but I encourage you to wait at least 24 hours to see the difference. As the cookie dough ages, it develops a more caramelised flavour, and the quintessential cookie flavour becomes more concentrated. Cookies made with longer-rested dough also brown a little more, which also contributes to the improvement in flavour.

1 Place the butter in a small saucepan and cook over a medium heat until browned. At first the butter will bubble and splatter, as the water cooks out, but once it settles it will start to foam. At this point keep an eye out for the appearance of brown flecks, as this is when the butter is browned. Pour into a small bowl and refrigerate for about an hour or until the butter is firm but still a little pliable.

2 Scrape the butter into the bowl of an electric stand mixer fitted with the paddle attachment. Add the sugars and beat together for about 2 minutes until fully combined and paste-like. Add the egg yolk and beat for 5 minutes, scraping the bowl down occasionally, until the mixture is very light and fluffy. Add the egg and the vanilla and beat for another minute or until fully combined. Add the flours, baking powder, bicarbonate of soda and salt to a large bowl and whisk together to combine. Add the flour mixture and mix just until a dough is starting to come together. Add the chocolate and mix until evenly distributed through the dough. The dough needs to be refrigerated for at least an hour before the cookies are baked, simply to control their spread and to make sure they have the desired texture, ideally, though, you should leave it for 24–72 hours (see Note).

Preheat the oven to 180°C/160°C Fan (350°F). Line two large baking trays (pans) with baking parchment.

4 Divide the dough into 12 equal portions and roll into balls. Place six balls on each tray and sprinkle with a little flaked sea salt. Bake in the preheated oven for about 13–15 minutes or until the edges of the cookies are golden brown. Remove and set aside to cool on the trays for 10 minutes before transferring to a wire rack to cool completely.

5 Kept in a sealed container, these will keep for 3–4 days. The rolled balls of dough can also be frozen for up to three months and baked straight from the freezer, adding an extra minute or so to the bake time.

CHOKLADBISKVIER

These classic Swedish cookies are not particularly hard to make but they are a bit fiddly and time consuming. Don't let that put you off. Shaped like small cones, they are made by combining an almond macaroon with chocolate buttercream. The recipe makes rather a lot, but if you need something to take to a party these will absolutely get you a return invitation. For the buttercream, I like to use a chocolate with a relatively high cocoa content, of around 80%, so that it isn't too sweet and has a robust chocolate flavour. If you want to make a coffee and chocolate version add a little instant espresso powder to the Swiss meringue as it is whisking.

MAKES 30

Macaroon

200 g (2 cups) ground almonds (almond flour)
200 g (1⅔ cups) icing (confectioner's) sugar
150 g egg whites (from about 4 large eggs)
¼ teaspoon almond extract (optional)
¼ teaspoon fine sea salt

Chocolate Swiss Meringue Buttercream

80 g egg whites (from about 2 large eggs)
large pinch fine sea salt
160 g (¾ cup + 1 tablespoon) caster (superfine) sugar
240 g (2 sticks + 1 tablespoon) unsalted butter, diced and at room temperature
125 g (4½ oz) dark chocolate (80% cocoa solids), melted and cooled

Coating

300 g (10½ oz) dark or milk chocolate, melted and preferably tempered

Note: The coating calls for a lot of chocolate but not all of it will be used – you need enough to allow for dunking. Any remaining can be left to set and used in another recipe.

1 Preheat the oven to 190°C/170°C Fan (375°F) and line two large baking trays (pans) with baking parchment.

2 For the macaroon, simply put everything in a large bowl and stir to form a sticky batter. To form the cookies, you can either pipe into small rounds or use a small mechanical ice cream scoop, depositing about 1 tablespoon of batter per cookie. Alternatively, you can also use two spoons to portion out the batter. Use wet fingers to neaten up the shape should you need to. The cookies will spread as they bake, so don't be tempted to put too many on a single tray.

3 Bake for 15–18 minutes or until golden brown. Remove from the oven and slide the parchment onto a wire rack so the cookies can fully cool.

4 To make the buttercream, place the egg whites, salt and sugar in a heatproof bowl and place over a pan of simmering water. Whisk gently until the mixture is hot to the touch and you can no longer feel any grains of sugar. Remove the bowl from the heat and, using an electric mixer, whisk until stiff and glossy and cooled to room temperature, 5–7 minutes. With the mixer still running, slowly add the butter, a couple pieces at a time. Once it is all added, continue mixing until a smooth silky buttercream texture has been formed. Scrape in the cooled melted chocolate and again mix until evenly combined.

5 Peel the cookies from the parchment and flip so they are bottom side up. Pipe, scoop or spoon a mound of buttercream onto each cookie and then use a small offset spatula to shape the buttercream into a cone shape. Place the finished cookies on a baking tray and refrigerate for about an hour or until the buttercream is firm.

»»»

6 You can coat the cookies in either tempered or melted chocolate. If you temper it, follow the instructions on page 30 and remove the cookies from the refrigerator whilst you temper the chocolate. If the cookies are coated straight from the refrigerator, the buttercream will be too cold and will cool the chocolate too fast, making it hard to apply.

7 Scrape the tempered, or melted chocolate, into a smaller bowl, then carefully dunk each cookie into the chocolate, coating just the buttercream. Give the cookie a little wiggle so any excess chocolate drips back into the bowl. Place, cookie side down, onto a baking tray and leave until the chocolate has set. If using melted chocolate transfer the finished cookies to the refrigerator to allow the chocolate to set.

8 If you temper the chocolate, the cookies can be stored in a sealed container for up to 4 days. If you melt it, they are best stored in the refrigerator and then brought out a couple hours before you want to serve them.

BROWN BUTTER COCOA RYE BROWNIES

I've used the same base brownie recipe, save for the odd tweak here and there, for over a decade, it's a recipe I love (it is the base of the S'mores Brownie recipe on page 98). But what happens when you make brownies without chocolate, a brownie made with only cocoa powder? After multiple tests and lots of tweaks this is what I came up with. It makes for a brownie that is rich and fudgy with an intensely strong cocoa flavour. My preference is to use dutched cocoa, for those rich roasted notes, but a natural cocoa will give a slightly brighter and more fruity finished flavour; the choice is yours. I also like to use rye flour, as it helps give the cocoa a backbone of flavour whilst at the same time imparting the finished brownie with a deeper, richer flavour and texture, but you can use plain (all-purpose) flour in its place.

MAKES 9

170 g (1½ sticks) unsalted butter, diced
75 g (¾ cup + 2 tablespoons) cocoa powder (dutched)
2 large eggs
100 g (½ cup) caster (superfine) sugar
125 g (½ cup + 1 tablespoon, packed) light brown sugar
½ teaspoon vanilla extract
½ teaspoon fine sea salt
75 g (¾ cup) wholemeal (wholewheat) rye flour
100 g (3½ oz/roughly a generous ½ cup) dark chocolate chips (optional)
flaked sea salt, for garnish

Tip: To ensure these have the glossy crust we all love in a brownie, the eggs and sugar need to be well whipped. Whipping helps to dissolve the sugar, which in turn helps to develop the shiny crust.

1 Preheat the oven to 170°C/150°C Fan (340°F). Lightly grease a 20 cm (8 in) square cake tin (pan) and line the base and sides with baking parchment.

2 Put the butter in a medium saucepan, and place over a medium heat to brown. At first, the butter will splatter, as the water cooks out, but it will then start to foam. It is at this stage you need to watch for the appearance of brown flecks as this is the sign the butter is browned. Once the butter is browned, remove the pan from the heat, tip in the cocoa and whisk to combine. Set aside for 2–3 minutes to cool slightly.

3 Add the eggs, sugars, vanilla and salt to a large bowl and, using an electric mixer, whisk for 2–3 minutes or until the eggs are thick and pale. With the mixer running, pour in the cocoa mixture and whisk for a minute or until everything is evenly combined. Add the flour and mix together until a smooth batter is formed, then add the chocolate chips, if using, and mix just until evenly distributed. Pour the batter into the prepared tin and spread evenly, sprinkling with a little flaked sea salt, if you like things with a sweet and salty kick.

4 Bake in the preheated oven for 20–25 minutes or until the brownies still seem a little underbaked in the centre. A toothpick inserted into the middle should come out with moist crumbs and even a little bit of moist batter, just not completely coated in unbaked batter. Remove and set aside to cool to room temperature, then transfer to the refrigerator for at least an hour until thoroughly chilled. This last stage of refrigeration is optional, but it helps to make a more dense and fudgy texture.

5 Kept in a sealed container, these will keep for 3–4 days.

DESSERTS

ROASTED WHITE CHOCOLATE BASQUE CHEESECAKE WITH DRUNKEN CHERRIES

All cheesecake is good cheesecake. But if you ask me about Basque Cheesecake, well, that holds an extra-special place in my heart. Not only is it incredibly easy to make, the intense heat used to cook it results in a deeply caramelised crust whilst maintaining an incredibly creamy centre. In this version, both brown sugar and caramelised white chocolate are used to really amplify this toasty goodness. Whatever you do, don't skip the boozy cherries; they're the perfect accompaniment to this dish.

SERVES 12

Cheesecake

200 ml (¾ cup + 1 tablespoon) whipping (heavy) cream
175 g (6 oz) caramelised white chocolate, melted
750 g (3⅓ cups) full-fat cream cheese, room temperature
200 g (scant 1 cup, packed) light brown sugar
½ teaspoon fine sea salt
4 large eggs
1 teaspoon vanilla bean paste
2 tablespoons plain (all-purpose) flour (use 1 tablespoon cornflour/cornstarch if you need to make this gluten free)

Drunken Cherries

50 ml (3½ tablespoons) water
50 g (¼ cup) caster (superfine) sugar
250 g (9 oz) fresh sweet cherries, stoned
50 ml (3½ tablespoons) amaretto liqueur

whipped cream, to serve

1. To make the cheesecake, start by making a ganache. Pour the cream into a saucepan, bring to a simmer, then remove from the heat and pour a third over the melted chocolate, stirring to combine. Mix in the remaining cream in two additions, stirring well until the ganache is smooth and silky. Set aside to cool.

2. Preheat the oven to 240°C/220°C Fan (475°F). Line a 20 cm (8 in) springform cake tin (pan) with a single layer of crumpled baking parchment. Don't worry about making this look perfect, ruffled edges are part of this cheesecake's charm.

3. Put the cream cheese in a large bowl and beat until smooth and creamy, either using a wooden spoon or some form of electric mixer, the choice is yours. Add the sugar and salt and mix until evenly combined. Add the eggs, one at a time, beating until fully combined before adding the next. Add the vanilla and the cooled ganache and mix until combined. Add the flour and mix briefly until evenly distributed.

4. Pour the batter into the prepared tin, transfer to the oven and bake for 35–40 minutes or until the top is dark and puffed but not quite burnt. Remove from the oven and set aside to cool for an hour before transferring to the refrigerator for at least 4 hours, preferably overnight, to chill thoroughly. As the cheesecake cools, it will sink; this is normal.

5. For the drunken cherries, put the water and sugar in a small saucepan and heat gently until the sugar has dissolved. Add the cherries and simmer for 3–4 minutes until the cherries are starting to soften but are still holding their shape. Spoon the cherries into a small jar or bowl, leaving the syrup in the pan. Cook the syrup for a further 2–3 minutes until thick and syrupy. Remove from the heat, stir through the amaretto, then pour atop the cherries. Kept in the refrigerator, these cherries will keep for a couple weeks, so long as the fruit stays submerged in the syrup.

6. Cut slices of the cheesecake and serve with a a spoonful of the drunken cherries and a dollop of whipped cream.

7. Kept refrigerated, the cheesecake will keep for up to 5 days.

PISTACHIO TIRAMISU

If you're the baker in your friendship group, there is something that goes unsaid. Each and every one of your friends is secretly hoping you'll arrive at their house holding a dessert. This twist on a classic tiramisu is made in a loaf tin (pan), making it incredibly easy to transport – and, therefore, a great choice when you're the designated dessert person. This tiramisu is made with white chocolate and pistachio, both of which work incredibly well with coffee. For the boozy element I've used amaretto, as the nuttiness boosts the flavour of the pistachios and also complements the coffee flavour.

SERVES 6–8

100 g (¾ cup) pistachios
100 g (3½ oz/roughly a generous ½ cup) white chocolate, roughly chopped
3 large eggs, separated
50 g (¼ cup) caster (superfine) sugar
250 g (1 generous cup) mascarpone
75 g (5 tablespoons) pistachio cream
½ teaspoon vanilla bean paste
pinch fine sea salt
125 ml (½ cup) whipping (heavy) cream
150 ml (scant ⅔ cup) espresso or strong black coffee
75 ml (5 tablespoons) amaretto liqueur
150 g (5½ oz/roughly 20 sponge fingers) savaoirdi sponge fingers (ladyfingers)

Note: The pistachio cream used here is akin to a pistachio Nutella. Unlike pure pistachio pastes or praline paste, it is made with a combination of pistachios, sugar and oil (sometimes with the addition of milk powder and an emulsifier such as sunflower lecithin). The best versions tend to be made with 45% pistachios.

1 Line a 450 g (1 lb) loaf tin (pan) with a double layer of cling film (plastic wrap), so that the entire inside of the tin is lined and the excess hangs over the sides. Add the pistachios and chocolate to the bowl of a food processor and briefly pulse until they resemble coarse breadcrumbs. This can also be done simply with a knife, should you prefer.

2 Put the egg yolks and sugar in a large bowl, place over a pan of simmering water and whisk constantly until thick and pale, 2–3 minutes. The finished texture should resemble a homemade mayonnaise. Remove the bowl from the heat and whisk through the mascarpone, pistachio cream and vanilla. Set aside.

3 In a separate bowl, whisk the egg whites and the salt until the meringue holds soft peaks. Add the cream to a large bowl and whisk until it holds soft peaks.

4 Add the whipped cream to the mascarpone mixture and fold together. Fold the meringue through the mascarpone cream mixture in three additions, trying to keep it as light as possible.

5 Pour the coffee and amaretto into a shallow bowl. Sprinkle a third of the pistachio/chocolate mixture into the bottom of the loaf tin. Spread a thin layer of the mascarpone cream atop the pistachio layer, then add a layer of sponge fingers, dipping them briefly into the coffee mixture first. Spoon just under half of the remaining cream atop the sponge finger layer and spread into an even layer. Repeat the layering of pistachios/sponge fingers/cream a second time. Finish by spreading the last portion of cream on top and sprinkling over the final third of the pistachio mixture.

6 Wrap the tiramisu with the overhanging cling film, so that it is fully sealed in the tin. Refrigerate for at least 4 hours.

7 To serve, unwrap the top layer of cling film so the base of the tiramisu is exposed. Carefully invert the tiramisu onto a serving platter and peel away the remaining cling film.

8 Kept refrigerated, the tiramisu will keep for 2–3 days.

SALTED DARK CHOCOLATE SORBET

As an avid fan of both chocolate and ice cream, you might be shocked to learn that I don't love chocolate ice cream. Too often it's missing the intensity of chocolate and is far too creamy. Instead, I skip the dairy altogether and make a sorbet. I know this isn't technically an ice cream, but it is silky, almost creamy and with an intense chocolate flavour, everything I want in a chocolate ice cream. For the cocoa powder, you can use either variety, dutched or natural, but the former is my preference for a deep chocolate flavour.

SERVES 6

165 g (¾ cup + 1 tablespoon) caster (superfine) sugar
pinch fine sea salt
85 g (1 cup) cocoa powder (dutched or natural)
600 ml (2½ cups) boiling water
2 tablespoons liquid glucose (corn syrup or golden syrup will also work)
125 g (4½ oz) dark chocolate (70% cocoa solids), finely chopped
1 teaspoon vanilla extract
2 tablespoons vodka, rum or any other strong alcohol
flaky sea salt, to serve

Note: The alcohol is optional but it helps to create a sorbet that is scoopable straight from the freezer. Use vodka for its neutral flavour or rum (or any other strong alcohol) for the subtle flavour it will add.

1. Put the sugar, salt and cocoa in a large heatproof jug and whisk together. Pour over the boiling water and combine, stirring until the sugar has dissolved. Add the glucose and chocolate and set aside for a couple minutes before stirring together with the whisk until the mixture is smooth and the chocolate is fully melted and combined. Add the vanilla and vodka and stir to combine. Cover and refrigerate for at least 4 hours but preferably overnight. The extended chill helps the sorbet churn quicker and gives a better finished texture.
2. Before you churn the sorbet, place a 450 g (1 lb) loaf tin (pan) in the freezer for a couple hours. You can use any freezer-safe container, but I prefer a metal loaf tin because when chilled it retains the cold temperature a little longer compared to plastic containers, which means the sorbet doesn't melt as quickly when you decant it from the ice cream machine. The downside is that loaf tins don't have lids, so you'll need to use cling film (plastic wrap) to seal.
3. Churn using an ice cream machine, following the manufacturer's instructions, until the sorbet has the texture of soft-serve ice cream. Scoop into the loaf tin and cover with cling film (or seal your container with its lid). Freeze for 4 hours, at which point it should be fully frozen.
4. Serve with a sprinkling of flaky sea salt.
5. Kept in the freezer, sealed well, it will keep for up to a month, though the texture will be at its best in the first 2 weeks.

'MILK' CHOCOLATE CRÈME BRÛLÉE WITH LIME BLACKBERRIES

Although I've called this a 'milk' chocolate dessert, it is actually made with dark chocolate. I know this is confusing, but when the dessert also includes a significant amount of dairy and sugar, the chocolate flavour ends up tasting much closer to milk chocolate than the dark chocolate you started out with. I like to serve it alongside a batch of lime-macerated blackberries.

SERVES 4

Crème Brûlée

400 ml (1⅔ cups) whipping (heavy) cream
100 ml (⅓ cup + 1 tablespoon) whole milk
1 teaspoon vanilla bean paste
4 large egg yolks
50 g (¼ cup) caster (superfine) sugar, plus extra to serve
100 g (3½ oz) dark chocolate (75–80% cocoa solids), finely chopped

Lime-macerated Blackberries

125 g (4½ oz) blackberries
1 tablespoon caster (superfine) sugar
1 tablespoon lime juice
lime zest, to garnish

1. Preheat the oven to 160°C/140°C Fan (325°F) and place four 175 ml (6 fl oz) ramekins in a deep roasting tin (pan).
2. Put the cream, milk and vanilla in a small saucepan and bring to a simmer. Meanwhile, add the egg yolks and sugar to a large jug and whisk until smooth and pale. When at a simmer, pour the cream mixture into the jug, whisking gently as you pour to prevent the yolks from scrambling. Once smooth, add the chocolate and set aside for a couple minutes before stirring together to form a smooth chocolate custard. If the custard is foamy use a large spoon to skim off this layer as best you can.
3. Pour the custard into the ramekins through a fine-mesh sieve. This will help break up any bubbles still in the mixture. Carefully pour boiling water into the roasting tin so that it comes about halfway up the sides of the ramekins. Transfer to the oven and bake for 30–35 minutes or until the custards are set around the edges but have a gentle wobble in the centre. Remove from the water and set aside to cool to room temperature before refrigerating for at least 4 hours.
4. While the custards are chilling, prepare the fruit topping. With a sharp pairing knife, cut the blackberries in half, sprinkle over the sugar and lime juice and stir gently to combine. Set aside until ready to serve the dessert, stirring occasionally to ensure everything is evenly coated in the syrup that will form.
5. When ready to serve, sprinkle each of the custards with a thin layer of sugar, about a teaspoon per custard, and use a blowtorch to melt and caramelise the sugar. Serve with the macerated blackberries.
6. When baked, the custards can be refrigerated for 2–3 days, but once the sugar has been added and blowtorched they are best served within a couple hours.

MILK CHOCOLATE LIQUORICE ICE CREAM

Look, you may hate black liquorice, many people do. If that's you, turn the page, this recipe isn't for you. This is for fellow fans of the dark stuff, who love the molasses-rich, aniseed-like flavour. Ever since I visited family in Canada, aged eighteen, I've had a love affair with liquorice ice cream. The version I had back then was paired with orange, and sold as 'tiger ice cream', but in this recipe the liquorice is partnered with milk chocolate for a rich and creamy finish.

SERVES 6

300 ml (1¼ cups) whole milk
450 ml (generous 1¾ cups) whipping (heavy) cream
1 teaspoon vanilla bean paste
125 g (4½ oz) soft black liquorice, diced
100 g (½ cup) caster (superfine) sugar
6 large egg yolks
20 g (¼ cup) cocoa powder (dutched)
pinch fine sea salt
50 g (1¾ oz) milk chocolate, finely chopped
2 tablespoons absinthe

Note: The absinthe gives the frozen ice cream a scoopable texture as well as boosting the flavour of the liquorice. If you don't have absinthe you can use any other high-proof alcohol, such as vodka, to the same effect.

1 Pour the milk, cream and vanilla into a large saucepan and add the liquorice. Place the pan over a low heat and cook, stirring occasionally, until the liquorice is fully melted. Meanwhile, put the sugar and egg yolks into a large bowl and whisk together for 30 seconds or so. Add the cocoa and salt and whisk until smooth and lump free. Pour the hot cream mixture over the yolks, stirring as you pour to prevent the yolks from scrambling. Pour the custard back into the saucepan, place over a low heat, and cook, stirring constantly, until the custard reaches between 75 and 80°C (167 and 176°F). The liquorice thickens this custard so it can be tricky to judge when it is fully cooked without checking the temperature. If cooking by eye, watch for the custard to thicken slightly.

2 While the custard is cooking, put the chocolate in the bottom of a large heatproof jug and, as soon as the custard is ready, pour it over the chocolate and leave for about 2 minutes before stirring together until smooth. Finish by pouring in the absinthe, stirring to combine. Press a sheet of cling film (plastic wrap) onto the surface of the custard and refrigerate for at least 4 hours, preferably overnight.

3 When chilled, pour the custard into an ice cream machine and churn according to the manufacturer's instructions. When it's the texture of soft-serve ice cream, scoop into a freezer-safe container with a lid. I like use to use a 450 g (1 lb) loaf tin (pan) that has been in the freezer for a few hours and cover it with cling film. Freeze for at least 4 hours before serving.

4 Homemade ice cream keeps for about a month but the texture is at its best within the first 2 weeks.

ROASTED STRAWBERRIES AND CREAM WITH WHITE CHOCOLATE MASCARPONE GANACHE

I am a big fan of prepare-ahead desserts and this particular dish is a firm summertime favourite, perfect for BBQs. All the elements can be made ahead and stored in the refrigerator for a couple days before serving. The only work that needs to be done at the time of serving is to very briefly whisk the ganache.

SERVES 4

Mascarpone Ganache

150 g (5½ oz) white chocolate, finely chopped
200 ml (¾ cup + 1 tablespoon) whipping (heavy) cream
250 g (1 cup + 1 tablespoon) mascarpone

Lemon Streusel

70 g (generous ½ cup) plain (all-purpose) flour
40 g (3 tablespoons) caster (superfine) sugar
zest ½ lemon
pinch flaked sea salt
50 g (3½ tablespoons) unsalted butter, diced

Roasted Strawberries

1 vanilla pod
365 g (12½ oz) strawberries, hulled and halved
3 tablespoons caster (superfine) sugar
zest and juice ½ lemon

Note: To give the roasted strawberries a different dimension, add either a couple of teaspoons of sumac, or a teaspoon of coarsely ground black pepper before roasting.

1 To make the ganache, put the chocolate in a large heatproof jug and melt in the microwave (see page 24). Pour the cream into a small saucepan and bring to a simmer. Pour a third over the chocolate and stir to combine (don't worry if it seems grainy or split at this point). Mix in the remaining cream in two additions, stirring well until a smooth and shiny ganache is formed. Add the mascarpone and stir until thoroughly combined. If you have one, finish with a brief blend using a stick blender, to ensure the ganache is thoroughly emulsified. Cover with cling film (plastic wrap) and refrigerate for at least 4 hours but up to 3 days.

2 To make the streusel, place the flour, sugar, zest and salt in a bowl and combine. Add the butter and use your fingertips to rub it into the flour until the mixture resembles breadcrumbs. Press into a ball of dough and refrigerate for at least 30 minutes or until needed.

3 For the finished dessert you have a choice: serve the strawberries whilst still hot or let them cool, which is my preference. Either way, both the strawberries and streusel can be baked at the same time and then served immediately or allowed to cool.

4 Preheat the oven to 190°C/170°C Fan (375°F).

5 Line a small, rimmed baking tray (pan) with baking parchment and crumble the streusel onto the tray. Slice the vanilla pod in half along its length and scrape out the seeds. In a small bowl toss together all the strawberry ingredients, including the vanilla seeds, until evenly coated. Scrape onto a second small, rimmed baking tray, spread in an even layer, then sprinkle over 2 tablespoons water. Bake both the strawberries and the streusel for an initial 8–10 minutes. The finished streusel should be lightly browned and should take 10 minutes, max. Remove the streusel once browned and set aside to cool fully. Continue cooking the strawberries for a rough total of 20–25 minutes or until the fruit is soft and coated in syrup. Remove and set aside until cooled to room temperature. Transfer both elements to small bowls, cover, and refrigerate until needed, up to 2 days.

6 To serve, remove the ganache from the refrigerator and whisk very briefly until it barely holds soft peaks. The addition of mascarpone means this will happen very quickly, so whisk with brevity and caution. Divide the ganache between four dessert bowls, top with strawberries and syrup and finish with a sprinkling of streusel.

CARAMELISED RICE PUDDING WITH PEARS AND ROASTED WHITE CHOCOLATE

Hot or cold, rice pudding is pure comfort. It is a taste of childhood and a simple but always satisfying dessert. I like to serve this version with caramelised pears and, to add a touch of indulgence, top it with caramelised white chocolate sauce and a pinch of flaked sea salt. To double down on the caramelised flavour, the rice pudding is made with caramelised sugar, which makes this whole thing caramel on caramel on caramel.

SERVES 4

Rice Pudding

75 g (¼ cup + 2 tablespoons) caster (superfine) sugar
10 g (scant 1 tablespoon) unsalted butter
large pinch flaked sea salt
200 ml (¾ cup + 1 tablespoon) whipping (heavy) cream
565 ml (2⅓ cups) whole milk
½ vanilla pod or 1 teaspoon vanilla bean paste
65 g (scant ½ cup) pudding rice (arborio or another short grain rice will work well too)

Pears

3 pears (Conference or Bosc), firm but ripe
30 g (2 tablespoons) unsalted butter, diced
50 g (scant ¼ cup, packed) light brown sugar
pinch flaked sea salt
1 tablespoon lemon juice

White Chocolate Sauce

100 ml (scant ½ cup) whipping (heavy) cream
60 g (2 oz/roughly ⅓ cup) caramelised white chocolate, melted
pinch flaked sea salt

1 Peel and core the pears, then cut into 2 cm (¾ in) chunks (the size doesn't need to be exact). Put the butter and sugar into a small frying pan and cook over a medium heat until the butter is fully melted. Add the pears, salt and lemon juice and give everything a good stir. Cook for about 10 minutes until the pears are tender, but still holding their shape, and the caramel mixture is reduced and syrupy. Pour into a small bowl, set aside until cool, then transfer to the refrigerator until needed. If you prefer, you can caramelise the pears as the rice pudding is cooking and serve them both hot.

2 To make the rice pudding, put the sugar in a large saucepan and cook over a medium heat until melted and caramelised to the colour of an old penny, a deep copper colour, then add the butter and salt, followed by the cream and milk. The sugar may seize and form hard chunks of caramel, but don't worry, they will melt as you cook the pudding. Scrape the seeds from the vanilla pod and add both the seeds and the pod itself to the saucepan. Pour in the rice and stir to combine. Bring the mixture to the boil, then reduce the heat to a simmer and cook, stirring occasionally, until the rice is cooked through and the liquid is reduced, about 40 minutes.

3 To make the sauce, pour the cream into a small saucepan, bring to a simmer, then remove from the heat and pour a third over the melted chocolate until fully combined. Add the remaining cream in two additions, stirring well until the sauce is smooth and silky.

4 If serving hot, the pudding is now ready. Divide the pears between four bowls and spoon the rice pudding on top. Pour on some of the sauce and sprinkle with a little flaked sea salt. If serving cold, refrigerate the pudding until thoroughly chilled, about 2–3 hours. Once chilled, stir to loosen, adding a little extra cream if needed, and then divide into bowls as above. Pour the sauce on top and sprinkle with a little flaked sea salt just before serving.

5 Kept refrigerated, the rice pudding will keep for 3–5 days, the pears for 2 days.

CHOCOLATE MOUSSE WITH CANDIED HAZELNUTS AND OLIVE OIL

I couldn't write a book on chocolate and not include a recipe for chocolate mousse. This is a classic version, light and airy but still incredibly rich and chocolatey – exactly the sort of mousse you'd expect to eat in a French bistro. To add another dimension, though, I've skipped the cream often served alongside and instead accompanied it with candied hazelnuts.

SERVES 6

Chocolate Mousse

250 g (9 oz) dark chocolate (70–80% cocoa solids), finely chopped
150 ml (scant ⅔ cup) whole milk
5 large eggs, separated
65 g (⅓ cup) caster (superfine) sugar
½ teaspoon vanilla bean paste
120 ml (½ cup) whipping (heavy) cream

Candied Hazelnuts

100 g (¾ cup) blanched hazelnuts
100 g (½ cup) caster (superfine) sugar
30 ml (2 tablespoons) water

To Serve

extra virgin olive oil
flaked sea salt

Note: Meringue and cream are much easier to fold into other mixtures when slightly under-whisked. If whisked until stiff peaks, they become dry and lose significantly more air when combined with something else.

1 To make the mousse, place the chocolate in a large heatproof bowl and melt, using either a bain-marie or the microwave (see page 24). Pour the milk into a medium saucepan, place over a medium heat and bring to a simmer. Meanwhile, put the egg yolks, 50 g (1¾ oz) of the sugar and the vanilla in a separate mixing bowl and whisk together until smooth and pale. When the milk is at a simmer, slowly pour it into the yolk mixture, stirring to prevent it scrambling. Pour the custard back into the saucepan, place over a low heat and cook until it reaches a temperature of 75–80°C (167–176°F) or thickens enough to coat the back of a spoon. Immediately pour the custard into a heatproof jug. Pour a third of the custard into the bowl of chocolate and stir to combine. Mix in the remaining custard in two additions, stirring until silky smooth.

2 Put the egg whites in a large bowl and, using an electric hand mixer, whisk until foamy. Slowly rain in the remaining sugar, continuing to whisk until the meringue holds soft peaks. In a separate bowl, but using the same mixer (there's no need to wash the attachments), whisk the cream to soft peaks.

3 Fold the meringue into the chocolate custard in three additions, keeping the mixture as light as possible. For the first addition, you can be a little bit more assertive, not worrying too much about retaining the airiness. This addition will loosen the chocolate mixture, making it easier to combine the remaining meringue and cream without losing too much air. Fold in the cream, until the mixture is streak free. Cover the bowl and refrigerate for at least 4 hours. If you're pushed for time, you can pour the mousse into individual bowls or glasses, where they'll set in about 2 hours.

4 Preheat the oven to 180°C/160°C Fan (350°F). Place the hazelnuts on a rimmed baking tray (pan) and toast in the oven for 10–12 minutes or until golden brown. Remove and set aside.

5 Put the sugar and water into a small saucepan and place over a medium heat. Once the mixture is bubbling and the sugar has dissolved, add the hazelnuts and remove from the heat. Stir continuously until the sugar has formed a white crust over the hazelnuts. Place the pan back on the heat and stir until the white crust has turned a golden caramel colour. Scrape out onto a baking tray lined with baking parchment and, using a wooden spoon or spatula, separate them so they don't stick together. Set aside to cool.

6 To serve, dip a large spoon in boiling-hot water and use to scoop the mousse into bowls. Top with the hazelnuts and finish with a drizzle of olive oil and a sprinkling of salt.

7 The mousse can be made up to 2 days in advance and refrigerated until needed. The candied hazelnuts can be made a couple days in advance, too, but they need storing in a sealed container and kept in a dry cool spot.

COFFEE AND TAHINI POTS DE CRÈME

This dessert features all my favourite toasty flavours combined. I am talking about a coffee-infused custard made with brown sugar, mixed with tahini and finished with a dose of caramelised white chocolate. Pot de crème is a form of baked custard that is very similar to crème brûlée. Apart from the obvious lack of caramelised sugar crust, the main difference between the two is the finished texture. Pot de crème is normally made with more milk than the cream-rich brûlée; the latter is also made with more egg yolks. Pot de crème is therefore a touch lighter and a little less rich.

MAKES 6

250 ml (generous 1 cup) whipping (heavy) cream, plus extra to serve
250 ml (generous 1 cup) whole milk
1 tablespoon coarsely ground coffee
4 large egg yolks
50 g (scant ¼ cup, packed) light brown sugar
¼ teaspoon fine sea salt
50 g (1¾ oz) caramelised white chocolate, finely chopped, plus extra for garnish
50 g (3 tablespoons) tahini

1 Pour the cream and milk into a saucepan, add the coffee and whisk to combine. Place over a medium heat, bring to a simmer, then remove the pan from the heat, cover with a lid and set aside for 30 minutes to infuse.

2 Place the pan back on the heat and bring back to a simmer. Meanwhile, put the egg yolks, sugar and salt in a large heatproof bowl and whisk together until smooth and pale. Pour the hot cream over the yolks, whisking as you pour to prevent them from scrambling. Once combined, add the chocolate and leave for a couple minutes before stirring together to combine. Pour in the tahini and stir to combine. Pour the custard through a fine-mesh sieve, straining out all the coffee granules, into a large jug. Cover and set aside for 20–30 minutes or until cooled to room temperature.

3 Preheat the oven to 160°C/140°C Fan (325°F).

4 Place six small glasses in a deep roasting tin (pan) and divide the custard between the glasses. Pour boiling water into the roasting tin so that it comes about halfway up the sides of the custards. Place into the oven and bake for 30–40 minutes or until the custards are set at the edge and have a slight wobble in the centre. Remove and allow to sit in the water for 30 minutes before transferring to the refrigerator for at least 4 hours.

5 To serve, top each custard with a thin layer of grated caramelised white chocolate and a dollop of whipped cream, should you so wish.

6 Once baked the custards can be refrigerated for up to 3 days before serving.

CHOCOLATE ORANGE MERINGUE TUMBLE

Whenever you need a crowd-pleasing dessert that will elicit plenty of oohs and aahs, this is the recipe to go for. Inspired by a dessert made by chef Jeremy Lee, at London's Quo Vadis, this is a giant pile of cocoa-swirled meringues sandwiched together with cream and dotted with orange segments. Table side, it is adorned with lashings of vanilla crème anglaise and a chocolate orange sauce, then finished with a generous scattering of chopped hazelnuts.

SERVES 10

Meringues

5 large egg whites (approximately 200 g/7 oz)
½ teaspoon cream of tartar
300 g (1½ cups) caster (superfine) sugar
2 teaspoons cocoa powder (dutched or natural)

Crème Anglaise

150 ml (scant ⅔ cup) whole milk
150 ml (scant ⅔ cup) whipping (heavy) cream
3 large egg yolks
1 teaspoon vanilla bean paste
50 g (¼ cup) caster (superfine) sugar

Chocolate Orange Sauce

75 g (2½ oz/roughly, a scant ½ cup) dark chocolate (60–65% cocoa solids), melted
1 tablespoon runny honey
100 ml (⅓ cup + 1 tablespoon) orange juice

To Assemble

300 ml (1¼ cups) whipping (heavy) cream, whipped to soft peaks
3 oranges, segmented
75 g (generous ½ cup) hazelnuts, roasted and roughly chopped

1 Preheat the oven to 120°C/100°C Fan (250°F) and line two large baking trays (pans) with baking parchment.

2 For the meringues, add the egg whites and cream of tartar to the bowl of a stand mixer, or use an electric hand mixer and a large mixing bowl. Whisk on medium speed until the egg whites are foamy, then, with the mixer still running, slowly rain in the sugar. Continue whisking until the meringue holds stiff glossy peaks. Dust over about half of the cocoa and fold very briefly until lightly swirled through the meringue. Spoon ten large dollops of meringue onto the prepared trays. Dust with the remaining cocoa and use a skewer to lightly swirl it into the meringue.

3 Bake the meringues for about an hour or until crisp and dry. When fully baked, they can be easily lifted from the baking parchment. Turn off the oven, but leave the meringues inside to cool down slowly. Once fully cooled, the meringues can be stored in an airtight container for 3–4 days.

4 For the crème anglaise, pour the milk and cream into a large saucepan, place over a medium heat and bring to a simmer. Meanwhile, put the egg yolks, vanilla and sugar in a mixing bowl and whisk together until pale. When the milk mixture has reached a simmer, remove it from the heat and pour over the yolk mixture, whisking as you pour to prevent the egg from scrambling. Pour the custard back into the saucepan and cook over a low heat, stirring constantly with a spatula, until the custard reaches between 75 and 85°C (167 and 176°F) or has thickened enough to coat the back of a spoon. Pour the custard into a large jug, cover and refrigerate until needed. The custard can be stored in the refrigerator for up to 4 days.

5 For the chocolate sauce, place the orange juice and honey in a small saucepan and bring to a simmer. With the melted chocolate in a jug, pour a third of the orange juice over the chocolate and stir to combine. Add the remaining orange juice mixture in two additions, stirring well until fully combined before adding more. Once all the juice has been combined you should have a silky-smooth sauce. Cover and set aside at room temperature until ready to use. If you want to make this in advance you can refrigerate it for up to a week, rewarming slightly until fluid.

»»»

6. To assemble the tumble, place four of the meringues onto a large serving platter (preferably one with a rim to encase the sauces), using the whipped cream as an edible glue. Top the first layer of meringues with another three, then two, then one, to create a tower of meringues. Randomly place the orange segments around the tumble.
7. At the table, pour over the two sauces, scatter over the hazelnuts and enjoy!
8. Once assembled the dessert should be served immediately.

A BIG CHOCOLATE CHIP PANCAKE, WITH WHIPPED SALTED MAPLE BUTTER

I love pancakes, but I hate making them, especially for big groups. Standing over the stove making a seemingly unending stack of pancakes isn't my idea of fun. I'd much rather be spending that time with my family or friends or doing practically anything else. Step forward this giant chocolate chip pancake recipe, which eliminates pretty much all the work and replaces it with a gloriously large pancake with a deliciously crisp crust that can be cut into wedges, so everyone gets a piece. To serve, I like to pair it with a whipped butter flavoured with maple syrup. The recipe makes more than you're likely to need but it stores well in the refrigerator and is a great topping for French toast, crumpets or just regular ol' toast. If you prefer, you can just make a simple salted whipped butter.

SERVES 4

Pancake

175 g (1⅓ cups) plain (all-purpose) flour
50 g (¼ cup) caster (superfine) sugar
2 tablespoons malted milk powder
½ teaspoon fine sea salt
1 teaspoon baking powder
½ teaspoon bicarbonate of soda (baking soda)
180 ml (¾ cup) whole milk
2 large eggs
50 g (3½ tablespoons) unsalted butter
75 g (scant ½ cup) chocolate chips, dark or milk chocolate

Whipped and Salted Maple Butter

150 g (1⅓ sticks) unsalted butter, room temperature
2 tablespoons whole milk
50 ml (3½ tablespoons) maple syrup, plus extra to serve
½ teaspoon flaked sea salt
¼ teaspoon vanilla bean paste

Note: Isn't this just a cake? Admittedly, cakes and pancakes, especially this giant pancake, are incredibly similar. One very big difference, though, is the level of sweetness and amount of fat. Pancake batter is considerably less sweet than most cakes and generally includes a lot less fat, giving the pancake a markedly different flavour and texture.

1. To make the maple butter, put the butter and milk in a large bowl and, using an electric mixer, whisk on low speed for 1–2 minutes or until the butter and milk are combined. Increase the speed and whisk until the butter is very soft and pale, about 5 minutes, then add the maple syrup, salt and vanilla and whisk just until fully combined. Scrape into a bowl and set aside until needed.
2. Preheat the oven to 190°C/170°C Fan (375°F).
3. In a large bowl, mix together the flour, sugar, malt powder, salt, baking powder and bicarbonate of soda. In a large jug, whisk together the milk and eggs. Melt 35 g (1 oz) of the butter and pour this into the milk mixture, whisking well to combine. Make a well in the flour mixture and pour in the milk mixture and chocolate chips. Stir together to form a batter. Don't worry about making it perfectly smooth, a few lumps are absolutely fine.
4. Place a 23–25 cm (9–10 in) non-stick or cast-iron frying pan that can subsequently go in the oven over a medium heat. Add the remaining butter and, once melted and foaming, pour in the batter. It should spread easily into an even layer but can be encouraged to do so with the back of a spoon. Immediately transfer the pan to the oven and bake for 20–25 minutes or until the pancake springs back to a light touch. Remove from the oven and set aside for 5 minutes before inverting onto a large plate.
5. Top the pancake with plenty of the whipped butter, and extra maple syrup should you wish, and cut into wedges to serve.
6. Best eaten on the day it is made, whilst still warm.

LAZY BAKED ALASKA

Baked Alaska traditionally consists of a cake base, an ice cream filling and a meringue topping that is placed in the oven, under the grill (broiler), until browned. This version is more of a quick assembly job; one that utilises a couple of shop-bought elements plus a couple of simple homemade ones. The recipe is very much a guide. Using the meringue and ice cream as your base, you can make versions with all manner of ingredients. Brownie offcuts for the base, for example, leftover caramel instead of chocolate sauce or even jam instead of the compote. Whilst I like to make this with vanilla ice cream it would also be wonderful with the Salted Dark Chocolate Sorbet (page 118) or the Milk Chocolate Liquorice Ice Cream (page 121).

SERVES 2

Blueberry Compote

50 g (1¾ oz) blueberries
2 teaspoons caster (superfine) sugar
1 tablespoon lemon juice

Milk Chocolate Sauce

20 g (½ oz) milk chocolate, 40% cocoa solids, finely chopped
30 ml (2 tablespoons) whipping (heavy) cream

Swiss Meringue

1 large egg white
50 g (¼ cup) caster (superfine) sugar
small pinch fine sea salt
¼ teaspoon vanilla bean paste

To serve

20 g (2 tablespoons) salted pretzels or salted peanuts, roughly chopped
2 large scoops vanilla ice cream

1. For the compote, put everything in a small saucepan, place over a medium heat and cook for 2–3 minutes or until the fruit has broken down and the liquid is thick and syrupy. Scrape into a small bowl and set aside until needed. It can also be refrigerated for a couple days before using, if needed.
2. For the chocolate sauce, place everything in a small bowl and heat in a microwave, using short 15-second bursts, until the cream is hot. Stir everything together to form a smooth sauce. Set aside until needed. The sauce will thicken as it cools, so stir to loosen when needed. The sauce can also be refrigerated for a couple days before using, but once refrigerated it will firm up and will need heating slightly to loosen.
3. When ready to serve, make the meringue topping. Add everything to a heatproof bowl and place over a pan of simmering water. Whisk until the mixture is hot to the touch and the sugar has fully dissolved. Remove and use an electric mixer to whisk until the meringue holds stiff glossy peaks, about 3–4 minutes.
4. To assemble, divide your pretzels/peanuts between two coupe/martini glasses or other small bowls. Top with a scoop of ice cream and use an ice cream scoop or spoon to press down on the ball of ice cream to create a small well. Add the compote and then the sauce atop the ice cream. Spoon or pipe over the meringue. Use a kitchen blowtorch to burnish the meringue until it's as dark as you want.
5. Serve immediately.

BONET

The French have Crème Caramel and the Spanish have Crema Catalana. Bonet, which comes from the Piedmont region, is the Italian member of this trio. A similarly baked custard, it takes a diversion when it comes to flavour, and instead of vanilla, the custard is made with a mix of cocoa, almond liqueur and amaretti cookies. The result is a more textured custard with deep cocoa notes and a strong flavour of bitter almond.

SERVES 8

Caramel

150 g (¾ cup) caster (superfine) sugar
25 ml (2 tablespoons) boiling water

Custard

4 large eggs
125 g (½ cup + 2 tablespoons) caster (superfine) sugar
1 teaspoon vanilla bean paste
50 g (⅔ cup) cocoa powder (dutched or natural)
¼ teaspoon fine sea salt
550 ml (scant 2⅓ cups) whole milk
50 ml (3½ tablespoons) amaretto
100 g (3½ oz) crisp amaretti, finely crushed (don't use the soft variety)

To Serve

40 g (1½ oz) crisp amaretti
whipped cream

Tip: If a layer of caramel sticks to the inside of the tin after the dessert has been un-moulded, dip the tin into very hot water until the caramel is liquid enough to pour over the dessert.

1. To make the caramel, put the sugar and water in a saucepan, place over a medium heat and cook, without stirring, until the sugar has dissolved and caramelised to a deep copper colour. Pour this caramel into the base of a 450 g (1 lb) loaf tin (pan), gently tipping it so the caramel evenly covers the base of the tin. Set aside until the caramel has set, 15 minutes or so.
2. Preheat the oven to 160°C/140°C Fan (325°F).
3. For the custard, put the eggs, sugar, vanilla, cocoa and salt in a large bowl and whisk gently, just until combined. Try not to aerate this mixture too much. Pour in the milk and amaretto and stir to combine. Then stir through the crushed amaretti.
4. Pour the custard into the loaf tin and transfer to a large roasting tin (pan). Fill the larger dish with boiling water so that it comes about halfway up the sides of the loaf tin. Carefully transfer to the oven and bake for about an hour or until the edges of the custard are set but there is still a gentle wobble in the middle. Remove the roasting tin from the oven and then carefully remove the loaf pan from the water bath, allowing the custard to cool to room temperature for 30 minutes before transferring to the refrigerator for at least 4 hours or until thoroughly chilled, preferably overnight.
5. To serve, run a knife around the sides of the loaf tin to release the custard. Carefully invert onto a large plate or platter, making sure it has a rim to contain the caramel, which will have liquified in the refrigerator. Crumble the remaining amaretti over the top and serve in slices with a little whipped cream.
6. Once baked, the custard can be refrigerated for up to 3 days before serving.

IRISH CREAM TRIFLE POTS

If you love a glass of Baileys at Christmas but the bottle then languishes at the back of the shelf for the rest of the year, this is the perfect recipe in which to use it before the festive season rolls around again. Made with chocolate cake, a white chocolate cream and an Irish cream custard it feels decidedly retro but it's also a guaranteed crowd-pleaser. I've given a recipe for the chocolate cake, but if you want to make this even easier you can use shop-bought instead. I like to serve these with some maraschino cherries but you can leave them out if you wish.

SERVES 6–8

Chocolate Cake

50 g (3½ tablespoons) unsalted butter, diced
150 ml (scant ⅔ cup) black coffee
1½ tablespoons cocoa powder (dutched or natural)
50 g (1¾ oz) dark chocolate (70% cocoa), finely chopped
170 g (¾ cup, packed) light brown sugar
¼ teaspoon fine sea salt
1 large egg
75 ml (5 tablespoons) buttermilk
140 g (1 cup + 2 tablespoons) plain (all-purpose) flour
1 teaspoon bicarbonate of soda (baking soda)

White Chocolate Cream

450 ml (1¾ cups + 2 tablespoons) whipping (heavy) cream
½ teaspoon vanilla bean paste
120 g (4¼ oz) white chocolate, chopped

Irish Cream Custard

350 ml (scant 1½ cups) whole milk
150 ml (scant ⅔ cup) Irish cream liqueur, plus extra for soaking the cake
75 g (¼ cup + 2 tablespoons) caster (superfine) sugar
4 large egg yolks
25 g (scant ¼ cup) cornflour (cornstarch)
pinch fine sea salt

1 Preheat the oven to 180°C/160°C Fan (350°F) and line a 450 g (1 lb) loaf tin (pan) with a strip of baking parchment, so that parchment overhangs the long sides of the pan, securing it in place with metal binder clips.

2 For the chocolate cake, put the butter and coffee into a saucepan and place over a medium heat until the butter is fully melted. Remove from the heat and add the cocoa and chocolate and stir until fully combined. Add the sugar and salt and mix to combine. Add the egg and buttermilk and whisk until smooth. Sift in the flour and bicarbonate of soda and whisk briefly, just until a smooth batter is formed.

3 Scrape the batter into the prepared loaf pan. Bake for about 35 minutes or until the cake springs back to a light touch and is starting to pull away from the sides of the tin. Remove from the oven and allow to cool in the tin for 10 minutes before using the parchment to lift the cake onto a wire rack to cool completely.

4 To make the white chocolate cream, put the cream and vanilla in a saucepan, place over a medium heat and bring to a simmer. Meanwhile, put the chocolate in a bowl. Pour half the hot cream over the chocolate and set aside for a couple minutes before stirring together to form a smooth ganache. Add the remaining cream, stirring until smooth. Cover and refrigerate until needed, at least 4 hours.

5 To make the custard, put the milk, Irish cream and half the sugar in a large saucepan, place over a medium heat and bring to a simmer. Meanwhile, put the remaining sugar, egg yolks, cornflour and salt in a bowl and whisk together until smooth. Pour over the hot milk mixture, whisking as you pour to prevent the eggs from scrambling. Pour the custard back into the pan and cook, whisking constantly, until the mixture is bubbling and has thickened. Cook for a further minute before scraping into a bowl. Press a sheet of cling film (plastic wrap) onto the surface of the custard, to prevent a skin from forming, and refrigerate until needed but at least 4 hours.

»»»

To Assemble

180 ml (¾ cup) Irish cream liqueur
200 g (1 cup) jarred maraschino cherries (optional)
cocoa powder or grated chocolate, for garnish

Note: I prefer to use dark maraschino cherries, sold in a rich cherry syrup, not the brightly coloured red cocktail cherries.

6 To assemble, slice the cake into small cubes and place into the base of 6–8 glasses. Drizzle a couple tablespoons of Irish liqueur into each glass, to moisten the cake, and then scatter over the maraschino cherries. Remove the custard from the refrigerator and beat until smooth. Divide between the glasses. Remove the cream from the refrigerator, whisk, just until the cream holds soft peaks, and spoon over custard. Finish with either a dusting of cocoa powder or a little grated chocolate.

7 The assembled trifles are best on the day they are made but benefit from a few hours' rest in the refrigerator before serving. The pre-made elements can all be made up to 2 days in advance.

CHOC ICES

A childhood favourite in the UK, choc ices consist of vanilla ice cream coated in chocolate. For this easy version, the ice cream is a no-churn affair dipped into dark chocolate to create a thin shell. Whilst you might be tempted to add all manner of other flavours, which you obviously can, I would encourage you to leave these unadorned and revel in their simplicity.

MAKES 8

Vanilla Ice Cream

375 ml (generous 1½ cups) whipping (heavy) cream
2 teaspoons vanilla bean paste
pinch of fine sea salt
200 g (⅔ cup) sweetened condensed milk

Chocolate Coating

150 g (5½ oz) dark chocolate, 60–70% cocoa solids, roughly chopped
150 g (5½ oz) milk chocolate, 40–45% cocoa solids, roughly chopped
3 tablespoons coconut oil (see Note page 75)

1 Lightly grease a 20 cm (8 in) square cake tin (pan) and line with two strips of baking parchment, so the sides and base are lined and a little extra parchment hangs over the sides. You'll be able to use this parchment to lift the ice cream from the pan once frozen.

2 Put all the ingredients for the ice cream in a large bowl and whisk together just until the mixture holds soft peaks. Scrape into the prepared tin and spread into an even layer. Wrap the pan well with cling film (plastic wrap) and freeze for at least 4 hours, preferably overnight.

3 To make the coating, melt both chocolates using either a double boiler or a microwave (see page 24), then mix in the coconut oil, stirring well until combined. The oil will keep this mixture fluid for hours, so it doesn't need using immediately; just be sure to leave it to cool for at least 30 minutes before using so it doesn't melt the ice cream. To make dipping the ice creams easier, pour the chocolate mixture into a tall glass that is just a little wider than the ice cream bars.

4 Remove the ice cream from the freezer and, using the baking parchment to aid you, carefully it remove from the tin. Cut the ice cream into eight bars. Line a small baking tray, one that fits into your freezer, with baking parchment. Insert a cocktail stick (toothpick) or skewer in one end of one of the bars and use it to dip the bar into the chocolate, making sure to coat it completely. Allow any excess chocolate to drip back into the glass. The ice cream will very quickly start to set the chocolate coating. Once it loses its shine, carefully set the bar onto the baking tray and gently remove the cocktail stick. Once all the bars have been dipped, transfer the tray to the freezer for 30 minutes before transferring the bars to a freezerproof container.

5 Kept frozen, the bars will keep for up to a month but the texture of the ice cream will be at its best in the first 2 weeks. The leftover chocolate can be stored in the refrigerator and reheated to use as a sauce for ice cream for up to 2 months.

MALTED CHOCOLATE PANNA COTTA

Inspired by the malted milkshakes that originated in American soda shops, this panna cotta is layered to create a visually impressive dessert that is actually much easier to make than you might imagine.

SERVES 4

Malt Layer

1½ sheets gelatine
150 ml (scant ⅔ cup) whipping (heavy) cream
100 ml (⅓ cup + 1 tablespoon) whole milk
25 g (2 tablespoons, packed) light brown sugar
2 tablespoons malted milk powder
½ teaspoon vanilla bean paste
pinch fine sea salt

Milk Chocolate Layer

1½ sheets gelatine
150 ml (½ cup + 2 tablespoons) whipping (heavy) cream
125 ml (½ cup) whole milk
15 g (1 tablespoon, packed) light brown sugar
½ teaspoon vanilla bean paste
pinch fine sea salt
50 g (1¾ oz) milk chocolate, chopped

To Serve

grated milk chocolate
a little whipped cream
cocktail cherries

1. For the malt layer, put the gelatine in a small bowl, cover with ice-cold water and set aside for 5 minutes or until softened. Put the cream, milk, sugar, malt powder, vanilla and salt in a small saucepan and whisk together, over a medium heat, until the malt has fully dissolved and the mixture is at a simmer. Remove from the heat. Lift the gelatine from the bowl, squeeze out any excess water, add to the cream mixture and stir to combine. Divide the mixture between four dariole moulds. Refrigerate for a couple hours or until set.
2. For the chocolate layer, put the gelatine in a small bowl, cover with ice-cold water and set aside for 5 minutes or until softened. Put the cream, milk, sugar, vanilla and salt in a small saucepan and stir until the mixture is at a simmer. Remove from the heat. Lift the gelatine from the bowl, squeeze out any excess water, add to the cream mixture and stir to combine. Add the chocolate to the still-hot cream mixture and leave for a couple minutes before stirring together to combine.
3. Divide the mixture between the four dariole moulds. Refrigerate again for a couple hours or until fully set.
4. To un-mould, dip the moulds into a bowl of hot water for a couple seconds then carefully invert onto a small serving plate. To serve, grate over a little milk chocolate and top with a dollop of whipped cream and a cocktail cherry.
5. Before being un-moulded, and if kept in the refrigerator, the panna cotta will keep for up to 5 days. If storing for an extended period, make sure to cover the panna cotta to prevent them absorbing any odours from the refrigerator.

DINNER PARTY CAKE, AKA DOUBLE BAKED FLOURLESS CHOCOLATE CAKE

This is my go-to dinner party dessert. It's simple, can be made ahead, and is an absolute showstopper, guaranteed to go down a storm. The cake batter is a pretty classic flourless one; the difference lies in the method used to bake it. Half is baked as usual, then the remaining batter is added on top. The cake then gets a brief second bake, just until the crust is set. The top layer remains as light and airy as a chocolate mousse whilst the bottom layer is closer to a fudge brownie. Because this is a flourless cake it also happens to be gluten free. Take the dessert to the next level and serve in a puddle of nutmeg-infused crème anglaise.

SERVES 8–10

Flourless Chocolate Cake

250 g (9 oz) dark chocolate (70–80% cocoa solids)
250 g (9 oz) unsalted butter, diced
6 large eggs, separated
120 g (½ cup + 1 tablespoon, packed) light brown sugar
120 g (½ cup + 2 tablespoons) caster (superfine) sugar
¼ teaspoon cream of tartar
¼ teaspoon fine sea salt

Nutmeg Crème Anglaise

300 ml (1¼ cups) whipping (heavy) cream
300 ml (1¼ cups) whole milk
1 whole nutmeg
6 large egg yolks
1 teaspoon vanilla bean paste
100 g (½ cup) caster (superfine) sugar

To Serve

cocoa powder

Note: You can also use a 23 cm (9 in) springform tin (pan) if that is what you have, but you'll end up with less-defined layers.

As the recipe does use a lot of eggs, you could skip making the custard, simply infuse the same amount of nutmeg into 600 ml (20 fl oz/2½ cups) whipping (heavy) cream and refrigerate until needed, using as a sauce or whipping to soft peaks.

1. Preheat the oven to 180°C/160°C Fan (350°F). Lightly grease a 20 cm (8 in) round springform cake tin (pan) and line the base and sides with baking parchment.

2. Melt the chocolate and butter in a bain-marie (see page 24). Remove from the heat and set aside to cool slightly. Put the egg yolks and brown sugar in a large bowl set over a pan of simmering water and, using an electric hand mixer, whisk for 2–3 minutes or until the mixture is pale and thick. Remove the bowl from the heat, pour in the chocolate mixture and fold together to combine.

3. Working quickly, wash the beaters of the mixer. Put the egg whites, caster sugar, cream of tartar and salt in another large bowl and whisk until the meringue holds soft peaks. Fold a third of the meringue into the chocolate batter, then the remainder in two additions, folding gently until the mixture is streak free.

4. Pour half the batter into the prepared tin, spreading gently into an even layer. Bake for 25–30 minutes or until risen and domed on top. Remove and allow to cool for 10 minutes. During this time the centre of the cake should cave in on itself a little. If it stays level, use a spoon to lightly compress the cake, creating a slight well. Scrape the remaining batter over the cake and gently spread into an even layer. Bake for 15 minutes. The top layer will remain very soft but it will have formed a thin crust.

5. Leave to cool to room temperature before transferring to the refrigerator and leaving for at least 6 hours, but preferably overnight.

6. To make the crème anglaise, pour the cream and milk into a saucepan. Grate about a third of a single nutmeg into the pan, stir to combine, then bring the mixture to a simmer over a medium heat. Meanwhile, put the egg yolks, vanilla and sugar in a mixing bowl and whisk until pale. Pour over the cream mixture, whisking as you do so, to prevent the eggs from scrambling. Pour the custard back into the saucepan, place over a low heat and cook, stirring constantly, until the custard thickens enough »»»

to coat the back of a spoon. To ensure the custard is fully cooked it needs to reach between 75 and 80°C (167 and 176°F). Pour the custard into a jug, cover with cling film (plastic wrap), to prevent a skin from forming, and refrigerate until thoroughly chilled, at least 2 hours. You can also serve the custard warm, but I absolutely love it cold, so this is my preference.

7 To serve, carefully un-mould the cake, very gently peel away the parchment from the sides, and dust with cocoa powder. To get the cleanest slices, dip a knife in very hot water, wiping it dry with a kitchen cloth after each slice. Serve the slices in a puddle of the crème anglaise.

8 The cake can be refrigerated for up to 3 days.

CHOCOLATE AND PASSION FRUIT SEMIFREDDO

If you like the idea of making ice cream at home but think you'd only do so once or twice a year, an ice cream machine can seem an expensive bit of kit. Thankfully, semifreddo, the original no churn ice cream, creates a delicious frozen treat without any specialist equipment. This version uses my favourite combination of passion fruit and chocolate to create the perfect summertime dessert.

SERVES 8

Semifreddo

300 ml (1¼ cups) whipping (heavy) cream
200 g (7 oz) dark chocolate (75–85% cocoa solids)
2 large eggs
2 large egg yolks
125 g (½ cup + 2 tablespoons) caster (superfine) sugar
2 tablespoons liquid glucose (or honey or corn syrup)
1 teaspoon vanilla bean paste

Passion Fruit Sauce

125 g (generous ½ cup) passion fruit pulp (from about 6 passion fruit)
50 g (¼ cup) caster (superfine) sugar
juice ½ lime
½ teaspoon cornflour (cornstarch)

To Serve

macadamias, toasted and roughly chopped
whipped cream

1. Line a 450 g (1 lb) loaf tin (pan) with a double layer of cling film (plastic wrap), leaving plenty hanging over the sides.
2. To make the semifreddo, pour the cream into a large bowl and whisk until it holds soft peaks. Set aside. Place the chocolate into a bowl and melt, using either a bain-marie or a microwave (see page 24). Set aside to cool a little, but don't let it sit for too long as it still needs to be slightly warm.
3. Put the eggs, egg yolks, sugar, glucose and vanilla in a large heatproof bowl, place over a pan of simmering water and cook, whisking with an electric hand mixer, until the mixture has tripled in volume. Remove the bowl from the heat and continue to whisk just until the mixture has cooled slightly, a minute or so. Pour in the chocolate and fold to combine.
4. Fold a third of the whipped cream into the chocolate mixture, then the remainder in two additions. Once streak free, pour into the prepared tin. Fold the excess cling film over the semifreddo so that it is fully sealed. Transfer to the freezer and leave until completely frozen, at least 6 hours but preferably overnight.
5. Scoop the passion fruit pulp into a small saucepan, add the sugar and heat for a couple minutes until the sugar has dissolved and the mixture has come to a simmer. Meanwhile, put the lime juice and cornflour in a small bowl and whisk together to form a slurry. Pour into the pan and cook, whisking constantly, until the mixture has thickened slightly and is bubbling. Cook for a further minute before scraping into a small bowl. Press a sheet of cling film onto the surface of the sauce, to prevent a skin from forming, and chill until needed. The amount of cornflour will seem incredibly small, but all we are doing is giving the sauce a little body, not trying to make it thicken like a pastry cream.
6. To serve, cut slices of the semifreddo and top with passion fruit sauce, a sprinkling of toasted macadamias and a dollop of whipped cream.
7. The semifreddo will keep for about a month in the freezer, but the texture will be at its best within the first week.

PASTRY

DARK CHOCOLATE CHOUX À LA CUSTARD

Choux à la crème, a choux bun filled with whipped cream, is a French classic. In this recipe, I have replaced the cream with an intense dark chocolate custard. My preference is to make this with a chocolate that contains 85% cocoa solids, which means it has a robust chocolate flavour that is balanced by the dairy and sugar. If your taste is for something a little sweeter, you can substitute this with one that contains around 70% cocoa solids; I wouldn't go much lower than this, because the sweetness will start to dominate.

MAKES 15

Choux Pastry

1 x Choux Pastry (page 228)

Craquelin

50 g (⅓ cup + 1 tablespoon) plain (all-purpose) flour
50 g (¼ cup) caster (superfine)
large pinch fine sea salt
50 g (3½ tablespoons) unsalted butter, diced

Filling

2 x Chocolate Pastry Cream, made with dark chocolate (85% cocoa solids) (page 232)

To Finish

icing (confectioner's) sugar

1 To make the craquelin, put the flour, sugar and salt in a bowl and mix to combine. Add the butter and rub together until a crumbly dough is formed. Gently press together to form a uniform dough with no lumps of butter. Place the dough between two sheets of baking parchment and roll out to a thickness of 2 mm (1⁄10 in). Freeze until needed.

2 Preheat the oven to 190°C/170°C Fan (375°F). Line a large baking tray (pan) with parchment.

3 Scrape the choux dough into a piping bag fitted with a small round piping tip, no more than 1 cm (½ in) wide. Pipe rounds, about 4–5 cm (2 in) in diameter, onto the tray, leaving plenty of space for the choux to expand.

4 Remove the craquelin from the freezer and peel back the top layer of parchment. Use a round cookie cutter, the same size as your rounds of choux, to cut out discs of the craquelin. Place a disc on top of each mound of choux.

5 Bake the choux buns for 30 minutes until golden. Turn off the oven and open the oven door briefly to release any steam. Close the door and allow the buns to cool slowly, in the oven, for 20–30 minutes.

6 Remove the pastry cream from the refrigerator and beat until smooth. Scrape into a piping bag fitted with a small round piping tip, no wider than 1 cm (½ in). Use a pairing knife to make a small hole on the bottom of each bun and pipe full of custard. Finish with a dusting of icing sugar.

7 Unfilled buns will keep for a couple days, but once filled they're best served that same day.

BLACKBERRY ANISE ÉCLAIR

Whilst the combination of dark chocolate and raspberry is incredibly popular, it isn't really one I enjoy; I find the balance of flavour is often wrong and the whole thing tastes too acidic. When it comes to pairing dark chocolate with a berry my preferred partner is blackberry. I also like to add a hint of liquorice, which helps bring together the flavours of the fruit and chocolate.

MAKES 10

Choux Pastry

1 x Choux Pastry (page 228)
a little beaten egg, or oil spray and icing (confectioner's) sugar

Blackberry Star Anise Jam

300 g (10½ oz) blackberries
225 g (1 cup + 2 tablespoons) caster (superfine) sugar
4 tablespoons lemon juice
3 star anise

Chocolate Filling

1 x Chocolate Pastry Cream, made with dark chocolate (85% cocoa solids) (page 232)

Chocolate Glaze

75 g (2½ oz) dark chocolate (60–70% cocoa solids)
20 g (1½ tablespoons) unsalted butter, diced
½ tablespoon liquid glucose (or corn syrup or honey)

To Finish

cocoa nibs or grated chocolate

Tip: Éclairs conform to the shape they're piped, which means the neater you can pipe them the better the finished shape will be. Try to use a steady hand and apply even pressure as you pipe.

1 To make the jam, put all the ingredients into a medium saucepan, place over a high heat and bring to a rolling boil. Cook for 10–15 minutes or until the jam reaches 104°C (219°F). You can also test the jam is fully cooked by spooning a little onto a plate which has been chilled in the freezer. Leave for a minute before pressing with your finger; if the jam wrinkles it is ready. If not, cook a little longer. Pour the jam into a sterilised jar and refrigerate until needed.

2 Preheat the oven to 220°C/200°C fan (425°F).

3 Line a large baking tray (pan) with baking parchment and, on the back of the parchment, draw ten 12 cm (5 in) lines to act as your template. Scrape the choux pastry into a piping bag fitted with a 16 mm (½ in) French star piping tip. If you don't have one of these, a round piping tip of roughly the same diameter will also work. Pipe ten éclairs, using the lines as a guide.

4 To ensure my éclairs rise evenly and don't crack, I spray a very thin layer of oil (the type used to line cake tins) over them and then dust with a thin layer of icing sugar. Alternatively, lightly brush them with a little beaten egg. Place the éclairs in the oven, close the door and immediately reduce the heat to 180°C/160°C Fan (350°F). Bake the éclairs for 35–40 minutes until golden. Turn off the oven and open the door briefly to allow any steam to escape. Allow the éclairs to slowly cool down, in the oven, for 30 minutes. Remove and allow to cool fully.

5 To assemble, make three small holes along the length of the bottom of each éclair. Remove the pastry cream from the refrigerator, beat until smooth and scrape into a piping bag fitted with a small round piping tip. Scrape the jam into a second piping bag, also fitted with a small round piping tip. Pipe a little jam into each hole of the éclair and repeat with the pastry cream, filling until the cream starts to escape, scraping off any excess.

6 To make the glaze, put all the ingredients in a small bowl set over a pan of simmering water and cook until everything is melted and smooth. Set aside until slightly thickened. Dip the top of each éclair into the chocolate, allowing any excess to drip back into the bowl. Sprinkle over a few cocoa nibs or grated chocolate.

7 Once assembled the éclairs are best on the same day, but all the elements can be made up to 2 days in advance, if needed.

SALTED PBJ TARTS

I may not have grown up eating peanut butter and jelly sandwiches, but the combination is one that I revisit often. In this recipe the peanut element is a salty peanut frangipane instead of peanut butter. The frangipane layer is topped first with raspberry jam and then a generous amount of whipped vanilla ganache.

MAKES 6

Pastry

6 x Sweet Pastry tart shells, partially baked (page 218)

Vanilla Ganache

½ sheet gelatine
125 g (4½ oz) white chocolate
300 ml (10 fl oz/1¼ cups) whipping (heavy) cream
½ vanilla pod

Salty Peanut Frangipane

60 g (scant ½ cup) salted peanuts
75 g (⅔ stick) unsalted butter, room temperature
75 g (¼ cup + 2 tablespoons) (caster (superfine) sugar
1 large egg
30 g (⅓ cup) ground almonds (almond flour)
½ tablespoon plain (all-purpose) flour

Filling and Decoration

180 g (generous ½ cup) raspberry jam
2 tablespoons salted peanuts, roughly chopped

Tip: If you want, you can break the work up over a couple days, making the pastry and vanilla ganache on day one and doing the baking and assembly on day two.

1 For the vanilla ganache, put the gelatine in a bowl of ice-cold water. Set aside for 5 minutes until softened. Put the chocolate in a large heatproof jug and melt, using the microwave (see page 24). Meanwhile, pour the cream into a saucepan. Slice the vanilla pod in half, along its length, scrape out the seeds and add to the pan. Bring the cream to a simmer, then remove from the heat. Lift the gelatine from the water, squeeze out any excess moisture, then stir into the cream until dissolved. Pour a third of the cream over the chocolate and stir to combine. Pour in the remaining cream, in two additions, stirring well until fully combined. If you have one, finish with a brief blend using a stick blender, to ensure the ganache is thoroughly emulsified. Cover with cling film (plastic wrap) and refrigerate for at least 4 hours.

2 Preheat the oven to 180°C/160°C Fan (350°F).

3 To make the frangipane, put the peanuts in a food processor and pulse until they are finely ground. Peanuts have a high oil content, so if you grind them for too long you'll get peanut butter. You won't end up with anything quite as fine as the ground almonds but that's okay. Put the butter and sugar in a mixing bowl and, using an electric mixer, beat together for about 5 minutes until light and fluffy. Add the egg and beat to combine. Finally, add the almonds, peanuts and flour and mix to form a smooth batter.

4 Divide the frangipane between the six tart shells, spread evenly, then bake for 12–15 minutes or until the frangipane is lightly browned. Remove and set aside to cool. The frangipane shouldn't quite reach the top edge of the pastry, as you'll need a little space for the jam layer. If it does, use a spoon to gently scrape away a thin layer.

5 Spoon 120 g (4¼ oz) of the jam over the frangipane, spreading it in an even layer. Remove the ganache from the refrigerator and whisk until it just starts to hold soft peaks. Scrape it into a piping bag fitted with a large round piping tip and pipe a large mound of the ganache atop each pastry. Using a small measuring spoon that has been dipped in hot water, press the top of the ganache mounds to create small divots. Fill these with the reserved jam. Decorate the sides with a little sprinkle of peanuts.

6 The assembled tarts are best on the day they're baked but can be refrigerated for 2–3 days. The pastry will soften as they sit.

COCOA ECCLES CAKES

Since my mum is a proud Lancastrian, Eccles Cakes, made with flaky pastry and filled with a sweet and syrupy currant mixture, were a big part of my childhood and a treat that I still very much enjoy today. This particular version is far from traditional, but the flavour of chocolate goes well with both the dried fruit and the spicing, lending extra depth.

MAKES 8

Pastry

½ x Cocoa Rough Puff Pastry (page 230)
flour, for dusting

Filling

200 g (1½ cups) dried currants
100 g (scant ½ cup, packed) light brown sugar
50 g (3½ tablespoons) unsalted butter, diced
2½ tablespoons cocoa powder (dutched or natural)
zest 1 orange
1 teaspoon freshly grated nutmeg
½ teaspoon ground cinnamon
1 teaspoon ground allspice
large pinch flaked sea salt

To Coat

1 large egg white, lightly beaten
demerara sugar

1. For the filling, put everything in a large saucepan, place over a low to medium heat and cook, stirring occasionally, until the butter is melted and the mixture is smooth and evenly combined. Pour into a bowl, cover, and refrigerate overnight.
2. On a lightly floured work surface, roll out the pastry into a 35 × 40 cm (13½ in x 15½ in) rectangle. Cut out eight circles of pastry with a diameter of 12 cm (4½ in). Remove the filling from the refrigerator and divide it into eight equal portions. Press these portions together to form eight 'pucks'. Place one puck on each circle of pastry. Brush the border of the pastry with a little water, then fold the pastry over the filling and press it together to seal. Flip the cakes over, so they are seam-side down, then roll or press lightly to flatten them into puck-shaped discs.
3. Brush each cake with a thin layer of egg white, add a generous sprinkling of demerara sugar, then use a sharp knife to cut three slashes. Place the cakes on a large baking tray (pan) lined with baking parchment and refrigerate for 30 minutes whilst you preheat the oven to 200°C/180°C Fan (400°F).
4. Bake the cakes for 20–22 minutes until the pastry is dry and crisp and there is syrup bubbling out of the vent holes. Remove and set aside until fully cooled.
5. Kept in a sealed container these will keep for at least a couple days, but I prefer them on the day they are made, still a touch warm. Despite the addition of cocoa powder, these are still delicious served alongside cheese, preferably of the Lancashire variety.

BISTRO PROFITEROLES

Choux pastry, ice cream and chocolate sauce, it doesn't get much simpler than that. It also creates a crowd favourite that has stood the test of time, profiteroles. To elevate them slightly, I like to add a layer of craquelin, which results in very neat, pleasingly sweet, crisp buns.

SERVES 4

Choux Pastry

50 ml (3½ tablespoons) water
20 ml (1½ tablespoons) whole milk
¼ teaspoon fine sea salt
¼ teaspoon caster (superfine) sugar
35 g (2½ tablespoons) unsalted butter, diced
35 g (4½ tablespoons) plain (all-purpose) flour
1 large egg

Craquelin

50 g (¼ cup) caster (superfine) sugar
50 g (¼ cup + 2 tablespoons) plain (all-purpose) flour
pinch of fine sea salt
50 g (3½ tablespoons) unsalted butter, diced

Chocolate Sauce

75 g (2½ oz) milk chocolate, finely chopped
75 g (2½ oz) dark chocolate, finely chopped
150 ml (scant ⅔ cup) whipping (heavy) cream
50 ml (3½ tablespoons) whole milk

To Serve

1 × 460ml (1 US pint) shop-bought vanilla ice cream

1 To make the craquelin, put the sugar, flour and salt in a bowl and combine. Add the butter and rub together until a crumbly dough is formed. Gently press together to form a dough with no lumps of butter. Place the dough between two sheets of baking parchment and roll out to a thickness of 2 mm (⅛ in). Freeze until needed.

2 Preheat the oven to 190°C/170°C Fan (375°F) and line a large baking tray (pan) with baking parchment.

3 To make the choux pastry, put the water, milk, salt, sugar and butter in a saucepan and place over a low heat. Cook until the butter is melted, then increase the heat and bring to a rolling boil. Add the flour all at once and stir vigorously to form a dough. Stir on the heat for 1–2 minutes or until a thin film forms on the bottom of the pan.

4 Tip the dough into a bowl and beat for a few minutes to cool slightly. Add the egg and beat until fully combined. The finished dough should have a slight gloss and when lifted from the bowl should fall from the spatula in a V-shaped ribbon.

5 Scrape the pastry into a piping bag fitted with a small round piping tip and pipe into 12 small 3 cm (1¼ in) wide rounds. Remove the craquelin from the freezer and use a 3 cm (1¼ in) round cookie cutter to cut out discs of the dough. Place one atop each round of pastry.

6 Bake in the preheated oven for 25 minutes until golden. Turn off the oven and briefly open the oven door to allow any steam to escape. Allow the buns to cool in the oven for about 25 minutes, this prevents them collapsing.

7 To make the sauce, put the two chocolates in a large jug and melt in the microwave (see page 24). Pour the cream and milk into a saucepan and place over a medium heat. Bring to a simmer, then remove the pan from the heat and pour a third of the liquid over the chocolate, stirring to combine. Add the remaining cream in two additions, stirring well until the mixture is smooth and silky. Use whilst still warm.

8 To serve, slice the choux buns in half and fill each with a small scoop of ice cream. Serve three buns per person and top with a generous pour of the chocolate sauce. If you want to make these in advance the baked choux buns can be stored in a sealed container for up to two days.

Images overleaf »

HAZELNUT AND MAPLE MILK CHOCOLATE TART

Another of my all-time favourite desserts is the maple tart served at Clamato in Paris. This simple tart consists almost solely of thickened maple syrup and a generous dollop of whipped cream. That delightful dessert inspired this combination of milk chocolate, hazelnut and maple, one I think you'll want to use time and time again. As this recipe has a lot of elements, I suggest making it over a couple days.

SERVES 10–12

Pastry

1 x Sweet Pastry tart shell, fully baked (page 218)

Hazelnut Frangipane

75 g (⅔ stick) unsalted butter, room temperature
75 g (¼ cup + 2 tablespoons) caster (superfine) sugar
½ teaspoon vanilla bean paste
1 large egg
1 large egg yolk
40 g (scant ½ cup) ground almonds (almond flour)
40 g (scant ½ cup) finely ground toasted hazelnuts
½ tablespoon plain (all-purpose) flour
¼ teaspoon baking powder
¼ teaspoon fine sea salt

Maple Filling

50 g (3½ tablespoons) unsalted butter
50 g (6 tablespoons) plain (all-purpose) flour
300 g (¾ cup + 2 tablespoon) maple syrup
35 ml (2 tablespoons) water
large pinch of flaky sea salt

Chocolate Topping

125 g (4½ oz) milk chocolate (preferably 50% cocoa solids), finely chopped
125 ml (4 fl oz/½ cup) whipping (heavy) cream
15 g (1 tablespoon) unsalted butter, diced
small handful chopped hazelnuts, for decoration

1 Preheat the oven to 180°C/160°C Fan (350°F).

2 For the frangipane, beat together the butter, sugar and vanilla until light and fluffy, about 5 minutes. Add the egg and beat to combine before mixing in the egg yolk. Add the remaining ingredients and beat until a smooth batter is formed. Scrape this into the tart case, spread into an even layer, and bake in the oven for 20–25 minutes or until the frangipane is set and feels firm to the touch. Remove and set aside until fully cooled. The frangipane should fill the tart about halfway full. If it has risen more than that, you can use a spoon to gently shave away any excess.

3 For the maple filling, put the butter in a medium-sized saucepan and place over a medium heat. Cook until the butter is melted, then add the flour and cook, stirring occasionally, for about 2 minutes. Pour in the maple syrup and water and cook on a low simmer for 15–20 minutes or until reduced and thickened to a caramel-like consistency. Pour into the tart case, spread into an even layer and refrigerate for a couple hours. Once chilled, sprinkle with a little flaky sea salt.

4 Put the chocolate in a large heatproof jug and melt, using the microwave (see page 24). Pour the cream into a small saucepan, place over a medium heat, bring to a simmer, then pour a third over the chocolate and stir to combine. Add the remaining cream in two additions, stirring together until smooth and silky. Add the butter and stir until fully combined. Pour the ganache atop the chilled maple layer and very gently spread to cover. Finish by scattering over some roughly chopped hazelnuts. Refrigerate until the ganache is set.

5 Kept refrigerated this tart will keep for 2–3 days. Whilst best stored refrigerated it will taste better if served after a couple hours at room temperature.

TAHINI MILK CHOCOLATE PARIS-BREST

Traditionally made with a hazelnut praline filling, my modern take on this French classic is filled with a tahini crème mousseline and a milk chocolate ganache. For additional texture, I like to add a sesame craquelin to the choux pastry, giving the finished pastry a fun and delicious black and white decoration.

SERVES 8–10

Choux Pastry

1 x Choux Pastry (page 228)

Sesame Craquelin

60 g (½ cup) plain (all-purpose) flour
60 g (¼ cup + 1 tablespoon) caster (superfine) sugar
1 tablespoon white sesame seeds
1 tablespoon black sesame seeds
large pinch fine sea salt
60 g (¼ cup) unsalted butter, diced

Tahini Crème Mousseline

250 ml (1 generous cup) whole milk
1 vanilla pod
75 g (¼ cup + 2 tablespoons) caster (superfine) sugar
75 g (⅓ cup, packed) light brown sugar
2 large egg yolks
25 g (3 tablespoons) cornflour (cornstarch)
75 g (generous ¼ cup) tahini
200 g (1¾ sticks) unsalted butter, room temperature

Milk Chocolate Filling

100 g (3½ oz) milk chocolate (preferably 40% cocoa solids), finely chopped
120 ml (½ cup) whipping (heavy) cream

To Finish

a little icing (confectioner's) sugar
a few sesame seeds

Tip: Both the butter and tahini crème should be at room temperature when combined. If either are too cold the mousseline may split.

1 To make the craquelin, put the flour, sugar, sesame seeds and salt in a bowl and combine. Add the butter and rub together until a crumbly dough is formed. Gently press together to form a uniform dough with no lumps of butter. Place the dough between two sheets of baking parchment and roll out to a thickness of 2 mm (⅛ in). Freeze until needed.

2 Preheat the oven to 190°C/170°C Fan (375°F). Line a large baking tray (pan) with baking parchment and, on the back, draw a circle with a diameter of 20 cm (8 in).

3 Scrape the pastry into a piping bag fitted with a small, 1 cm (½ in), round piping tip and pipe two rings of pastry, one just inside the circle template and one just outside, ensuring both are touching all the way around. Pipe a third ring on top of the first two, along the seam. Remove the craquelin from the freezer and cut out a ring the same size as the choux and place atop the pastry.

4 Bake in the oven for 35–40 minutes or until golden brown. Briefly open the oven door to allow any steam to escape, then turn off the oven and allow the choux pastry to cool down slowly inside for about 30 minutes.

5 For the mousseline filling, pour the milk to a large saucepan. Cut the vanilla pod open along its length and scrape out the seeds. Add both the seeds and the pod itself to the milk, place over a medium heat and bring to a simmer. Remove from the heat and cover, setting aside for 30–60 minutes to infuse.

6 Place the pan back on the heat, add the caster sugar and bring to a simmer. Meanwhile, put the brown sugar, egg yolks and cornflour in a large bowl and whisk until smooth. Pour over the hot milk, whisking as you pour to prevent the yolks from scrambling. Remove the vanilla pod. Pour the custard back into the pan and cook, whisking constantly, until the mixture has thickened and is bubbling. Cook for a further minute then scrape into a bowl and whisk through the tahini. Cover and set aside for about an hour, to cool to room temperature. Ideally the tahini crème will have a temperature of about 20°C (68°F). If you want to make this ahead of time you can refrigerate it for up 3 days, but you must ensure it is brought up to temperature before using. »»»

7 Add the butter to the bowl of a stand mixer and, with the paddle attachment, beat for 5 minutes or until light and creamy. Add the tahini custard, a little at a time, beating until fully combined before adding more. Once all the tahini custard has been added, switch to the whisk attachment and mix for 5 minutes until light and fluffy.

8 For the chocolate filling, put the chocolate in a small bowl and melt, using either a bain-marie or microwave (see page 24). Pour the cream into a small saucepan, bring to a simmer, then pour a third over the chocolate, stirring to combine. Add the remaining cream in two additions, stirring well to form a smooth and silky ganache. Leave at room temperature until a pipe-able consistency.

9 Scrape the two fillings into separate piping bags, fitted with a 2 cm (1 in) star-shaped tip for the mousseline and a small round piping tip for the chocolate ganache. Use a serrated knife to slice the choux ring in half, horizontally. Pipe most of the chocolate filling into the base, then pipe all of the mousseline on top, in any style you prefer. Place the other half of choux back on top of the filling and dust with a little icing sugar. Pipe the remaining chocolate on top of the choux pastry and sprinkle with a few extra sesame seeds.

10 Once assembled the Paris-Brest is best consumed on the same day.

BAKED CHOCOLATE TARTS WITH HONEYED ORANGES

If you've ever made a simple ganache-filled tart, you'll find these baked chocolate tarts are a step up. Made with eggs, a mix of dark and milk chocolate and then baked, the resulting filling is both luxurious and silky. It is partnered with fragrant honeyed orange segments and a simple vanilla whipped cream.

MAKES 6

Pastry

6 x Sweet Pastry tart shells, fully baked (page 218)

Chocolate Filling

125 g (4½ oz) dark chocolate (60–70% cocoa solids), finely chopped
100 g (3½ oz) milk chocolate (40–50% cocoa solids), finely chopped
125 ml (generous ½ cup) whipping (heavy) cream
125 ml (generous ½ cup) whole milk
50 g (¼ cup, packed) light brown sugar
1 large egg
pinch fine sea salt

Honeyed Oranges

2 large oranges
1 tablespoon runny honey

Topping

180 ml (¾ cup) whipping (heavy) cream
¼ teaspoon vanilla bean paste
1 tablespoon caster (superfine) sugar

1 Preheat the oven to 160°C/140°C Fan (325°F) and line a baking tray (pan) with baking parchment.

2 For the filling, put the chocolates in a large heatproof jug and melt, using the microwave (see page 24). Pour the cream, milk and sugar into a saucepan and bring to a simmer. Remove the pan from the heat and pour a third over the chocolate and stir to combine. Add the remaining cream mixture in two additions, stirring together until smooth and silky. Lightly beat the egg and salt with a fork, then add to the chocolate mixture and, using a spatula, stir until smooth to form the custard. Try to incorporate as little air as possible to ensure the silkiest texture.

3 Place the tart shells on the baking tray and pour in the custard, filling them completely to the top. Carefully transfer to the oven and bake for 10–12 minutes until the edges are just set and the centres are still wobbly. Remove and set aside until fully cooled.

4 Peel and segment the oranges, place in a small bowl and set aside for the moment. Take the remaining orange flesh, squeeze into a small saucepan, extracting as much juice as possible, and add the honey. Bring to the boil over a medium heat, then reduce the heat slightly and cook at a simmer for 4–5 minutes or until the liquid has reduced to a syrupy consistency. Pour this over the orange segments and stir to combine.

5 For the topping, put everything into a large bowl and whisk until the cream holds medium peaks. Spoon cream onto each of the tarts, then spoon over some of the honeyed oranges.

6 Without the toppings, the tarts will keep for 2 days. They are best stored in the refrigerator but brought to room temperature before serving. Add the toppings just before you want to serve the tarts.

BLACK BOTTOM COCONUT CREAM PIE

When people say they don't like coconut I nod my head and pretend I understand but, honestly, I don't get it. Coconut is delicious! When paired with chocolate, we're talking a top-tier flavour pairing! On the surface, this appears to be just a classic coconut cream pie, but it is hiding a delicious secret – under the layers of whipped cream and toasted coconut custard lies a silky chocolate ganache, making it completely irresistible!

SERVES 8

Pastry

½ x Flaky Pie Dough (page 220), fully baked as a single pie crust

Chocolate Filling

100 g (3½ oz) dark chocolate (60% cocoa solids), finely chopped
180 ml (¾ cup) whipping (heavy) cream
15 g (1 tablespoon) unsalted butter, diced and at room temperature

Coconut Custard

80 g (1 cup) desiccated (dried shredded) coconut
400 ml (13½ fl oz) can coconut milk
1 teaspoon vanilla bean paste
3 large egg yolks
1 large egg
125 g (½ cup + 2 tablespoons) caster (superfine) sugar
40 g (5 tablespoons) cornflour (cornstarch)
large pinch fine sea salt
2 tablespoons dark rum (optional)

Topping

150 ml (scant ⅔ cup) whipping (heavy) cream
¼ teaspoon vanilla bean paste

1 For the filling, put the chocolate in a heatproof bowl or jug and melt (see page 24). Put the cream into a small saucepan and bring to a simmer. Remove from the heat, pour a third over the chocolate and stir to combine. Add the remaining cream in two additions, stirring well to form a silky smooth ganache. Add the butter and stir until smooth. If you have one, finish with a brief blend using a stick blender, to ensure the ganache is thoroughly emulsified. Pour the ganache into the pie crust and spread into an even layer. Refrigerate until the ganache is set, about an hour.

2 For the coconut custard, put the coconut into a large saucepan, place over a medium heat and cook, stirring occasionally, until it is golden. Remove a couple tablespoonfuls and set aside for the garnish. Pour in the coconut milk and vanilla bean paste and bring to a simmer. Meanwhile, put the egg yolks, egg, sugar, cornflour and salt in a large bowl and whisk until smooth. Pour the hot coconut milk over the egg mixture, whisking as you pour to prevent the eggs from scrambling. Pour the custard back into the saucepan and cook, whisking constantly, until the mixture has thickened and is bubbling. Cook for a further minute then scrape back into the bowl. Pour in the rum, if using, and whisk to combine. Allow the custard to cool for 5 minutes before pouring into the pie and spreading into an even layer. Press a piece of cling film (plastic wrap) onto the surface of the custard, to prevent a skin from forming, and refrigerate for a couple hours.

3 To serve, put the cream and vanilla in a large bowl and whisk until the cream holds soft peaks. Spread over the pie and scatter with the reserved coconut.

4 Kept refrigerated, the pie will keep for up to 3 days.

RUSTIC PLUM AND HAZELNUT GALETTE

If, when making pastry, a lattice crust or a crimped decorative border are words that make you recoil in horror, then this simple galette is probably more your speed. The flaky pastry is filled with a hazelnut and cocoa frangipane and then topped with plenty of sliced plums. Don't worry about it being picture perfect; a rustic appearance makes it look more inviting.

SERVES 8

Pastry

½ x Cocoa Rough Puff Pastry (page 230)
flour, for dusting
beaten egg, for egg wash
demerara sugar, for garnish

Cocoa and Hazelnut Frangipane

50 g (3½ tablespoons) unsalted butter, room temperature
50 g (¼ cup) caster (superfine) sugar
1 large egg
¼ teaspoon vanilla bean paste
50 g (½ cup) finely ground hazelnuts
15 g (3 tablespoons) cocoa powder (dutched or natural)
¼ teaspoon fine sea salt

Plum Filling

5 plums, ripe but firm
1 tablespoon caster (superfine) sugar
15 g (1 tablespoon) unsalted butter, diced into small pieces

1 To make the frangipane, place the butter and sugar in a large bowl and, using an electric mixer, beat together for 5 minutes or until light and fluffy. Add the egg and vanilla and beat to combine. Don't worry if the mixture looks a little curdled, it'll come back together once the remaining ingredients are added. Add the hazelnuts, cocoa and salt and beat until a smooth batter is formed. Set aside.

2 For the filling, slice the plums in half and remove the stones (pits). Slice each half in two and then each quarter into four slices.

3 To assemble, line a large baking tray (pan) with baking parchment. Roll out the pastry on a lightly floured work surface into a circle roughly 35 cm (13 in) in diameter. Lift onto the lined tray, allowing the excess pastry to hang over the sides for the moment. Spread the frangipane mixture in a 25 cm (10 in) wide circle over the pastry, leaving a 5 cm (2 in) border around the edge. Arrange the plum slices in concentric circles on top of the frangipane. Sprinkle the sugar over the plums and finish by dotting the pieces of butter randomly over the top of the plums. Fold the pastry border up and over the plums and then transfer the galette to the refrigerator for 30 minutes whilst you preheat the oven.

4 Preheat the oven to 190°C/170°C Fan (375°F) and, if you have one, place a baking stone or steel on the centre rack. This will help ensure the base of the pastry is beautifully crisp.

5 Just before baking, brush the pastry border with the beaten egg and sprinkle liberally with demerara sugar. Bake in the oven for about 45 minutes. Check after 20 minutes and if the pastry or filling is browning too quickly, lightly tent the galette with foil to prevent it from burning. The galette is baked when the pastry feels firm and crisp.

6 Remove from the oven and allow to cool before serving. You can serve it whilst still a little warm with custard or ice cream. Store by wrapping the baking tray with foil and refrigerating for 2–3 days, gently reheating in the oven before serving, or simply serve it cold.

COCOA CARDAMOM PALMIERS

These are not your average palmiers. Made with my Cocoa Rough Puff Pastry, they're laminated with cardamom sugar and finished with a coating of white chocolate, resulting in an incredibly flaky treat. Traditionally, they are made with a double swirl, resulting in a pastry that supposedly looks like elephant ears, another name given to this recipe. In this version they're baked as simple squares.

MAKES 16

75 g (⅓ cup) granulated sugar
1 teaspoon finely ground cardamom
pinch fine sea salt
½ x Cocoa Rough Puff Pastry (page 230)
flour, for dusting

To Coat

200 g (7 oz) white chocolate, preferably tempered (see page 30)

1. In a small bowl, whisk together the sugar, cardamom and salt.
2. On a lightly floured work surface, roll out the pastry into a square roughly 24 cm (9½ in) wide, then cut it into three 8 cm (3 in) strips. Brush or spray the top of the first strip with a very small amount of water, just enough to moisten the surface. Sprinkle over 2 teaspoons of the cardamom sugar. Brush or spray the top of the second strip with water, as before, and place it, moistened side down, on top of the sugar on the previous strip. Repeat a second time so that you have three layers of pastry. Wrap the pastry in cling film (plastic wrap) and roll lightly to compress, which will help the layers to stick together. Refrigerate for an hour.
3. Preheat the oven to 190°C/170°C Fan (375°F) and line two large baking trays (pans) with baking parchment.
4. Slice the stacked pastry into 16 strips, each roughly 15 mm (½ in), and dip both cut sides in the remaining sugar. Place eight on each of the baking trays, cut side up, setting them well apart to allow for spreading. Bake for 25–28 minutes until dry and crisp, rotating the trays halfway through baking. Remove from the oven and set aside until fully cooled.
5. If you want to elevate these even further, you can coat them in tempered white chocolate. Place the chocolate in a bowl and dip the palmiers halfway in, allowing any excess chocolate to drip back into the bowl. Place them back on the baking tray and leave until the chocolate has fully set, at least 30 minutes.
6. Kept in a sealed container these will be good for a couple days. If you want to avoid tempering the chocolate, you can dip the palmiers in melted white chocolate, but they will need storing in the fridge and they'll be best served on the day they're made.

LEMON CRUNCH TARTS

These beautiful tarts are all about the contrast in texture and flavour: a sharp and silky lemon cream (an adaption of lemon curd) is partnered with a crispy caramelised white chocolate layer hiding underneath. Together they combine to make a lemon tart like you've never had before.

MAKES 6

Pastry

6 x Sweet Pastry tart shells, fully baked (page 218)

Lemon Cream

75 ml (5 tablespoons) lemon juice
zest 2 lemons
1 large egg
1 large egg yolk
75 g (¼ cup + 2 tablespoons) caster (superfine) sugar
115 g (1 stick) unsalted butter, diced and at room temperature

Caramelised Crunch Layer

40 g (1¼ cups) puffed rice cereal
85 g (3oz/roughly ½ cup) caramelised white chocolate, plus a little extra for garnishing
¼ teaspoon flaked sea salt

1. To make the lemon cream, put the lemon juice, zest, egg, yolk and sugar in a metal bowl set over a pan of boiling water, making sure the bowl isn't touching the water, and whisk to combine. Cook, stirring constantly with the whisk, until the mixture has reached 80–82°C (176–179°F). This can take up to 10 minutes. Remove the bowl from the heat and pour the curd through a fine-mesh sieve (to remove the zest) into a large jug. Set aside until the temperature of the curd has cooled to 50–60°C (122–140°F), about 10 minutes.
2. Add the butter, a piece or two at a time, using a stick blender to combine, then cover the curd with cling film (plastic wrap) and refrigerate until thoroughly chilled, about 4 hours.
3. Preheat the oven to 190°C/170°C Fan (375°F).
4. For the crunch layer, pour the puffed rice cereal onto a rimmed baking tray (pan) and bake for 7–8 minutes until lightly toasted and smelling nutty and almost popcorn-like. Remove and set aside to cool.
5. Melt the chocolate in a microwave or bain-marie (see page 24) then pour in the toasted cereal and the salt and mix thoroughly until the cereal is evenly coated. Spoon the mixture into the cooled tart shells, gently compacting it into even layers that fill the tarts roughly halfway. Spoon over the lemon cream, spreading it into even layers that are flush with the rim of the tart shells. Refrigerate for at least an hour before serving.
6. To serve, use a microplane to grate a thin layer of caramelised white or milk chocolate on top of the tarts.
7. Stored in the refrigerator in an airtight container, these will last for a couple days after assembly.

CHERRY BERRY BLACK FOREST PIE

This pie is what happens if you take the flavours of a classic Black Forest Gâteau and swap the cake element for a flaky pie crust. This crust is filled with a mixture of cherries and blackberries and then topped with a moreish streusel. To serve, you can either make a vanilla whipped cream or add another chocolate element in the form of White Chocolate Whipped Ganache (page 234), made without the gelatine.

SERVES 8–10

Pastry

½ x Flaky Pie Doughl (page 220), partially baked, as a single crust pie shel

Streusel

135 g (generous 1 cup) plain (all-purpose) flour
45 g (½ cup) cocoa powder (dutched)
115 g (½ cup + 1 tablespoon) caster (superfine) sugar
¼ teaspoon flaked sea salt
135 g (9½ tablespoons) unsalted butter, melted

Fruit Filling

450 g (1 lb) blackberries
450 g (1 lb) cherries, pitted and halved
165 g (¾ cup + 1 tablespoon) caster (superfine) sugar
5 tablespoons cornflour (cornstarch)
juice ½ lemon
1 teaspoon vanilla bean paste

whipped cream or Whipped White Chocolate Ganache (page 234), to serve

1. For the streusel, add the flour, cocoa, sugar and salt to a small bowl and whisk to combine. Pour in the butter and stir with a fork until a crumbly streusel mixture is formed. Press together to form a ball of dough. Refrigerate for at least an hour before using. The streusel can be made up to three days in advance.
2. For the filling, add the fruit to a large bowl and scatter over 120 g (4¼ oz) of the sugar. Stir together and set aside for at least an hour to macerate, longer if possible. If using frozen fruit allow to thaw fully before macerating, noting that as the fruit defrosts it will also release a lot of liquid. In a small bowl whisk together the remaining sugar and the cornflour.
3. Preheat the oven to 180°C/160°C Fan (350°F).
4. Once the fruit is sat in a generous puddle of juice, pour the mixture through a fine-mesh sieve into a saucepan, setting the fruit aside for now. Cook the liquid over a medium heat until reduced to 50–60 ml (3–4 tablespoons). Remove the pan from the heat and add the lemon juice and vanilla bean paste and stir to combine. Add the cornflour mixture and whisk to form a slurry. Pour this mixture over the fruit and stir to combine.
5. Pour the filling into the partially baked pie crust and spread into an even layer. Remove the streusel from the refrigerator and crumble over the filling. Bake the pie for 50–60 minutes or until the fruit filling is bubbling around the edges of the pie. Remove the pie from the oven and set aside until fully cooled.
6. Serve with a dollop of whipped cream or Whipped White Chocolate Ganache (page 234).
7. Best served on the day it is made, but if refrigerated it is good for up to 3 days after baking.

LIME AND COCONUT MILK CHOCOLATE TWICE-BAKED CROISSANTS

If an almond croissant is your go-to bakery order, this lime and coconut version might just be your new favourite pastry. Not only does it have a punchier flavour than the traditional almond version, the addition of milk chocolate means it tastes like a cross between an almond croissant and a pain au chocolat.

MAKES 4–6 PASTRIES

Croissants

6 small or 4 large croissants, stale
1 x Cocoa Nib Simple Syrup (page 235)

Lime Coconut Frangipane

100 g (7 tablespoons) unsalted butter, room temperature
100 g (½ cup) caster (superfine) sugar
zest of 2 limes
1 large egg
¼ teaspoon vanilla bean paste
large pinch fine sea salt
50 g (½ cup) ground almonds (almond flour)
50 g (generous ½ cup) desiccated (dried shredded) coconut
60 g (2 oz/roughly ⅓ cup) roughly chopped milk chocolate

Topping

40 g (½ cup) desiccated (dried shredded) or flaked coconut (un-toasted)

Note: For a more intense lime flavour, make the Cocoa Nib Syrup with the juice of 2 limes in place of an equal amount of water. If you don't want to make a flavoured syrup, you can also make a simplified version using just sugar and water.

1. Preheat the oven to 180°C/160°C Fan (350°F).
2. To make the frangipane, beat together the butter, sugar and lime zest for about 3 minutes or until light and creamy. Add the egg and vanilla and beat briefly, just until combined. Add the salt, almonds and coconut and mix to form a cake-like batter.
3. Slice the croissants in half, horizontally, and brush both cut sides liberally with the cocoa nib syrup. Spoon or pipe a layer of the frangipane across the base of each croissant, using about two-thirds of the frangipane. Sprinkle the chocolate over the frangipane, then cover with the top halves of the croissants. Pipe or spread the remaining frangipane over the tops of the croissants, spreading it into a thin layer. Scatter the reserved coconut atop the croissants.
4. Place the croissants on a baking tray (pan) lined with baking parchment and bake for 15–18 minutes or until the frangipane and coconut topping is golden. Remove and set aside to cool before serving.

VANILLA PECAN TART

If you like your desserts with lots of texture, this is the recipe for you. Rich and warming, the toasted pecans are turned into a praline paste and layered inside a crisp, flaky tart shell, topped with a silky white chocolate cream. This is pure elegance and sophistication.

SERVES 10–12

Pastry

flour, for dusting
½ x Cocoa Flaky Pie Dough (page 220)
1 large egg yolk, lightly beaten

Pecan Praline

100 g (1 cup) pecans
100 g (½ cup) caster (superfine) sugar
¼ teaspoon fine sea salt
25 g (1 oz) milk chocolate, melted

White Chocolate Filling

120 ml (½ cup) whole milk
120 ml (½ cup) whipping (heavy) cream
½ vanilla pod or 1 teaspoon vanilla bean paste
1 sheet gelatine
250 g (9 oz) white chocolate, finely chopped
2 large egg yolks
10 g (2 teaspoons) caster (superfine) sugar

Decoration

grated milk chocolate

1 Preheat the oven to 180°C/160°C Fan (350°F).

2 To make the praline, scatter the pecans across a parchment-lined rimmed baking tray (pan) and toast in the oven for about 10 minutes or until lightly browned. Remove and set aside to cool. Add the sugar to a saucepan, place over a medium heat and cook the sugar until it has melted and caramelised, turning the colour of an old penny, a deep copper colour. Pour the sugar over the pecans and set aside for at least 30 minutes or until set solid. Break the praline into small pieces, place into the bowl of a food processor and blitz until it has broken down into a thin, pourable consistency. This can take up to 10 minutes. If your food processor is feeling hot, turn it off and allow it cool down for a few minutes before continuing. Pour the praline into a bowl and stir through the salt and chocolate. Set aside.

3 On a lightly floured work surface, roll out the pastry to a thickness of 3–4mm (⅛ in) and carefully drape into a 23 cm (9 in) loose-bottomed tart tin (pan), trimming off any excess. Dock the base with a fork and refrigerate for at least 30 minutes.

4 Line the tart shell with a crumpled layer of baking parchment and fill with baking beans. Bake in the preheated oven for about 25 minutes, then carefully lift out the baking beans. Bake the tart shell for a further 5–10 minutes or until the base is dry and crisp. If the pastry has puffed up, gently press it down with the back of a spoon. Brush the inside of the tart shell with the beaten egg yolk, then bake for a further 2 minutes or until the egg is fully set. This keeps the pastry crisp after the filling has been added. Set aside to cool.

5 Pour the praline paste into the base of the tart shell and spread in an even layer. Transfer to the freezer while you make the filling. The praline layer doesn't need to be fully frozen, just set enough that the white chocolate filling can be poured on without disturbing it.

6 To make the filling, pour the milk and cream into a saucepan. Cut the vanilla pod in half, lengthways, and scrape out the seeds. Add both the seeds and the pod itself to the pan. Place over a medium heat, bring to a simmer, then cover, remove from the heat and leave to infuse for 30 minutes.

7 Put the gelatine in a small bowl, cover with ice-cold water, then set aside for 5 minutes until softened. Put the chocolate in a large

heatproof jug and melt in the microwave (see page 24). Place the milk and cream back on the heat and return to a simmer. Meanwhile, whisk together the egg yolks and sugar until pale. Pour the hot cream mixture over the egg yolks, whisking as you do so to prevent the yolks from scrambling. Remove the spent vanilla pod and then pour the custard back into the pan, place over a low heat and cook, stirring constantly, until the custard thickens enough to coat the back of a spoon or reaches 75–80°C (167–176°F). Pour the custard over the chocolate. Remove the gelatine from the water and squeeze out as much liquid as you can. Add it to the custard and stir until silky smooth.

8 Remove the tart from the freezer, pour over the filling and decorate with grated milk chocolate. Transfer to the refrigerator and refrigerate for at least 4 hours or until the chocolate mixture is set.

9 Slice into portions and serve. Kept refrigerated, the tart will keep for up to 2 days.

EARL GREY MILK CHOCOLATE MILLEFEUILLE

Earl Grey will always make me think of my parents, who drink almost nothing else. This fragrant tea, made with bergamot alongside the black tea leaves, works incredibly well when paired with creamy milk chocolate.

MAKES 8

Pastry

½ x Cocoa Rough Puff Pastry (page 230)

Earl Grey Milk Chocolate Filling

225 ml (¾ cup + 3 tablespoons) whole milk
1 vanilla pod
50 g (¼ cup) caster (superfine) sugar
25 g (3 tablespoons) cornflour (cornstarch)
pinch fine sea salt
3 large egg yolks
75 g (2½ oz) milk chocolate (preferably 40% cocoa solids)
25 g (2 tablespoons) unsalted butter, diced
200 ml (¾ cup + 1 tablespoon) whipping (heavy) cream

Notes: The perfect baking tray for this recipe is known as a half sheet pan and measures 45 × 33 cm (17 × 13 in). If this size doesn't fit in your oven, which can be the case with some European ovens, you can use a slightly shorter but slightly wider baking tray, simply rolling out the pastry so it fits what you have. Just make sure the pastry is rolled to a thickness of roughly 3 mm (⅛ in).

The Earl Grey custard can be made up to step 1 and refrigerated 3 days in advance.

1 Pour the milk into a large saucepan. Cut the vanilla pod in half, along its length, and scrape out the seeds. Add both the seeds and the pod itself to the pan, place over a medium heat, bring to a simmer, then remove from the heat, cover with a lid, and set aside to infuse for an hour. Place the pan back on the heat and bring back to a simmer. Meanwhile, put the sugar, cornflour and salt in a bowl and whisk together. Add the egg yolks and whisk until the mixture is smooth and pale, about 30 seconds. Pour over the hot milk, whisking as you pour to prevent the yolks from scrambling. Remove the spent vanilla pod, then pour the custard back into the pan and cook, whisking constantly, until the custard is very thick and has started to bubble. Cook for a further minute then scrape into the bowl. Add the chocolate and butter and stir with the whisk until fully combined, smooth and lump free. Cover with cling film (plastic wrap) and refrigerate for at least an hour.

2 Preheat the oven to 200°C/180°C Fan (400°F).

3 Remove the pastry dough from the refrigerator and, on a lightly floured work surface, roll out into a rectangle slightly larger than 28 × 40 cm (11 × 16 in) then use a sharp knife to trim to size. Place the pastry on a large baking tray (pan) lined with baking parchment. Place a sheet of baking parchment on top of the pastry and place a second baking tray on top. Weigh this down with a loaf tin (pan) filled with baking beans, to keep the pastry from puffing up too much. Bake in the preheated oven for 25 minutes.

4 After the first 15 minutes give the pastry a quick check. If the pastry appears to have puffed up, press down on the top baking tray to gently compress it. After the initial 25 minutes are up, carefully remove the loaf tin and top baking tray and bake the pastry for a further 5 minutes, until crisp and dry. Remove and set aside until fully cooled.

5 Using a serrated bread knife, cut the pastry into three rectangles, cutting along the long length of pastry. Remove the filling from the refrigerator and beat until loose. In a separate bowl, whisk the cream until it holds soft peaks. Fold a quarter of the cream into the filling, then the remainder in three additions. Spread or pipe half the chocolate cream over one of the pastry rectangles, then place a second piece of pastry on top. Spread the remaining pastry cream atop this layer of pastry and finish by laying on the final piece of pastry. Using the absolute sharpest knife you have, cut the long rectangle of millefeuille into eight portions.

6 Best served on the day made.

BLUEBERRY TARRAGON WHITE CHOCOLATE CHEESECAKE TART

When I need a simple crowd-pleasing dessert, a no-bake cheesecake fits the bill perfectly. This white chocolate version uses Biscoff biscuits for a toasty, almost caramelised flavour in the crust and it is topped with a blueberry compote infused with a little tarragon for a beautiful herbal aniseed flavour.

SERVES 10–12

Biscuit Base

- 250 g (9 oz) Lotus Biscoff biscuits (cookies)
- 125 g (1 stick + 1 tablespoon) unsalted butter, melted and cooled
- ½ teaspoon flaked sea salt

White Chocolate Cheesecake

- 150 g (5½ oz) white chocolate, finely chopped
- 115 g (4 oz/½ cup) full-fat cream cheese
- 115 g (4 oz/½ cup) mascarpone
- 125 ml (½ cup) whipping (heavy) cream
- 1 teaspoon vanilla bean paste

Blueberry and Tarragon Compote

- 350 g (12 oz/roughly 2½ cups) blueberries
- 50 g (¼ cup) caster (superfine) sugar
- juice ½ lemon
- 2 tablespoons finely chopped fresh tarragon
- 1 tablespoon cornflour (cornstarch)

1 For the biscuit base, finely crush the Biscoff using either a food processor or by placing the biscuits in a freezer bag and beating with a rolling pin until finely ground. Tip the crumbs into a bowl, add the butter and salt and stir until throughly combined. Tip this mixture into the base of a 23 cm (9 in) loose-bottomed tart tin (pan) and spread, gently pressing it into an even layer. Use a flat-bottomed glass to compact the crust across the base and up the sides of the tin. Refrigerate whilst you make the cheesecake.

2 Put the chocolate in a small bowl and melt, using either a microwave or bain-marie (see page 24). Set aside for about 10 minutes until cool but still fluid. Place the chocolate and all of the remaining cheesecake ingredients in a large bowl and whisk until thick and holding soft peaks. Scrape atop the biscuit base and spread into an even layer.

3 To make the compote, place 250 g (9 oz) of the blueberries, the sugar, lemon juice and tarragon in a saucepan, along with 50 ml (3½ tablespoons) water and bring to the boil over a medium heat. Once at a rolling boil, cook for 3–4 minutes until the fruit is starting to break down and the liquid is slightly reduced. In a small bowl whisk together the cornflour and 2 tablespoons of the liquid from the pan. Pour this slurry into the saucepan and cook, stirring constantly, for a further minute or until you have a jam-like consistency. Scrape the compote into a bowl, cover, and refrigerate until needed.

4 When ready to serve, remove the compote from the refrigerator and stir through the remaining blueberries. Spoon atop the cheesecake, spreading over most of it, but leaving a small border around the edge.

5 Kept refrigerated, the cheesecake will keep for up to 2 days.

BREADS

SOUR CHERRY CUSTARD BUNS WITH COCOA STREUSEL

There are several recipes in this chapter that happily slot into the 'sweet bread for brunch' category, but this may be my favourite. I treat the brioche a little bit like a tart crust, adding a vanilla pastry cream, a sour cherry compote and a sweet and salty cocoa streusel to make an incredibly delicious dish.

MAKES 10

Dough

500 g (4 cups) strong white bread flour
7 g (2¼ teaspoons) fast-action dried yeast (instant yeast)
10 g (½ teaspoons) fine sea salt
30 g (2 heaped tablespoons) caster (superfine) sugar
250 ml (1 cup) whole milk
2 large eggs
100 g (7 tablespoons) unsalted butter, diced and at room temperature
1 large egg, lightly beaten, to coat

Pastry Cream

300 ml (1¼ cups) whole milk
1 teaspoon vanilla bean paste
4 large egg yolks
125 g (½ cup + 2 tablespoons) caster (superfine) sugar
30 g (¼ cup) cornflour (cornstarch)

Cocoa Streusel

80 g (⅔ cup) plain (all-purpose) flour
25 g (⅓ cup) cocoa powder (dutched)
65 g (⅓ cup) caster (superfine) sugar
¼ teaspoon flaked sea salt
80 g (5½ tablespoons) unsalted butter, melted

Sour Cherry Filling

100 g (3½ oz/roughly ½ cup) fresh or frozen sour cherries
2 tablespoons caster (superfine) sugar
juice ½ lemon
1 teaspoon cornflour (cornstarch)

1 To make the dough, put the flour, yeast, salt and sugar in the bowl of a stand mixer and mix briefly to combine. With the dough hook attached, pour in the milk and the eggs and mix together to form a shaggy dough, then, with the mixer on medium/low speed, knead for about 10 minutes or until the dough is smooth and elastic and no longer sticking to the sides of the bowl. Add the butter and continue kneading until fully combined and the dough is once again smooth and elastic, a further 5–10 minutes or so. If you take a little of the dough you should be able to carefully stretch it thin enough to almost see through it. Tip the dough out onto the work surface, shape into a ball, then place it, seam side down, in a lightly greased bowl. Cover and set aside for 20 minutes before transferring to the refrigerator to proof fully overnight. At this point you can leave the dough for up to 2 days before using it. If you want to use the dough on the same day, place it in a lightly greased bowl, cover with cling film (plastic wrap) and set aside until doubled in size, about an hour. If making and using the dough on the same day, be aware that the dough will be a little stickier and harder to handle.

2 To make the pastry cream, put the milk and vanilla in a large saucepan, place over a medium heat and bring to a simmer. Meanwhile, put the egg yolks, sugar and cornflour into a large bowl and whisk until smooth. When the milk has reached a simmer, pour onto the yolk mixture, stirring with the whisk as you do so. Pour the custard back into the pan and cook, whisking constantly, until the custard is bubbling and has thickened. Continue to cook for a further minute before scraping into a clean bowl. Cover with cling film and refrigerate until thoroughly chilled. The pastry cream can be made up to a day in advance.

3 For the streusel, put the flour, cocoa, sugar and salt in a bowl and whisk to combine. Pour in the butter and stir with a fork until a crumbly streusel mixture is formed. Press together into a ball and refrigerate for at least an hour before using. The streusel can be made up to 3 days in advance.

4 For the filling, stone the cherries, if using fresh ones, and place in a saucepan along with the sugar and lemon juice and stir to combine. If using frozen cherries, simply stir everything together to combine. Cook over a medium heat for about 2 minutes or until the fruit has released lots of juice and the mixture is starting to bubble. Meanwhile, mix together the lemon juice and cornflour to form a slurry. Scrape this into the pan and cook, stirring »»» constantly, for a further minute or so until the liquid has thickened and formed a gel-like texture. Scrape into a bowl, cover with cling film, and refrigerate until needed. The filling can be made and refrigerated up to 2 days in advance.

5 Tip the dough out onto the work surface, knock back and divide into 10 equal portions. Form each piece into a neat ball and place on two large parchment-lined baking trays (pans), spaced well apart, then press each ball into a flat 7.5 cm (3 in) wide 'puck'. Lightly cover the buns with cling film and set aside until they have doubled in size, about an hour if the dough was at room temperature, up to 2 hours if the dough was refrigerated.

6 About half an hour before the buns are ready to bake, preheat the oven to 180°C/160°C Fan (350°F).

7 Remove the fillings and toppings from the refrigerator. Beat the pastry cream until smooth. Use your fingers to press a depression in the centre of each of the proofed buns, about 4–5 cm (2 in) wide. Spoon pastry cream into the depression and top with the cherry compote. Brush the border of the buns with beaten egg, then crumble the streusel topping over this border.

8 Bake for 18–20 minutes or until the brioche is golden brown. Remove and set aside to cool. These are best on the day made but they can also be frozen for up to a month and refreshed in a hot oven for 5 minutes.

HAZELNUT BUNS WITH SALTED BUTTER CRAQUELIN

If you've made choux pastry before, it's very possible you've come across craquelin, a thin dough that is sometimes added to choux before baking. What you may not know is that it can also be used with bread. The thin dough browns as it bakes, giving these brioche buns a light crisp top, a wonderfully textural element in an otherwise very soft recipe. Whilst these buns are delicious served simply as they are, I couldn't resist adding a caramelised white chocolate and hazelnut cream filling.

MAKES 6

Brioche Dough

250 g (2 cups) strong white bread flour
5 g (scant 1 teaspoon) fine sea salt
7 g (2¼ teaspoons) fast-action dried yeast (instant yeast)
15 g (1 tablespoon) caster (superfine) sugar
120 ml (½ cup) whole milk
1 large egg
50 g (3½ tablespoons) unsalted butter, room temperature

Craquelin

75 g (scant ⅔ cup) plain (all-purpose) flour
75 g (⅓ cup, packed) light brown sugar
pinch flaked sea salt
75 g (⅔ stick) unsalted butter, diced

Caramelised White Chocolate Filling

150 g (5½ oz) caramelised white chocolate
300 ml (1¼ cups) whipping (heavy) cream
100 g (⅓ cup + 1 tablespoon) smooth hazelnut paste/butter (see Note)

Decoration

chopped hazelnuts, to decorate (optional)

1. To make the craquelin, put the flour, sugar and salt in a bowl and combine. Add the butter and rub together until a crumbly dough is formed. Press together to form a uniform dough with no lumps of butter. Place the dough between two sheets of baking parchment and roll out to a thickness of 2 mm (⅛ in). Freeze until needed.
2. For the filling, place the chocolate into a heatproof bowl and melt, using either a bain-marie or the microwave (see page 24). Pour the cream into a saucepan, place over a medium heat and bring to a simmer. Remove from the heat and pour a third of the cream over the chocolate, stirring to combine. Add the remaining cream in two additions, stirring well until smooth and silky. Add the hazelnut butter and stir until smooth and everything is evenly combined. Cover and refrigerate for at least 4 hours before using.
3. For the brioche, add the flour, salt, yeast and sugar to the bowl of a stand mixer and briefly mix to combine. With the dough hook attached, add the milk and egg and mix together to form a shaggy dough. On medium/low speed, knead until the dough is smooth and elastic, about 10 minutes. Add the butter and knead for a further 5–10 minutes or until the dough is again smooth and elastic. If you want to make this in advance, place the dough in a lightly greased bowl, cover with cling film and set aside for 20 minutes before transferring to the refrigerator to rest for up to 2 days. If using immediately, place in a lightly greased bowl, cover with cling film and set aside until doubled in size, about an hour.
4. Tip the dough out onto the work surface, knock back and divide into six equal portions, roll each piece into a neat ball and place on a large parchment-lined baking tray (pan). Lightly cover the buns with cling film and set aside until they have doubled in size, about 60 minutes if the dough was at room temperature, up to 2 hours if the dough was refrigerated.
5. Peheat the oven to 180°C/160°C Fan (350°F).
6. Remove the craquelin from the freezer and, using a 7 cm (2 in) round cookie cutter, cut out six discs, then place one on top of each ball of dough. Bake in the preheated oven for 18–20 minutes or until the craquelin and the visible dough are both golden brown. Remove and set aside until fully cooled. To assemble, slice

Note: Hazelnut paste is a smooth paste made from 100% hazelnuts, with no additional sugar. When it contains sugar it should be referred to as 'praline paste'. I like to use versions made specifically for baking, as they are incredibly smooth, but you can also use 'hazelnut butter', which should also be made with 100% hazelnuts, but tends not to be quite as smooth as the paste.

the buns in half. Remove the filling from the refrigerator and whisk just until it holds soft peaks. It can very easily become grainy and over-whisked, so it is best to do this by hand rather than use an electric mixer. Spoon some of the filling atop the base of each bun then sandwich with the tops, pressing together until the cream is just peaking out of the sides. Sprinkle a few chopped hazelnuts over any cream that is peeking out the sides of the buns.

7 Best served on the day made.

VANILLA CUSTARD BUNS WITH MILK CHOCOLATE GLAZE

This recipe is inspired by the Danish Fastelavnsboller, which translates as festival bun. The festival in question is the Danish equivalent of Shrove Tuesday or Mardi Gras. The bun comes in all manner of shapes and sizes and pinning down an exact definition is tricky, but generally it is a sweet, cream-filled bun, at least in Denmark (it varies across other Scandinavian countries). Here, I've filled them with a vanilla pastry cream, which is lightened with whipped cream and then finished with a shiny milk chocolate glaze. To make them as light and as soft as possible, I use a cooked flour paste, commonly referred to as tangzhong, which helps the buns retain moisture and ensures a pillowy soft result.

MAKES 6

Milk Bread

250 g (2 cups) strong white bread flour
135 ml (½ cup + 1 tablespoon) whole milk
5 g (1 scant teaspoon) fine sea salt
5 g (2 teaspoons) fast-action dried yeast (instant yeast)
25 g (2 tablespoons) caster (superfine) sugar
1 large egg, plus one for the egg wash
50 g (3½ tablespoons) unsalted butter, diced and at room temperature

Vanilla Cream Filling

225 ml (scant 1 cup) whole milk
½ vanilla pod
3 large egg yolks
50 g (¼ cup) caster (superfine) sugar
25 g (3 tablespoons) cornflour (cornstarch)
pinch fine sea salt
20 g (1½ tablespoons) unsalted butter, diced
100 ml (scant ½ cup) whipping (heavy) cream

Milk Chocolate Glaze

50 g (1¾ oz) milk chocolate
35 ml (2½ tablespoons) whipping (heavy) cream
1 tablespoon golden syrup, liquid glucose or corn syrup
pinch fine sea salt

1 To make the vanilla cream filling, pour the milk into a medium saucepan and place over a medium heat. Cut the vanilla pod in half lengthways, scrape out the seeds and add both the seeds and pod itself to the milk. Bring to a simmer, place a lid on the pan, remove from the heat and set aside for an hour to infuse. Put the pan back on the heat and return to a simmer. Meanwhile, put the egg yolks, sugar, cornflour and salt in a large bowl and whisk until smooth. Pour over the hot milk, whisking as you do so to prevent the yolks from scrambling. Pour the custard back into the saucepan and return to the heat. Cook, whisking constantly, until the custard is bubbling and thick. Once the custard is bubbling, cook for a further minute before scraping into a bowl and whisking in the butter. Once smooth, remove the vanilla pod (saving it for another use, see page 22), cover with cling film (plastic wrap) and refrigerate until needed.

2 To make the milk bread, first make the tangzhong paste. Put 20 g (2½ tablespoons) of the flour and 80 ml (2½ fl oz) of the milk in a small pan, place over a medium heat and cook, stirring constantly, until the mixture forms a thick paste. Scrape this into a small bowl, pour over the remaining milk and set aside for 5 minutes.

3 Put the remaining flour with the salt, yeast and sugar into the bowl of a stand mixer fitted with the dough hook, mixing briefly to combine. Pour in the remaining milk, flour paste and egg and mix on low speed to form a shaggy dough, then knead, on medium/low, for about 10 minutes until smooth and elastic. Add the butter and continue kneading until the butter has been fully absorbed and the dough is once again smooth and elastic and no longer sticking to the sides of the bowl, this can take up to 10 minutes. Shape the dough into a ball and place, seam side down, in a lightly greased bowl. Cover with cling film (plastic wrap) or a damp tea towel and set aside until doubled in size, about 60–90 minutes. You can also let the dough rise for 20 minutes before transferring to the refrigerator for up to 2 days, if you want to prepare the dough ahead of time. »»»

4 Tip out the dough and press down to knock out all the air. Divide it into six equal portions, then roll each piece into a neat ball by folding the edges of the dough back onto itself. Doing this a few times will create a ball with a taut skin. Place the balls, seam side down, onto a large parchment-lined baking tray (pan). Lightly cover with cling film or a damp tea towel and set aside until doubled in size, about 60 minutes (longer if the dough was refrigerated).

5 Preheat the oven to 200°C/180°C Fan (400°F).

6 Brush the buns with the beaten egg, then bake for 12–15 minutes or until golden brown. Remove and set aside until cooled to room temperature.

7 Remove the pastry cream from the refrigerator and beat with a spatula until silky and smooth. In a large bowl, whisk the cream to soft peaks. Gently fold a third of the cream into the pastry cream, then, when fully combined, fold in the remaining cream in two additions. Spoon the mixture into a piping bag fitted with a 1 cm (½ in) round piping tip. Use a small paring knife to make a hole in the base of each bun, then push the piping tip into the middle of the bun and pipe full of cream, enough so that it starts to push out of the hole. Repeat with all the buns.

8 For the glaze, put the chocolate in a small heatproof bowl and melt, using the microwave (see page 24). Pour the cream, golden syrup and salt into a small saucepan, place over a medium heat, bring to a simmer, then remove from the heat and pour a third over the chocolate, stirring to combine. Add the remaining cream mixture in two additions, stirring well to form a smooth silky glaze. Set the glaze aside until thickened – about 30–60 minutes. Dip each of the buns into the glaze, allowing any excess to dip back into the bowl. Set aside until the glaze has set, about 30 minutes.

9 These will keep for up to 3 days, but once filled are best served on the same day.

DOUBLE CHOCOLATE NO-KNEAD LOAF

This dramatically dark loaf is adapted from the iconic Jim Lahey no-knead bread. For me, the intense, not too sweet, flavour beautifully encapsulates everything I love about dark chocolate. Obviously, I wouldn't use it for any savoury applications, but it is great served on its own, lightly toasted, spread with salted butter or with Whipped and Salted Maple Butter (page 132) or either of the homemade chocolate spreads on page 245, but it really comes into its own when used to make French toast or bread and butter pudding.

MAKES 1 LARGE LOAF

200 g (1⅔ cups) strong white bread flour
200 g (1⅔ cups) plain (all-purpose) flour
30 g (6 tablespoons) cocoa powder (natural or dutched)
3 tablespoons, packed, light brown sugar
1 g (¼ teaspoon) fast-action dried yeast (instant yeast)
8 g (1½ teaspoons) fine sea salt
125 g (4½ oz/roughly ¾ cup) dark chocolate, roughly chopped
350 ml (scant 1½ cups) water, at a temperature of 20–25°C (68–77°F)

1 This needs a large mixing bowl as the dough will rise significantly overnight. Put the flours, cocoa, sugar, yeast and salt in the bowl and whisk to combine. Brown sugar and cocoa powder can have a tendency to form clumps so you may need to sift them. Add the chocolate and stir briefly stir to distribute.

2 Make a well in the centre of the mixture, pour in the water and use your hands, or a wooden spoon, to stir together to form a very sticky dough. You do not need to knead this dough at all, just mix until there are no dry spots. Cover the bowl with cling film (plastic wrap) and set aside at room temperature for 12–18 hours.

3 The dough is ready when it has risen significantly and the surface is pock-marked with lots of little holes. It will also have gone from being slightly rounded on top to having more of a flat, level top. Turn out onto a work surface liberally dusted with flour and, with floured hands, fold the four sides of the dough over and into the centre to form a ball. Flip over, so the seam is resting on the work surface, and use cupped hands to gently drag the dough towards yourself, developing tension on the surface of the dough. Carefully lift the dough, using a dough scraper to help, and transfer it, seam side down, to a sheet of baking parchment. Cover the dough with a large bowl and leave for 2 hours.

4 Half an hour to an hour before the dough has finished proofing, place a large, lidded, cast-iron pot in an oven that has been preheated to 250°C/230°C Fan (475°F). When ready to bake, the dough should have doubled in size and, if gently poked with a floured finger, an indentation should slowly spring back but not all the way. If it springs back quickly and fills in completely it has not yet finished proofing and, conversely, if it holds the indentation and doesn't spring back at all, it has possibly over-proofed.

5 Remove the pot from the oven and take off the lid. Using a razor blade or very sharp knife, slash a large cross on the top of the dough, then immediately lift it, using the parchment as a sling, and carefully place it inside the pot. Place the lid back on and bake for 20 minutes, then reduce the temperature to 220°C/200°C Fan (400°F) and remove the lid, allowing any steam to escape. Bake for a further 20 minutes, with the lid removed,

until the crust is crisp. Normally, you partially judge the doneness of a loaf through its colour, but as this loaf is much darker this is tricky. I like to bake it as dark as possible without it burning, which takes a total of 40–45 minutes. Remove the loaf from the oven and set onto a wire rack to cool for at least an hour.

6 Homemade bread should stay fresh for 2–3 days, but if you want to store it longer, cut it into slices and place in the freezer, where it will keep for up to 2 months.

BLACKBERRY AND WHITE CHOCOLATE SCONES

People living in the UK are likely to consider these an affront to their much-loved traditional scones. Borrowing more from the American-style scone, these fruity numbers are jam-packed with blackberries and chunks of white chocolate, and then cut into triangles – much like you'd find in coffee shops and bakeries across the US. Definitely not traditional, but absolutely delicious nonetheless.

MAKES 8

365 g (scant 3 cups) plain (all-purpose) flour
2 teaspoons baking powder
½ teaspoon bicarbonate of soda (baking soda)
¼ teaspoon fine sea salt
40 g (3 tablespoons) caster (superfine) sugar
zest 1 lemon
100 g (7 tablespoons) unsalted butter, diced and chilled
100 ml (scant ½ cup) buttermilk, plus extra for brushing the tops of the scones
2 large eggs
1 teaspoon vanilla extract
250 g (9 oz/roughly 1⅔ cups) frozen blackberries
100 g (3½ oz/a scant ⅔ cup) roughly chopped white chocolate
demerara sugar, for garnish

Tip: Using the blackberries whilst they are still frozen prevents them breaking down during the folding process.

1 Preheat the oven to 200°C/180°C Fan (400°F) and line a large baking tray (pan) with baking parchment.

2 Put the flour, baking powder, bicarbonate of soda, salt, sugar and zest in a large bowl and stir to combine. Add the butter and rub into the flour until it is in pea-sized pieces. In a large jug, whisk together the buttermilk, eggs and vanilla. Drizzle in this mixture, stirring together with a knife until a shaggy dough is formed. You can also do the previous step using a food processor; simply add the dry ingredients and the butter to the bowl of a processor and pulse until a coarse crumbly mixture is formed. Pour in the liquid ingredients and pulse briefly, just until a shaggy dough is formed. Tip out the dough onto a work surface and scatter over a third of the blackberries and chocolate, pressing them gently into the dough. Using a dough scraper, fold the dough in on itself, enclosing the fruit and chocolate. Press flat and repeat this process twice more until everything has been mixed into the dough.

3 Press the dough into a 20 cm (8 in) round circle, then cut it into eight triangles. Transfer the scones to the prepared baking tray, brush the tops with a little extra buttermilk, sprinkle liberally with demerara sugar and bake for 18–20 minutes or until golden brown. Remove from the oven and allow to cool before serving.

4 Kept in a sealed container these will keep for 2–3 days, but are best enjoyed as fresh as possible. The scones can also be frozen for a couple months once cut into triangles. Simply allow them to thaw for 30 minutes, whilst the oven preheats, glaze with buttermilk and garnish with demerara and then bake as normal.

COCOA NIB AND VANILLA RING DOUGHNUTS

Not all chocolate recipes need to punch you in the face with flavour, they can also be delicate and subtle, like this perfectly pillowy ring doughnut coated in a vanilla bean cocoa nib sugar. If you want to double down on the chocolate, serve them with a chocolate dipping sauce or a mug of hot chocolate.

MAKES 10–12

Brioche Doughnut Dough

500 g (4 cups) strong white bread flour, plus extra for dusting
50 g (scant ¼ cup, packed) light brown sugar
10 g (1½ teaspoons) fine sea salt
7 g (2¼ teaspoons) fast-action dried yeast (instant yeast)
3 large eggs
200 ml (1 cup + 1 tablespoon) whole milk
150 g (1⅓ sticks) unsalted butter, diced and at room temperature
vegetable oil, for deep frying

Vanilla Bean Cocoa Nib Sugar

200 g (1 cup) caster (superfine) sugar
2 tablespoons Cocoa Nib Vanilla Powder (page 255)

1 To make the dough, put the flour, sugar, salt and yeast in the bowl of a stand mixer and briefly mix to combine. With the dough hook attached, add the eggs and milk and mix to form a shaggy dough, then, on low/medium speed, knead the dough for 10–15 minutes until it is smooth and elastic and no longer sticking to the sides of the bowl. With the mixer still running, slowly add the butter until it is fully absorbed and the dough is once again smooth and elastic. This can take up to 10 minutes. Form the dough into a ball and place, seam side down, in a lightly greased bowl. Cover with cling film (plastic wrap) and set aside for 20 minutes before transferring to the refrigerator to proof slowly overnight. At this point the dough can be refrigerated for up to 2 days.

2 The following day, remove the dough from the refrigerator and roll out on a lightly floured work surface until it's a thickness of about 1 cm (½ in). Using a 7.5 cm (3 in) round cookie cutter, cut out as many doughnuts as you can. Use a 2.5 cm (1 in) round cutter to remove the middle from each doughnut. Place each ring doughnut on an individual square of baking parchment, then place on a large baking tray (pan). Place the doughnut 'holes' on a separate parchment-lined tray. Lightly cover both trays with a damp tea towel or cling film (plastic wrap). Gently re-knead the scraps and roll out as before, cutting out as many doughnuts as you can. You should end up with around 10–12.

3 Set the doughnuts aside for 60–90 minutes or until doubled in size. Place a large saucepan over a medium/low heat and fill three-quarters full with vegetable oil. Bring the oil to around 170°C (338°F), then reduce the heat to low, to maintain the temperature. Working with two doughnuts at a time, carefully lift them into the oil, using the parchment as a sling. Fry for 3–4 minutes, flipping halfway through cooking, until golden brown. Once the doughnuts are in the oil they should slip off their parchment slings easily; you can then remove the parchment with some tongs and discard. Use a slotted spoon to transfer the doughnuts to a baking tray lined with a paper towel to absorb any excess oil.

4 In a large bowl, whisk together the sugar and cocoa nib powder. Toss the doughnuts, whilst they are still hot, in the sugar until fully coated. Remove and set aside whilst you fry the remaining doughnuts and doughnut holes.

5 Fried doughnuts are best served as close to frying as possible, but at least on the same day.

Images overleaf »

CHOCOLATE CHIP BRIOCHE

I rarely use chocolate chips, but this is one recipe where I will happily do so. This recipe is my version of the Belgian Cramique, a classic breakfast loaf that is traditionally made in two flavours, raisin or chocolate. Unsurprisingly, I've opted for chocolate. I serve it with a little butter, dunked into coffee.

SERVES 4–6

335 g (2⅔ cups) strong white bread flour, plus extra for dusting
150 ml (½ cup + 2 tablespoons) whole milk
7 g (2¼ teaspoons) fast-action dried yeast (instant yeast)
5 g (1 scant teaspoon) fine sea salt
50 g (¼ cup) caster (superfine) sugar
2 large eggs, plus one for egg wash
65 g (4½ tablespoons) unsalted butter
135 g (4¾ oz/roughly ¾ cup) dark chocolate chips, or roughly chopped bar

1. Make a paste by putting 35 g (1¼ oz) of the flour and 100 ml (3½ fl oz) of the milk into a small saucepan and cooking over a low heat, stirring constantly, until a thick paste has been formed, 1–2 minutes. Scrape into a small bowl, pour over the remaining milk and set aside to cool for 5 minutes.
2. Put the remaining flour, yeast, salt and sugar into the bowl of a stand mixer fitted with the dough hook, mixing briefly to combine. Pour in the remaining milk, flour paste and egg and mix on low speed to form a shaggy dough, then knead, on medium/low, for about 10 minutes until smooth and elastic and no longer sticking to the sides of the bowl. Add the butter and continue kneading until fully absorbed and the dough is smooth and elastic and no longer sticking to the sides of the bowl (up to 10 minutes).
3. Tip the dough out onto the work surface, shape into a ball and place, seam side down, in a lightly greased bowl. Cover with cling film (plastic wrap) and set aside for 20 minutes before transferring to the refrigerator to proof fully overnight.
4. The following day, remove the dough from the refrigerator, turn out onto a lightly floured work surface and roll into a 30 cm (12 in) square. Scatter over two-thirds of the chocolate chips in an even layer, pressing them down so they stick into the dough. Fold the four corners of the dough into the centre, creating a smaller square, then scatter over the remaining chocolate chips, pressing them in. Fold the four corners into the centre once again, then flip the whole thing over so that the smooth side of the dough is facing up. Cup your hands and use them to lightly drag the dough towards yourself, creating tension on the skin of the dough and rounding out the shape, then lift and turn the dough and repeat the process, so that the dough becomes a taut, round ball. Transfer onto a large parchment-lined baking tray (pan). Cover lightly with a damp tea towel or cling film (plastic wrap) and set aside until the dough has doubled in size, this can take up to 2 hours.
5. Preheat the oven to 190°C/170°C Fan (375°F).
6. Brush the fully proofed dough with a beaten egg and then, just before baking, use a razor blade or very sharp knife to score a line around the circumference of the dough. Bake for 25–30 minutes or until the loaf is golden brown. Remove and allow to cool for an hour before enjoying.
7. The loaf will keep for 3–4 days, if stored in a sealed container.

CHOCOLATE ORANGE MORNING BUNS

San Francisco's Tartine bakery is widely credited with the creation of morning buns and they make theirs with croissant dough and a sugar infused with orange and cinnamon. To get buns on the counter for their early morning customers, bakers work through the night to ensure freshly baked buns. At home, no one is getting up that early to ensure freshly baked pastries for friends and family. Or is that just me? Instead, make them first thing in the morning and they'll be ready in time for a relaxed brunch.

MAKES 12

Dough

1 x Cocoa Croissant Dough (page 223)
flour, for dusting

Filling

100 g (3½ oz) dark chocolate (65–70% cocoa solids), roughly chopped
150 g (1⅓ sticks) unsalted butter, diced
2 tablespoons cocoa powder (dutched)
60 g (scant ¼ cup, packed) light brown sugar
¼ teaspoon fine sea salt
zest 2 large oranges

Coating

100 g (½ cup) caster (superfine) sugar or Vanilla Bean Cocoa Nib Sugar (page 197)

Note: You can easily halve the recipe, but you'll need to roll the ½ batch of croissant dough into a 30 × 30 cm (12 × 12 in) square rather than a cylinder.

1 Remove the croissant dough from the refrigerator and, on a lightly floured work surface, roll out into a rectangle 60 × 30 cm (24 × 12 in). Gently fold in half, place on a baking tray (pan) lined with baking parchment, cover with cling film (plastic wrap) and refrigerate for 30 minutes to relax the dough.

2 Put the chocolate and butter in a heatproof bowl set over a pan of simmering water and heat, stirring occasionally, until fully melted. Remove the bowl from the heat and mix in the remaining ingredients. Set aside until the mixture is thick and spreadable but not fully set.

3 When the chocolate mixture is ready, remove the dough from the refrigerator and unfold. Using a small offset spatula, spread the filling evenly over the dough, then, starting from one of the long edges, roll it up into a 60 cm (24 in) cylinder. Divide this cylinder into 12 equal-sized buns.

4 Lightly grease a 12-hole muffin tin (pan), place the buns, cut side up, into the holes and lightly cover with cling film. To proof, place a roasting tin (pan) in the bottom of the oven and pour in very hot, but not boiling, water, close the door and leave for 20 minutes. The aim is to create a humid environment where the temperature measures 24–28°C (75–82°F). Any higher and the butter is liable to melt into the dough, any lower and the dough will take longer to proof. After 20 minutes, add the buns to the oven and leave for 2–3 hours to proof. You'll know they're ready when they've puffed up and they look as if they are full of air. You should also see the layers starting to separate.

5 Just before they've finished proofing, remove the buns and water and heat the oven to 180°C/160°C Fan (350°F). Bake the buns for about 30 minutes until browned and the edges are crisp. Allow the buns to cool for 2 minutes before carefully inverting onto a wire rack. Allow to cool a little, just enough so that you can handle them, then toss in the sugar. Do this while the buns are still warm to ensure the sugar sticks.

6 These are best served on the day they're made.

Images overleaf »

TOASTED CHOCOLATE SANDWICH

When I was a teenager I did an exchange trip to France, staying with a family just outside Nantes. That trip was special for many reasons but my biggest revelation was being introduced to the idea of chocolate served on bread, a momentous discovery, I'm sure you'd agree. Whilst this recipe is more indulgent than the version I had all those years ago, it is a sense memory that remains with me all these years later. The original used stale bread and a piece of dark chocolate and was served as an afterschool snack; this version takes it a little further and turns it into the sweet equivalent of a cheese toastie (grilled cheese).

SERVES 1

2 slices white bread, preferably sourdough, cut to a thickness of 2 cm (¾ in)
15 g (1 tablespoon) unsalted butter, softened
25 g (1 oz/roughly 2 heaped tablespoons) roughly chopped dark chocolate
pinch flaked sea salt

1. Butter one side of both bread slices. Place a frying pan over a medium heat and, when hot, add the slices, buttered side down. Cook for a few minutes or until the bread has started to brown. Lay the chocolate on one of the slices, then sandwich together with the second slice, browned side facing up. Cook for a further couple minutes, flipping halfway, until the bread is a rich golden brown and the chocolate has melted. Remove from the heat, cut in half, and sprinkle with a little salt.
2. Enjoy whilst the sandwich is still warm and the chocolate melted.

PEAR AND MILK CHOCOLATE DANISH

Bakeries are full of incredible Danishes, each bakery seemingly trying to outdo the next in terms of intricacy of design and flavour. This recipe sticks with simplicity with a filling that consists of a fresh pear compote enriched with lots of vanilla and kept bright with a little lemon, finished with a generous amount of whipped milk chocolate ganache.

MAKES 12

Pastry

1 x Cocoa Croissant Dough (page 223)
flour, for dusting
1 egg, lightly beaten, for egg wash

Pear Filling

400 g (14 oz) pear, peeled and diced (weighed after dicing)
juice 1 lemon
1 teaspoon vanilla bean paste or ½ vanilla pod
50 g (¼ cup) caster (superfine) sugar
1 teaspoon cornflour (cornstarch)

Milk Chocolate Ganache

1 x Whipped Milk Chocolate Ganache (page 234)

Decoration

cocoa nibs

Note: This recipe can be easily halved, though for the croissant dough I still use a full batch regardless and then freeze the extra un-proofed discs of pastry on a baking tray (pan) lined with baking parchment. Once frozen, the discs can be transferred to a container and kept for up to a month. To use, proof as per the recipe, which from frozen will take about 8 hours. You can also defrost them slowly in the refrigerator overnight and then proceed to proof as normal.

1. I like to make both fillings the day before assembling the pastries, to reduce the amount of work required in one single day, but, strictly speaking, the whipped ganache needs to be made only 4 hours in advance and the pear mixture can be made whilst the pastries are proofing.
2. For the pear filling, add all the ingredients to a small saucepan, place over a medium heat, cover and cook for 5 minutes or until the pear is tender but still holding its shape. Spoon 100 g (3½ oz) of the mixture into a small jug and, using a stick blender, purée until smooth. Add the cornflour to the purée and whisk until smooth. Add this mixture back into the pan with the remaining pear and stir to combine. Return the pan to the heat and cook, stirring constantly, until the mixture is bubbling and has thickened slightly. Scrape into a bowl, cover and refrigerate until needed.
3. Make the ganache according to the recipe on page 234 and refrigerate overnight, or for at least 4 hours.
4. Remove the croissant dough from the refrigerator and, on a very lightly floured work surface, roll out into a rectangle measuring at least 30 × 40 cm (12 × 16 in) to a thickness of 5 mm (⅛ in). Using a 10 cm (4 in) round cookie cutter, cut out 12 discs of pastry and place on two large baking trays (pans) lined with baking parchment. Lightly cover with cling film (plastic wrap) and proof in a warm spot, 24–28°C (75–82°F), for 2–3 hours or until the pastry is puffed and you can see some separation of the layers on the sides. (See the Croissant Dough recipe on page 223 for tips on proofing.)
5. Just before the Danishes have finished proofing, preheat the oven to 180°C/160°C Fan (350°F).
6. To create the well for the fillings a 5 cm (2 in) wide divot needs to be made in the centre of each pastry. You can do this by using your fingers to press down in the middle of each disc, but my preference is to weigh down the pastries with mini pudding basins or dariole moulds, 5 cm (2 in) wide at the base, filled with rice. You can also create 5 cm (2 in) wide foil parcels filled with rice.
7. Brush the outer edge of the pastries with a little beaten egg and bake for 15 minutes. Remove the foil parcels or moulds and bake for 5 minutes or so more or until the pastry is set. Remove from the oven and set aside until fully cooled.

8 To assemble, spoon the pear filling into the well of each Danish. Whisk the ganache until it just holds soft peaks, do not over-whisk. Spoon or pipe a little atop each pastry and finish by sprinkling over a few cocoa nibs.

9 These are best served on the day they are made.

OVERNIGHT CITRUS PECAN STICKY BUNS

This sticky bun, a twist on a classic yeasted bun, is filled with a cinnamon butter that is spiked with orange zest and baked atop a pool of caramel sauce and pecans. When I've got friends or family staying I like to whip up a batch the night before and allow them to rise slowly overnight, in the refrigerator, so that I can make my houseguests the absolute best brunch the following day.

MAKES 12

Cocoa Brioche

460 g (3⅔ cups) strong white bread flour, plus extra for dusting
40 g (½ cup) cocoa powder (dutched or natural)
50 g (¼ cup) caster (superfine) sugar
10 g (1½ teaspoons) fine sea salt
7g (2¼ teaspoons) fast-action dried yeast (instant yeast)
250 ml (generous 1 cup) whole milk
2 large eggs, plus one for egg wash
75 g (⅔ stick) unsalted butter, diced and at room temperature

Pecan Caramel Topping

150 g (1½ cups) pecans, roughly chopped
150 g (1⅓ sticks) unsalted butter, diced
200 g (scant 1 cup, packed) light brown sugar
large pinch fine sea salt
75 ml (5 tablespoons) orange juice (from 1–2 oranges)

Filling

150 g (⅔ cup, packed) light brown sugar
2 tablespoons ground cinnamon
60 g (½ stick) unsalted butter, very soft
zest 2 oranges

Note: I prefer to use a metal baking tin (pan) for this recipe. You could also use a glass dish but they'll take a few minutes extra to bake.

1 To make the brioche, put the flour, cocoa, sugar, salt and yeast in the bowl of a stand mixer and whisk to combine. If the cocoa is lumpy it is best to sift it into the bowl. Pour in the milk and the eggs and, with the dough hook attached, mix together to form a shaggy dough. On medium/low speed, knead the dough for about 10 minutes or until smooth and elastic. Add the butter and continue to knead until it has been fully combined and the dough is once again smooth and elastic. Turn out the dough onto a work surface, shape into a ball, place in a lightly greased bowl, seam side down, and cover with cling film (plastic wrap). Leave at room temperature for 20 minutes before transferring to the refrigerator for up to 2 days. You can also proof the dough at room temperature but as it is highly enriched it is much easier to handle once chilled, even if just briefly. If you want to make and use the dough on the same day, allow it to proof fully at room temperature (this will take about an hour), knock it back and then place the dough on a baking tray (pan) lined with baking parchment. Wrap well in cling film (plastic wrap) and freeze for 20 minutes or until the dough is firm but still pliable.

2 Preheat the oven to 180°C/160°C Fan (350°F). Lightly grease a 23 × 33 cm (9 × 13 in) brownie tin (pan) and line the base with baking parchment.

3 To make the topping, scatter the pecans on a rimmed baking tray and toast for 10–12 minutes or until golden and fragrant. Remove and tip into the prepared brownie tin, spreading into an even layer. Put the remaining ingredients in a saucepan, place over a medium heat and cook until everything is melted and bubbling. Pour this caramel over the pecans. Set aside.

4 Place the filling ingredients in a bowl and mix everything together to form a thick paste. On a lightly floured work surface, roll out the dough into a large 45 cm (18 in) square. Dollop on the filling and spread evenly so the entire surface of the dough is covered in a thin layer. Roll up the dough so you have a long sausage, then cut into 12 equal pieces and place, cut side up, in the tin, on top of the pecan caramel. Cover with cling film (plastic wrap) and refrigerate overnight, to allow the buns to proof slowly. You can also proof them at room temperature for about an hour at room temperature, if baking them on the same day.

5. Remove the buns from the refrigerator and leave for up to an hour before baking, to allow them to come to room temperature and to finish proofing if not already doubled in size. If already doubled in size, allow the buns to come to room temperature for 30 minutes whilst you preheat the oven.
6. Preheat the oven to 180°C/160°C Fan (350°F), then bake the buns for about 25 minutes or until they feel set and are browning around the edges. Allow to cool in the tin for 10 minutes before carefully inverting onto a large baking tray or serving platter. If you turn them out any earlier the caramel will be a little loose and will run off the buns.
7. The finished buns are best on the day they're made, but can be served up to two days after baking.

GIANT MANGO AND LIME RUM BABA

Long before Italians soaked sponge (lady) fingers in Marsala to make tiramisu, the French were soaking cakes in rum to make rum baba. Made with an enriched dough, similar to a brioche dough, but with a higher level of hydration, this requires piping rather than shaping. Once baked the baba is relatively dry and acts like a sponge, soaking up lots of syrup. The baba has a debated history, but what we do know is that it's an extremely old recipe, dating back to at least 1835 (the baba itself is likely much older, but the addition of rum can be traced to this date). The French folk from that time might be shocked by this highly untraditional version, but I like to think they'd be won over by the beautiful tropical flavours.

SERVES 12

Baba Dough

275 g (2 cups + 2 tablespoons) strong white bread flour
1 tablespoon caster (superfine) sugar
5 g (1 scant teaspoon) fine sea salt
7 g (2¼ teaspoons) fast-action dried yeast (instant yeast)
70 ml (5 tablespoons) whole milk
3 large eggs
75 g (⅔ stick) unsalted butter, diced and at room temperature, plus extra for greasing

Lime Vanilla Rum Syrup

zest and juice 2 limes
2 teaspoons vanilla bean paste
250 g (1¼ cups) caster (superfine) sugar
300 ml (1¼ cups) water
100 ml (scant ½ cup) dark rum (or a coconut rum)

To Serve

1 x Milk Chocolate Crémeux (page 236)
300 ml (1¼ cups) whipping (heavy) cream, whipped to soft peaks
2 ripe mangoes, peeled and diced
zest 1 lime

1. To make the baba dough, put the flour, sugar, salt and yeast in the bowl of a stand mixer and briefly mix to combine. Add the milk and one of the eggs and, with the dough hook attached, mix to form a shaggy dough. Knead on medium speed for 10 minutes or until smooth and elastic. Add the remaining eggs and knead for 2–3 minutes until fully combined. Add the butter, mix until combined, then continue kneading for around a total of 10 minutes or until the dough, whilst wet, is stretchy and elastic.

2. This dough is very loose and tricky to handle. To make it easier to use, scrape the dough into a piping bag fitted with a wide piping tip (if using a disposable bag simply cut a 2.5 cm/1 in opening). Grease a 2.4 litre (10 cup) bundt tin (pan) with softened butter or a spray oil. Pipe the batter into the tin, piping around the central column so that the batter is evenly distributed. Cover the tin with cling film (plastic wrap) and allow the baba to rise for about an hour or until doubled in size.

3. Preheat the oven to 200°C/180°C Fan (400°F).

4. Bake the baba for about 30 minutes or until golden brown. Remove and allow to cool in the pan for 5–10 minutes before carefully inverting onto a wire rack to cool completely.

5. For the syrup, put the zest, vanilla, sugar and water in a saucepan, place over a medium heat and bring to a rolling boil. Reduce the heat and cook at a low simmer for about 5 minutes. Remove from the heat, add the lime juice and rum, stir to combine, then strain to remove the zest and use immediately whilst still hot.

6. To soak the baba, use a serrated knife to cut the baba into slices. Place the slices on a rimmed baking tray (pan) and pour over the syrup. Leave for a couple minutes before flipping the slices so they're evenly coated. Leave until all the syrup has been absorbed.

Tip: When you cut the flesh from the mango you will be left with the skins and a stone (pit). Both have plenty of flavour still to give. Rather than letting this go to waste, you can use them when making the syrup, adding at the start of the process, increasing the water to 350 ml (scant 1½ cups) and cooking at a low simmer for 10 minutes. The finished syrup will have a strong, enhanced mango flavour.

7 Serve slices of baba with a spoonful of crémeux, a spoonful of whipped cream, a scattering of diced mango, finished with a little fresh lime zest.

8 Once baked, the baba can be stored for a couple days before using, just ensure the syrup is hot when the baba is sliced and soaked with it.

STRAWBERRY CREAM CHEESE BUNS

These buns, made in a similar way to cinnamon buns, are filled with chocolate and then topped with a strawberry whipped cream. To add a strong flavour of strawberry without the need to make a purée, I like to use freeze-dried strawberries.

MAKES 12

Cocoa Brioche

460 g (3⅔ cups) strong white bread flour
40 g (½ cup) cocoa powder (dutched or natural)
50 g (¼ cup) caster (superfine) sugar
10 g (1½ teaspoons) fine sea salt
7 g (2¼ teaspoons) fast-action dried yeast (instant yeast)
250 ml (1 cup + 1 tablespoon) whole milk
2 large eggs, plus one for egg wash
75 g (⅔ stick) unsalted butter, diced and at room temperature

Chocolate Filling

100 g (3½ oz) dark chocolate (60–70% cocoa solids)
140 g (1¼ sticks) unsalted butter, diced
1 tablespoon cocoa powder (dutched or natural)
30 g (2 tablespoons, packed) light brown sugar
large pinch fine sea salt

Strawberry Cream Topping

400 ml (1⅔ cups) whipping (heavy) cream
20 g (4 tablespoons) powdered freeze-dried strawberries, plus extra to decorate
1 tablespoon caster (superfine) sugar

1 To make the brioche, put the flour, cocoa, sugar, salt and yeast in the bowl of a stand mixer and whisk to combine. If the cocoa is lumpy, it is best to sift it into the bowl. Add the milk and eggs and, with the dough hook attached, mix together to form a shaggy dough. On medium/low speed, knead the dough for 10 minutes or until smooth and elastic. Add the butter and continue to knead until the butter has been fully combined and the dough is, once again, smooth and elastic. Turn out the dough onto a work surface, shape into a rough ball, place in a lightly greased bowl, cover and leave at room temperature for 20 minutes before transferring to the refrigerator for up to 2 days. You can proof this dough at room temperature but as it is highly enriched it is much easier to handle once chilled. If making these entirely on the same day you can allow the dough to proof fully, for about an hour, at room temperature, knock it back and then place it on a baking tray (pan) lined with baking parchment. Wrap well in cling film (plastic wrap) and freeze for 20 minutes or until the dough is firm but still pliable.

2 Just before you want to assemble the buns, make the chocolate filling. Put all the ingredients in a saucepan, place over a low heat and cook, stirring constantly, until the butter and chocolate are fully melted. Remove from the heat and set aside.

3 Remove the dough from the refrigerator and, on a lightly floured work surface, roll out into a 50 × 30 cm (20 × 12 in) rectangle. Spread the chocolate filling in an even layer over the entire surface of the dough. Leave until the filling feels tacky, then, starting at one of the longer edges, roll up the dough so that you have a 50 cm (20 in) long sausage. Divide this into 12 equal slices and place, cut side up, in a 23 × 33 cm (9 × 13 in) brownie tin (pan) lined with baking parchment. For a more refined look, proof and bake these inside 9 cm (3½ in) English muffin rings set on top of two baking trays lined with baking parchment. Cover and set aside for 60–90 minutes or until the buns have doubled in size.

4 Preheat the oven to 190°C/170°C Fan (375°F).

5 Lightly brush the buns with beaten egg and bake for about 25 minutes (20 minutes if using muffin rings) or lightly browned and the buns feel set. Remove and set aside until cooled.

6 For the strawberry topping, put everything into a large bowl and whisk until the cream holds soft peaks. Spoon or pipe the cream atop the buns and sprinkle with a little extra strawberry powder.

COCOA SWIRL MILK BREAD

Perfectly square loaves of soft and squishy milk bread will always make me think of Japan, where this style of bread is ubiquitous. This version is made with two doughs, one plain and one with cocoa, rolled up together for a dramatic and incredibly appealing swirl when sliced into. The bread itself is milky and lightly sweetened, with a subtle flavour from the cocoa. It is baked in a pullman loaf tin (pan), a straight-sided tin with a lid. To get a perfectly square loaf use the lid, for a rounded finish, bake without it.

MAKES 1 LARGE LOAF

350 g (12 oz/2¾ cups) strong white bread flour, plus extra for dusting
300 ml (1¼ cups) whole milk
5 g (scant 1 teaspoon) fine salt
5 g (1¾ teaspoons) fast-action dried yeast (instant yeast)
2 tablespoons, packed, light brown sugar
50 g (3½ tablespoons) unsalted butter, diced and at room temperature
3 tablespoons cocoa powder (dutched)
2 tablespoons boiling water
1 egg, lightly beaten, for egg wash

Note: This recipe can be made with either natural or dutched cocoa powder. I prefer to use dutched as it gives a nice contrast of colour and a deeper, richer flavour.

Tip: Spritzing with water helps the two doughs adhere together and prevents air-pockets forming between the layers when baked.

1. Make a tangzhong paste by putting 25 g (1 oz) of the flour and 75 ml (2½ fl oz) of the milk in a small saucepan, placing it over a medium heat and cooking, stirring constantly, until a thick paste is formed. Scrape the paste into a jug and pour over the remaining milk. Set aside for 5 minutes.
2. Put the remaining flour, salt, yeast and sugar in the bowl of a stand mixer and whisk to combine. Add the milk and tangzhong mixture and, with the dough hook attached, mix to form a shaggy dough. On medium speed, knead the dough for 10 minutes or until smooth and elastic. Add the butter and knead until fully combined and the dough is again smooth and elastic and forming a ball around the dough hook, up to 10 minutes. Meanwhile, whisk together the cocoa and boiling water, making a thick paste.
3. Turn out the dough and divide into two equal portions; this is best done by weight. Return one portion to the mixer bowl, add the cocoa paste and knead briefly until throughly combined, about 2 minutes. Form both pieces of dough into rounds, then place in separate, lightly greased bowls. Cover with cling film (plastic wrap) and set aside until doubled in size, 60–90 minutes.
4. Preheat the oven to 210°C/190°C Fan (410°F) and lightly grease a 23 × 10 × 10 cm (9 × 4 × 4 in) pullman loaf tin and line with parchment.
5. On a lightly floured work surface, roll out the plain dough into a 23 × 23 cm (9 × 9 in) square. Repeat with the cocoa dough. Lightly spritz the plain dough with water and lay the cocoa dough on top.
6. Roll this dough into a 28 × 23 cm (11 × 9 in) rectangle, then, starting from one of the shorter sides, roll up into a 23 cm (9 in) sausage. Place this, seam side down, in the prepared tin, cover with cling film (plastic wrap) or a damp tea towel and set aside until doubled in size, 60–90 minutes.
7. If baking with the pullman tin lid, skip the egg wash and simply slide on the lid. If you want a rounded top, brush the loaf with a little beaten egg just before baking.

8 Bake for 30 minutes if baking without the lid, 35 minutes if using the lid, until a deep golden brown. Remove from the oven, remove the lid, if using, and cool the bread in the tin for a couple minutes before turning out onto a wire rack to cool completely.

9 Kept covered the bread will keep for up to 3 days. You can also freeze the bread for up to a month.

BUILDING BLOCKS

SWEET PASTRY

This is my go-to recipe when making tarts; sweet and crisp, it is the perfect foil for all manner of fillings. I have provided two versions, one vanilla and one cocoa, both of which can be used interchangeably in any recipe that calls for sweet pastry.

Makes enough for 1 large (23 cm/9 in) tart or 6 individual (10 cm/4 in) tarts

Vanilla Sweet Pastry

200 g (scant 1⅔ cups) plain (all-purpose) flour, plus extra for dusting
25 g (scant ¼ cup) icing (confectioner's) sugar
¼ teaspoon fine sea salt
115 g (1 stick) unsalted butter, diced and chilled
1 large egg yolk
¼ teaspoon vanilla bean paste
½ tablespoon water

Cocoa Sweet Pastry

170 g (1⅓ cups) plain (all-purpose) flour
30 g (¼ cup + 2 tablespoons) cocoa powder (dutched or natural)
50 g (scant ½ cup) icing (confectioner's) sugar
115 g (1 stick) unsalted butter, diced and chilled
1 large egg yolk
1 tablespoon ice-cold water

1 Put the flour, cocoa (if making the cocoa version), sugar and salt in the bowl of a food processor and pulse to combine. Add the butter and pulse until the mixture resembles coarse sand. Add the egg yolk and vanilla (if making the vanilla version), and pulse until evenly mixed. Add the water and pulse just until the dough starts to hold together. Squeeze a little of the pastry in your hands, if it crumbles instead of holding together, the dough may need a little extra water.

2 Alternatively, place the flour, cocoa (if using), sugar and salt in a large bowl and whisk to combine. As cocoa can be lumpy, it is best to sift it into the bowl. Add the butter and rub it into the flour mixture with your hands. Mix together the egg yolk, vanilla if using, and water and drizzle into the flour mixture, using a knife to stir until the pastry starts to hold together.

3 Tip out the dough onto a work surface and use your hands to bring it together into a uniform dough. If making a large tart, press into a flat disc, wrap well in cling film (plastic wrap) and refrigerate until needed. If making individual tarts, form the dough into a thick sausage shape, wrap in cling film and refrigerate until needed. At this stage the dough can be refrigerated for 2 days or frozen for up to 2 months.

To Bake

4 Remove the dough from the refrigerator and, if making individual tarts, cut into six even slices or leave whole if making a large tart. If baking individual tarts the dough can normally be rolled immediately, if making a large tart allow the dough to warm up at room temperature for 5 minutes. Roll out the dough on a lightly floured work surface to a thickness of about 3 mm (1/10 in). Use to line either a single 23 × 3.5 cm (9 in) tart tin (pan) or six 10 cm (4 in) individual tart tins/rings, trimming off any excess pastry. The scraps can be formed back together and then refrigerated or frozen for use at another time. Chill the pastry case or cases, on a large baking tray (pan) lined with baking parchment, in the refrigerator for 30 minutes before baking.

5 Preheat the oven to 190°C/170°C Fan (375°F).

6 Dock the tart case(s) with a fork, line with a piece of crumpled baking parchment and fill with baking beans or rice. Bake for 20 minutes if making individual tarts and 25 minutes if making a single tart. Carefully remove the baking beans and transfer the tart(s) back to the oven for an additional 5–10 minutes or until the base of the pastry is golden. If adding a filling that requires baking, keep this second bake a little shorter, just until the base is dry and starting to brown but not fully baked.

7 If adding a wet filling, brush the inside of the finished tart cases with a beaten egg yolk before baking for another 2 minutes or so. The egg yolk will set and create an almost waterproof layer, slowing down the rate at which the pastry softens.

FLAKY PIE DOUGH

This pie dough is incredibly flaky and has a toasty flavour, with a hint of bitterness from the cocoa, which also gives the baked pastry a dramatically dark colour.

Makes enough for one 23 cm (9 in) double crust pie or two 23 cm (9 in) single crust pies

300 g (scant 2½ cups) plain (all-purpose) flour, plus extra for dusting
½ teaspoon fine sea salt
2 tablespoons caster (superfine) sugar
50 g (⅔ cup) cocoa powder (dutched or natural)
225 g (2 sticks) unsalted butter, chilled and diced
160 ml (⅔ cup) ice-cold water

1 In a large bowl, whisk together the flour, salt and sugar. Sift in the cocoa and whisk to combine. Add the butter and, using your fingertips, press and rub the butter into large flat flakes. Make a well in the centre of the flour and drizzle in the water a little at a time, tossing, squeezing and pressing with your hands to combine. Keep adding the water, a little at a time, until the dough is still a little shaggy but is mostly coming together. You may need slightly more or slightly less water than specified. Turn out onto a work surface and use your hands to press together into a rectangle of dough. Wrap in cling film (plastic wrap) and refrigerate for an hour. This rest allows the flour to hydrate and makes the rolling out much easier.

2 On a lightly floured work surface, roll out the dough into a rectangle measuring roughly 25 × 45 cm (10 × 18 in). Cut into four smaller rectangles, stack atop each other and then repeat this process a second time. Wrap the dough in cling film and refrigerate for 20 minutes. Repeat the rolling out and stacking process one final time. Before refrigerating, roll the dough slightly, just to compress the pieces together, divide in half and wrap each piece in cling film. Refrigerate or freeze the dough until needed. If resting in the refrigerator, leave for at least 2 hours before using, but preferably overnight.

3 Each piece of dough is enough for a single 23 cm (9 in) crust pie and together they'll make a single double crust pie. Refrigerated the pie dough will keep for 2–3 days but frozen it will keep for up to 2 months.

Blind Baking A Pie Crust

4 To form a single crust pie, roll out one of the portions of pastry on a lightly floured work surface until about 30 cm (12 in) in diameter. Carefully drape into a 23 cm (9 in) pie plate. Trim the pastry so that there is about 2.5 cm (1 in) of pastry hanging over the edge of the pie plate. Tuck and roll this excess pastry under itself to form a rope of dough that sits on the rim of the pie plate. Crimp this border as desired. Dock the base of the pastry with a fork and refrigerate for an hour before baking.

5 To fully bake the pie crust, preheat the oven to 200°C/180°C Fan (400°F). Line the pie crust with a large piece of crumpled baking parchment and fill with baking beans or rice. You can brush the crimped crust with egg wash should you wish, but with a cocoa crust I often skip this. Place the pie on a baking tray (pan) and bake for about 20 minutes. Remove the pie from the oven, carefully lift out the baking beans, then return to the oven and bake for a further 12–15 minutes or until the base is dry and crisp. Remove and set aside until fully cooled.

6 To par-bake, prior to adding a filling that requires additional baking, do as above, baking for an initial 20 minutes before removing the baking beans and baking for just 5–8 minutes, until set. If the filling requires a prolonged bake (such as for a fruit pie) cover the border with foil, as the cocoa pastry can become a touch bitter if browned too much.

COCOA CROISSANT DOUGH

Nothing feels more like culinary wizardry than biting into a homemade croissant or pain au chocolat. That something so incredibly delicious can be made at home seems miraculous! This recipe isn't for the faint of heart, but if you're at all similar to me, you may actually find making a batch of croissant dough a relaxing, almost meditative process. You can use either a natural or dutched cocoa, though my preference is for the latter. Both add a wonderful colour and a subtle flavour.

MAKES 12

Dough

- 460 g (3⅔ cups) strong white flour (11–12% protein content), plus extra for dusting
- 40 g (½ cup) cocoa powder (dutched or natural)
- 60 g (¼ cup + 1 tablespoon) caster (superfine) sugar
- 10 g (3 teaspoons) fast action dried yeast (instant yeast) or 22 g (2½ tablespoons) fresh yeast
- 10 g (1½ teaspoons) fine sea salt
- 130 ml (generous ½ cup) water, room temperature
- 130 ml (generous ½ cup) whole milk, room temperature
- 30 g (2 tablespoons) unsalted butter, melted and cooled to room temperature
- 1 egg, lightly beaten, to egg wash

To Laminate

- 280 g (2½ sticks) unsalted butter, chilled

For Pains Au Chocolat

- 24 dark chocolate batons (see Resources, page 250)

Note: To make a traditional pain au chocolat, without the cocoa, simply use 500 g (1 lb 2 oz) flour and no cocoa powder.

Pictured: Pear & Milk Chocolate Danishes (page 206).

1 The day before you want to laminate and, potentially, use the finished croissant dough, make the base dough. Put the flour, cocoa (sifting it if it has any lumps), sugar, dried yeast (if using) and salt into the bowl of a stand mixer and whisk to combine. If using fresh yeast, combine the water and milk in a separate bowl, crumble in the yeast, and whisk until dissolved. Add the water and milk (or the fresh yeast mixture) and butter to the flour mixture and, with the dough hook attached, knead for 1–2 minutes on low speed to form a shaggy dough, then knead for 5–6 minutes or until the dough is uniform. Don't worry too much about fully developing the gluten, as this will happen during the lamination process. Turn the dough out onto a work surface and shape it into a ball and cover, leaving for it for 20–30 minutes until it has puffed up a little but not by more than 50%. Knock back the dough and press into a flat square. Using minimal flour, roll the dough into a 20 × 40 cm (8 × 16 in) rectangle, then place on a baking tray (pan) lined with baking parchment and wrap well with cling film (plastic wrap). Transfer the dough to the freezer for 30 minutes to stop the yeast in its tracks, then move to the refrigerator to rest for a minimum of 8 hours and up to 24 hours.

2 The following day, take a large sheet of baking parchment and draw a 20 × 20 cm (8 × 8 in) square on one side, then turn the paper over. Lay slices of the chilled butter in a relatively even layer, using the drawing as a template. Fold the excess paper over the butter, creating a 20 × 20 cm (8 × 8 in) packet of fully enclosed butter. Using a rolling pin, bash the butter to soften it slightly and make it more pliable, then roll out the butter to form a square conforming to the shape of the template – try to make it as neat and even as possible. At this stage the butter should still be relatively cool but very pliable; you should be able to bend it without cracking. The temperature on an instant-read thermometer should be 11-16°C (52-61°F). »»»

3 The most important part of laminating croissant dough is ensuring the butter and the dough have a similarly pliable texture before they are combined. If the butter is too cold it will be brittle and will crack when rolled, resulting in uneven lamination. If the butter is too warm it will either leak out of the pastry or it will melt into the dough, resulting in a croissant that is lacking in layers and is more bready in texture.

4 Remove the dough from the refrigerator and place it on a lightly floured work surface with one of the shorter sides facing you. Roll it out, extending the size slightly to a 20 × 45 cm (8 × 18 in) rectangle, then unwrap the butter square and set it in the centre of the dough. Fold the ends of the dough up and over the butter, pinching the seam closed so the butter is fully encased. Turn the dough 90 degrees so the seam on top of the dough is now pointing away from you.

5 Lightly flour the dough, then use a rolling pin to gently press it several times along its length. This motion helps to flatten the dough slightly and keeps the shape neat and even when you start rolling. Using even pressure, roll the dough into a 20 × 65 cm (8 × 25 in) rectangle, trying to keep the shape as neat and accurate as possible. Trim the ends, to retain a sharp edge. Brush off any excess flour and perform the first of two folds, known as a double or book fold. Take the top edge of the dough and fold it to the middle of the dough. Fold the bottom edge of the dough into the middle to meet the other edge. Fold this entire package in half, like closing a book. Brush off any excess flour and refrigerate the dough for 20 minutes, wrapping well in cling film.

6 Put the dough on a lightly floured work surface with the spine of the pastry book on your right hand side, pointing away from you. Lightly flour the dough and roll it out to 20 × 65 cm (8 × 25 in) as before, brushing off any excess flour. Repeat the double fold as before, then wrap up and refrigerate again for at least 45 minutes before using in your chosen recipe.

7 To make pain au chocolat, roll out the finished dough so that it measures 30 × 50 cm (12 × 20 in). If at any point you find the dough resisting, place it on a baking tray, cover, and refrigerate for 20 minutes. Cut the dough into two 15 × 50 cm (6 × 10 in) rectangles and then each rectangle into six smaller rectangles measuring roughly 8 × 15 cm (3 × 6 in). To shape the pain au chocolat, place a chocolate baton along the short edge of each piece of dough then begin to roll up. Once the baton is fully encased, add a second baton and continue rolling up. Repeat until all twelve are formed.

8 If you want to bake these the following day, place on a baking tray lined with baking parchment, wrap well with cling film and refrigerate. If you want to bake immediately, proceed straight to the final proof. You can also freeze the pastries at this point. To bake frozen pastries, defrost them, still wrapped up, in the refrigerator overnight and then proof as follows.

9 To proof, place a roasting tin (pan) in the bottom of the oven and pour in very hot, but not boiling, water, close the door and leave for 20 minutes. The aim is to create a humid environment where the temperature measures 24–28°C (75–82°F). Any hotter and the butter will start to melt, any cooler and the pastries will take an incredibly long time to proof. Line two large baking trays with baking parchment and place six pains au chocolat on each tray. Put in the oven and proof for 2–3 hours; normally 2½ hours should be sufficient. When ready to bake, the pastries will have doubled in size, the layers may appear to be separating and if you gently shake the trays they should jiggle. Remove from the oven whilst you heat it to 190°C/170°C Fan (375°F). Brush the finished pastries with beaten egg, then bake for 15–18 minutes until well risen and browned. Remove from the oven and allow to cool fully before enjoying.

Images overleaf»

CHOUX PASTRY

This pastry is synonymous with French baking, being used in many traditional recipes, such as éclairs and Paris-Brest. Whilst never strictly necessary, when making choux I often add a layer of craquelin to the pastry before baking. This thin dough is made like a crumble or streusel but rolled out until thin. As the pastry bakes the craquelin melts onto the choux, ensuring it rises to its maximum potential. The craquelin then sets and creates a crisp outer layer, adding even more texture to the pastry.

Enough for 15 choux buns or 10 éclairs

Classic Choux Pastry

70 g (½ cup + 1 tablespoon) plain (all-purpose) flour
100 ml (⅓ cup + 1 tablespoon) water
40 ml (2½ tablespoons) whole milk
½ teaspoon fine sea salt
½ teaspoon caster (superfine) sugar
70 g (5 tablespoons) unsalted butter, diced
2 large eggs, lightly beaten

Cocoa Choux Pastry

55 g (6½ tablespoons) strong white bread flour
15 g (3 tablespoons) cocoa powder (dutched or natural)
110 ml (⅓ cup + 3 tablespoons) water
45 ml (3 tablespoons) whole milk
½ teaspoon fine sea salt
2 teaspoons caster (superfine) sugar
70 g (5 tablespoons) unsalted butter, diced
2 large eggs, lightly beaten

1. Sift the flour, and cocoa (if making the cocoa version), onto a piece of baking parchment or into a small bowl. Put the water, milk, salt, sugar and butter in a saucepan, place over a low heat until the butter is melted, then increase the heat and bring to a rolling boil. Add the flour, and cocoa, if using, all at once, stirring vigorously with a spatula to form a dough. Continue to stir on the heat for 1–2 minutes or until a thin film has formed on the bottom of the pan. If using a non-stick pan, this film may not develop but what actually matters is that the temperature of the dough is raised.

2. Tip the dough into a bowl and beat for a few minutes to cool slightly. Add the eggs, a little at a time, beating until fully combined before adding more. You want to add enough egg so that the finished dough is smooth, a little glossy and, when lifted from the bowl, falls from the spatula in a V-shaped ribbon. If too little is added the choux won't rise, if too much is added it will rise but then collapse. Scrape the pastry into a piping bag fitted with a piping tip and use as per your recipe.

3. Choux pastry can be made up to 24 hours in advance, stored in the refrigerator until needed. Make sure it is covered well with a layer of cling film (plastic wrap) so that it doesn't develop a skin. If you find piping tricky, chilling the pastry also thickens it up slightly, making it a little easier to handle.

Craquelin

50 g (¼ cup) caster (superfine)
50 g (⅓ cup + 1 tablespoon) plain (all-purpose) flour
pinch of fine sea salt
50 g (3½ tablespoons) unsalted butter, diced and chilled

4 To make the craquelin, put the sugar, flour and salt in a bowl and whisk to combine. Add the butter and rub into the flour until a crumbly dough is formed, then use your hands to gently press into a uniform dough with no lumps of butter. Roll out between two sheets of baking parchment until a thickness of 2 mm (1⁄10 in). Transfer to the freezer until needed. At this point the craquelin can be frozen for up to a month (if freezing for more than a day it is best to wrap the tray in cling film (plastic wrap).

5 When you are ready to pipe your choux pastry, remove the craquelin from the freezer and cut into the desired shape(s). If adding to round choux buns, cut into discs using a cookie cutter, cutting them the same size as the piped rounds of pastry. If adding to éclairs, cut into small rectangles, roughly the same length and width as the piped éclairs.

6 Craquelin becomes very soft if left at room temperature, so use it quickly before it has a chance to warm up.

COCOA ROUGH PUFF PASTRY

This makes a lot of pastry, but if you're going to the effort of making homemade rough puff, you might as well make enough to freeze some for another time. A gloriously flaky pastry, rough puff is slightly easier to make than traditional puff pastry. The key to making both, though, is to keep everything cold. Use ice-cold water and, if it's particularly warm, chill your other ingredients and even your equipment, if necessary. You'll notice the recipe includes a little bit of vinegar; this is used to stop the pastry oxidising whilst in the refrigerator, but it also makes for a slightly easier rolling-out process.

Makes 1.15 kg (2 lb 8 oz) pastry, enough for two of the recipes in this book

400 g (3 ¼ cups) plain (all-purpose) flour, plus extra for dusting
70 g (¾ cup) cocoa powder (dutched or natural)
40 g (3 tablespoons) caster (superfine) sugar
10 g (1½ teaspoons) fine sea salt
340 g (3 sticks) unsalted butter, chilled and diced into 1.5cm (½ in) cubes
2 tablespoons apple cider vinegar
240 ml (1 cup) ice-cold water

1. Sift the flour and cocoa into a large bowl and stir together with the sugar and salt. Add the butter and toss through the flour so that it is coated in flour. Mix the vinegar with the water, then drizzle in two-thirds, stirring with a knife. Add the remaining water in smaller increments, mixing until the dough is starting to come together and there is almost no dry flour remaining. You may need slightly more or slightly less water than specified. It won't form a ball of dough at this stage, but it should be shaggy with no dry pockets of flour. Tip onto a work surface and use a dough scraper to press into a neat square. Lift the dough onto a large piece of cling film (plastic wrap), two layers if needed, and fold over lightly. Roll into a rectangle that is roughly 20 × 25 cm (8 × 10 in). Rolling inside cling film helps hold the shaggy dough together and stops you adding any extra flour. Refrigerate for 30 minutes.

2. The dough now needs to be rolled out and folded multiple times; each fold is known as a turn or fold. As with traditional puff pastry this rough puff dough is folded a total of six times. This might seem excessive, but you'll be rewarded with the flakiest of pastries.

3. On a lightly floured work surface, roll out the dough into a rectangle measuring 20 × 60 cm (8 × 23 in). Brush away any excess flour, then fold the top third of the rectangle down towards you to cover the middle third of the dough. Then fold the bottom third up and over the other two layers; effectively folding the dough in thirds, like a business letter. Turn the dough 90 degrees so that the open ends of the dough are at the top and bottom, facing towards and away from you. Repeat this rolling out and folding process a second time, then wrap in cling film and refrigerate for 20 minutes.

4. Repeat this process twice more, refrigerating after each double set of folds, so that the dough is laminated a total of six times. Chill the dough for at least an hour before using, preferably overnight, after which it will be easier to roll out.

CHOCOLATE SWISS MERINGUE BUTTERCREAM

There are many styles of frosting and buttercream, but Swiss meringue is the one I use the most. For me, it has the best of everything: sweetness, texture, ease of use and adaptability. Made with egg white, it has a wonderfully silky texture with just the right level of sweetness and works well in most situations. For my favourite chocolate buttercream, I make a classic Swiss meringue buttercream and simply add melted chocolate. I have experimented with a mixture of chocolate and cocoa powder but I chose the simpler route, using a dark chocolate with around 80–85% cocoa content. This may seem high, and you may worry about the sweetness level, but I find this to be the best way to balance sweetness whilst also achieving a prominent chocolate flavour.

Enough to generously coat a 20–23 cm (8–9 in) three-layer cake

- 160 g egg whites (from 4 large egg whites)
- ¼ teaspoon cream of tartar (or a few drops of lemon juice)
- ¼ teaspoon fine sea salt
- 320 g (scant 1⅔ cups) caster (superfine) sugar
- 450 g (1 lb, 4 sticks) unsalted butter, diced and at room temperature
- 250 g (9 oz) dark chocolate (80–85% cocoa solids), melted and cooled

1. Put the egg whites, cream of tartar, salt and sugar in a large heatproof bowl and place over a pan of simmering water. Cook, stirring with a whisk, until the mixture is hot to the touch and you can no longer feel any grains of sugar. Remove the bowl from the heat and transfer the mixture to a stand mixer fitted with the whisk attachment. Whisk until the mixture is at room temperature and the meringue is stiff and glossy. This can take up to 5 minutes. With the mixer still running, add the butter a couple pieces at a time, mixing until combined before adding more. Once all the butter has been combined the mixture should have a buttercream-like texture. Pour in the chocolate and mix until fully combined.
2. To get the silkiest possible texture, switch to the paddle attachment and mix on the lowest speed for a few minutes, eliminating any excess air bubbles and ensuring the smoothest possible buttercream.

Troubleshooting

Whilst relatively simple to make, there are two things that can go wrong. Thankfully, they're easy problems to fix.

Split Buttercream: If, when you add the butter, the buttercream appears to be curdled or split this is usually down to the butter being too cold. Simply continue mixing and, as the butter warms up, the buttercream will come together.

Loose Buttercream: If, when you've added the butter, the buttercream seems too loose, almost like wet paint, it is likely the meringue was still too warm and has partially melted the butter. In this situation, stop adding butter and pop the bowl in the refrigerator for 10–15 minutes then continue mixing, it should come back together with ease.

CHOCOLATE PASTRY CREAM

Pastry cream is a true staple, and although it's incredibly simple to make, because it is used in so many recipes it is important to learn how to do so properly. As the custard is thickened with cornflour (cornstarch), scrambling the eggs is less likely than with a thin custard such as crème anglaise, making it a much more user-friendly technique. The two biggest tips are firstly to whisk continuously once the custard is added to the hot pan and, secondly, to continue cooking it for a minute or so after it is bubbling and thickened, as this ensures the amylase enzyme in the eggs is deactivated. If this step is skipped, the thickening powers of the cornflour can be affected, resulting in a thinner custard than required.

Dark Chocolate Pastry Cream

- 100 g (scant ½ cup, packed) light brown sugar
- 20 g (2½ tablespoons) cornflour (cornstarch)
- 15 g (3 tablespoons) cocoa powder (dutched or natural)
- 300 ml (1¼ cups) whole milk
- 3 large egg yolks
- ¼ teaspoon fine sea salt
- 15 g (1 tablespoon) unsalted butter, diced
- 100 g (3½ oz) dark chocolate (65–85% cocoa solids, depending on recipe), finely chopped

White Chocolate Pastry Cream

- 80 g (⅓ cup + 1 tablespoon) caster (superfine) sugar
- 30 g (¼ cup) cornflour (cornstarch)
- 300 ml (1¼ cups) whole milk
- 1 teaspoon vanilla bean paste
- 3 large egg yolks
- ¼ teaspoon fine sea salt
- 15 g (1 tablespoon) unsalted butter, diced
- 100 g (3½ oz) white chocolate (around 40% cocoa butter), finely chopped

1. Sift half the sugar, all the cornflour and cocoa (if making the dark chocolate version) into a large bowl and whisk to combine. Put the milk, vanilla (if making the white chocolate version) and the remaining sugar in a saucepan, whisk to combine, place over a medium heat and bring to a simmer. Add the egg yolks and salt to the bowl with the cornflour mix and whisk until the mixture is smooth.
2. Pour the hot milk mixture over the egg mixture, whisking to combine. Pour this mixture back into the saucepan and place back on the heat. Cook, whisking constantly, until the custard is very thick and is bubbling. Continue cooking for another minute before scraping into a bowl. Add the butter and chocolate and whisk to combine. Cover with cling film (plastic wrap) and refrigerate until needed.
3. Pastry cream can be made a day in advance and refrigerated until needed.

Note: Depending on which recipe the pastry cream will be used in, you can use chocolate with a varied percentage of cocoa. Generally I use either a 60–70% dark chocolate for an everyday pastry cream or I use a chocolate with 85% cocoa solids when I want something a little more intense and grown up, as in my Dark Chocolate Choux a la Custard recipe on page 151.

WHIPPED GANACHE

These simple ganaches are some of the most useful recipes you'll find in this book. They're very easy to adapt and can be both the centrepiece of a simple dessert or one element of a more complex dish. Whilst you can amend the amount of cream to chocolate as needed, I have used a ratio that results in ganaches that whip incredibly easily with less risk of turning too thick and grainy; they could simply be called chocolate whipped creams. If you want a denser result, use a little less cream. I have also included a suggested amount of gelatine; this is used to stabilise the whipped ganache and is a useful addition if you are preparing a dish ahead of time and need it to hold for a number of hours. If using and serving immediately, it can be dispensed with.

Whipped White Chocolate Ganache

- 400 ml (1⅔ cups) whipping (heavy) cream
- ½ vanilla pod
- 1 sheet of gelatine (optional)
- 165 g (5¾ oz) white chocolate (30% cocoa butter), or caramelised white chocolate

Whipped Dark Chocolate Ganache

- 1 sheet gelatine (optional)
- 400 ml (1⅔ cups) whipping (heavy) cream
- ½ teaspoon vanilla bean paste
- 125 g (4½ oz) dark chocolate (65–70% cocoa solids), finely chopped

Whipped Milk Chocolate Ganache

- 1 sheet gelatine (optional)
- 400 ml (1⅔ cups) whipping (heavy) cream
- ½ teaspoon vanilla bean paste
- 150 g (5½ oz) milk chocolate (40–45% cocoa solids), finely chopped

Note: I like to use a vanilla pod for the white chocolate ganache as it adds a strong depth of flavour, but you can use 1 teaspoon vanilla bean paste instead. You can also skip the vanilla element entirely, if you prefer.

1 To make the white chocolate ganache, pour the cream into a saucepan. Cut the vanilla pod lengthways in half and scrape out the seeds. Add both the seeds and pod itself to the cream. Place the pan over a medium heat and bring the cream to a simmer. Cover, remove from the heat and set aside for 30–60 minutes to infuse.

2 For all three ganaches, put the gelatine, if using, in a small bowl and cover with ice-cold water. Set aside for 5 minutes.

3 For the dark and milk chocolate ganaches, put the cream and vanilla bean paste in a saucepan, place over a medium heat and bring to a simmer. If making the white chocolate version, simply place the pan back on the heat. Add the chocolate to a large heatproof jug and melt in a microwave or bain-marie (see page 24). Once at temperature, remove the pan from the heat and remove the vanilla pod, if using. Remove the gelatine from the water, squeeze to remove as much liquid as possible, add to the cream and stir to combine. Pour a third of the cream over the chocolate, stirring well to combine. Add the remaining cream in two additions, stirring well to form a silky, smooth ganache, then, using a stick blender, give the mixture a brief blend to ensure the ganache is thoroughly emulsified.

4 Cover the surface with cling film (plastic wrap) to prevent a skin from forming and refrigerate for at least 4 hours before using.

5 To use, scrape the ganache into a large bowl and whisk until the desired texture. As the chocolate thickens the cream, this will be a very quick process, so, to ensure the best texture, it is better to whisk by hand, rather than use an electric mixer.

6 Once refrigerated, but before whipping, the ganache can be stored for 2–3 days. Once whipped, use immediately.

COCOA NIB SIMPLE SYRUP

The cocoa nibs give this simple syrup a subtle cocoa flavour. It can be used in a whole host of recipes, from cocktails, to cakes and brioche. If a recipe calls for this syrup and you don't have any cocoa nibs on hand you can also use a traditional simple syrup made with equal parts sugar and water, just bringing to a simmer to dissolve the sugar. You can also replace some or all of the water with a citrus juice such as lemon or lime.

100 g (½ cup) caster (superfine) sugar
150 ml (scant ⅔ cup) water
2 tablespoons cocoa nibs

1. Put the sugar, water and cocoa nibs in a small saucepan, place over a medium heat and bring to the boil. Reduce the heat to a simmer and cook for about 5 minutes until slightly reduced and syrupy. Pour into a jar, seal and store in the refrigerator for up to two weeks before using.

COCOA NIB VANILLA POWDER

Vanilla pods are expensive, so this is one of my favourite ways to get as much value from each pod as possible. The powder can be added as an alternative to vanilla extract or vanilla bean paste, it can also be mixed through with sugar when adding a coating to things like doughnuts.

2 spent vanilla pods
2 tablespoons cocoa nibs

1. If the vanilla pods have been submerged in liquid, rinse thoroughly in water to remove any coating. This is especially important if they were infused in cream. Place the pods on a wire rack and leave for a couple days, at room temperature, until completely dry and very brittle. You can also dehydrate them by putting in a very low oven, just keep an eye on them so they don't brown and become bitter.
2. Put the vanilla pods and cocoa nibs in a spice grinder and pulse until a fine powder is formed. Pour into a small jar and seal. Store in a dry cool spot for up to 6 months.

CHOCOLATE CRÉMEUX

Crémeux is a French technique that instead of using cream to make a ganache uses crème anglaise, a thin custard. The resulting ganache, unsurprisingly, has a particularly silky texture that is simply incredible. These crémeux are excellent used as a filling for cakes or tarts but can also be used as the centre of a simple dessert.

Dark Chocolate Crémeux

265 g (9½ oz) dark chocolate (60–75% cocoa solids), finely chopped
200 ml (¾ cup + 1 tablespoon) whipping (heavy) cream
200 ml (¾ cup + 1 tablespoon) whole milk
3 large egg yolks
75 g (¼ cup + 2 tablespoons) caster (superfine) sugar

Milk Chocolate Crémeux

300 g (10½ oz) milk chocolate (40–50% cocoa solids), finely chopped
200 ml (¾ cup + 1 tablespoon) whipping (heavy) cream
200 ml (¾ cup + 1 tablespoon) whole milk
3 large egg yolks
65 g (⅓ cup) caster (superfine) sugar

1 For both versions, melt the chocolate either using a bain-marie or the microwave (see page 24).

2 Pour the cream and milk into a saucepan, place over a medium heat and bring to a simmer. Meanwhile, put the egg yolks and sugar in a bowl and whisk until pale. Pour the hot cream mixture over the egg mixture, whisking as you do so to prevent the yolks from scrambling. Pour the custard back into the pan, place over a low heat and cook, stirring constantly, until the custard reaches a temperature of 75–80°C (167–176°F) or thickens enough to coat the back of a spoon. Remove and pour into a jug. Pour a third of the custard over the chocolate. Stir with a whisk or spatula until smooth and silky. Add the remaining custard in two additions. Finish by giving the mixture a brief blend using a stick blender, to ensure it is fully emulsified. Pour the crémeux into a shallow container and cover with cling film (plastic wrap) and refrigerate for at least 4 hours before using, preferably overnight.

WHITE CHOCOLATE CRÉMEUX

As white chocolate is made without cocoa solids, this cremeux is much softer and less stable, so I like to make this with the addition of gelatine. I also whip it once chilled, making it a variation of a whipped ganache.

1 sheet gelatine
250 g (9 oz) white chocolate (30% cocoa butter), finely chopped
120 ml (½ cup) whipping (heavy) cream
120 ml (½ cup) whole milk
2 large egg yolks
25 g (2 tablespoons) caster (superfine) sugar

1. Put the gelatine in a small bowl, cover with ice-cold water and set aside for 5 minutes to soften. Put the chocolate in a large heatproof jug and melt in the microwave (see page 24).
2. Pour the cream and milk into a saucepan, place over a medium heat and bring to a simmer. Meanwhile, put the egg yolks and sugar in a large bowl and whisk to combine. Pour over the hot cream, whisking as you do so to prevent the yolks from scrambling. Pour the custard back into the pan and cook, stirring constantly, until it reaches a temperature of 75–80°C (167–176°F) or thickens enough to coat the back of a spoon. Lift the gelatine from the bowl, squeezing out any excess water, add to the saucepan and stir to combine. Pour the custard into a jug. Pour a third of the custard over the chocolate, stir to combine. Add the remaining custard in two additions. Finish by giving the mixture a brief blend using a stick blender, to ensure it is fully emulsified. Pour the crémeux into a shallow container and cover with cling film (plastic wrap) and refrigerate for at least 4 hours before using, preferably overnight.

A Note On Gelatine

I prefer to use gelatine sheets rather than powder, and I list them by sheet rather than weight because all gelatine sheets are designed to set the same amount of liquid regardless of their strength (known as bloom). Thus one sheet of gold grade gelatine will set the same amount of liquid as one sheet of platinum grade gelatine.

If you're unable to get sheet gelatine, for every one sheet you can instead use 2 g powdered gelatine dissolved in 1 tablespoon ice-cold water. Once the powdered gelatine and water are mixed together, leave for a few minutes before using.

A LITTLE SWEET TREAT

THREE SIMPLE TRUFFLES

Homemade chocolate truffles are one of my favourite edible gifts, guaranteed to put the biggest smile on the face of anyone lucky enough to be the recipient. Below are three favourites that offer something more than a classic ganache. When making them, you have a couple choices when it comes to how they're finished. My preference is to coat them in tempered chocolate, matching the chocolate to the filling. This is, admittedly, a lot of work, so if you prefer you can simply roll them in cocoa powder or something textural, such as desiccated dried (shredded) coconut, finely chopped nuts or biscuit crumbs.

Browned Butter White Chocolate Truffles

Makes 15

30 g (2 tablespoons) unsalted butter, diced
200 g (7 oz) white chocolate (30% cocoa butter), finely chopped
70 ml (5 tablespoons) whipping (heavy) cream
large pinch flaked sea salt

1. First brown the butter by putting it in a small saucepan and placing over a medium heat. The butter will first melt and then start to splutter as the water cooks out. Once the spluttering settles the butter will start to foam and it is at this point you need to keep an eye out for flecks of brown appearing. When they do, pour the browned butter into a small bowl and refrigerate until it is firm but spreadable.

2. To make the ganache, place the chocolate and cream in a heatproof bowl and using either a bain-marie or a microwave, heat until the chocolate has almost fully melted (see page 24). Remove the bowl from the heat and stir until a smooth ganache is formed. Add the butter and salt and stir until the ganache is smooth and lump free (see page 26 for tips on making ganache). Cover and refrigerate until firm.

3. Spoon into small portions of ganache, each weighing roughly 20 g (¾ oz), then roll into balls. If the truffles feel particularly soft you can refrigerate them briefly before coating in tempered chocolate (see page 243). If rolling them in something dry, such as cocoa powder or desiccated (dried shredded) coconut, do this as soon as the truffles have been rolled, as the slightly warmed chocolate will help the coating to stick.

4. If not coating them in tempered chocolate, they are best stored in the refrigerator, in a sealed container, where they'll keep for up to two weeks. They will, however, taste better served at room temperature.

Earl Grey Milk Chocolate Truffles

Makes 15

200 g (7 oz) milk chocolate (40% cocoa solids), finely chopped
115 ml (½ cup) whipping (heavy) cream, plus a little extra
2 Earl Grey tea bags, or 2 tablespoons loose leaf Earl Grey tea
15 g (1 tablespoon) unsalted butter, diced and at room temperature

1. Place the chocolate into a heatproof bowl and melt either using a bain-marie or in a microwave (see page 24). Put the cream and tea bags in a small saucepan, place over a medium heat and bring to a simmer. Remove from the heat and set aside for 5 minutes to infuse. Remove the tea bags from the cream, pressing them with the back of a spoon before you discard them to extract as much cream as possible and ensure you get maximum flavour payoff. As some cream will be lost in this process, top up with a little extra cream to bring back up to 115 ml (4 fl oz). If using loose leaf tea, follow the same process but pour the infused cream through a fine-mesh sieve, pressing to extract as much of the cream and flavour as possible. Top up with extra cream if needed.

2. Pour the infused cream back into the saucepan and return to a simmer. Pour a third of the cream over the chocolate and stir to combine. Pour in the remaining cream, in two additions, stirring well to form a silky smooth ganache (see page 26 for tips on making ganache). Add the butter and stir until combined and the ganache is silky and perfectly smooth. If you have one, finish by giving the mixture a brief blend using a stick blender, to ensure the ganache is fully emulsified. Cover and refrigerate until firm.

»»»

3 Spoon into small portions of ganache, each weighing roughly 20 g (¾ oz), then roll into balls. If the truffles feel particularly soft, you can refrigerate them briefly before coating in tempered chocolate (see opposite). If rolling them in something dry, such as cocoa powder or biscuit crumbs, do this as soon as the truffles have been rolled, as the slightly warmed chocolate will help the coating to stick.

4 If not coating them in tempered chocolate they are best stored in the refrigerator, in a sealed container, where they'll keep for up to two weeks. They will, however, taste better served at room temperature.

Salted Caramel Dark Chocolate Truffles

Makes 30

225 g (8 oz) dark chocolate (70–75% cocoa solids), finely chopped
200 g (1 cup) caster (superfine) sugar
200 ml (¾ cup + 1 tablespoon) whipping (heavy) cream
20 g (1½ tablespoons) unsalted butter, diced
large pinch flaked sea salt

1. Place the dark chocolate in a heatproof bowl and melt, using either a bain-marie or a microwave (see page 24). Put the sugar in a medium saucepan, place over a medium heat and cook until the sugar has melted and caramelised, turning the colour of old penny, a deep copper colour. Meanwhile, pour the cream into a separate saucepan and bring to a simmer. Once the sugar has caramelised add the butter and salt and pour in half the hot cream. Take care, as the caramel will erupt and bubble up, creating a lot of extremely hot steam. Once the bubbling has subsided slightly, pour in the remaining cream. Remove the pan from the heat and stir until the caramel is smooth. Allow to cool for a few minutes. Pour a third of the caramel over the chocolate, stirring to combine. Add the remaining caramel in two additions, stirring well until the ganache is smooth and silky. If you have one, finish by giving the mixture a brief blend using a stick blender, to ensure the ganache is fully emulsified (see page 26 for tips on making ganache). Cover the ganache with cling film (plastic wrap) and refrigerate until firm.
2. Spoon into small portions of ganache, each weighing roughly 20 g (¾ oz), then roll into balls. If the truffles feel particularly soft you can refrigerate them briefly before coating in tempered chocolate (see opposite). If rolling them in something dry, such as cocoa powder or nuts, do this as soon as the truffles have been rolled, as the slightly warmed chocolate will help the coating to stick.
3. If not coating them in tempered chocolate they are best stored in the refrigerator, in a sealed container, where they'll keep for up to two weeks. They will, however, taste better served at room temperature.

250 g (9 oz) chocolate (any type), tempered (see page 30)

TO COAT IN TEMPERED CHOCOLATE

This amount of chocolate is enough to temper 30 truffles, but even if only making 15 I would still temper 250 g (9 oz) chocolate. Using an amount of this size stops the chocolate cooling too quickly and gives you enough chocolate so that coating is easy. Any leftover tempered chocolate can be stored in a sealed container and reused for another recipe. Keep your leftover tempered chocolate in a dark cool spot.

Method 1

Spoon a little of the tempered chocolate onto the tips of the fingers of one hand and place a truffle on top. Roll the truffle in the chocolate until fully coated, then carefully place on a baking tray (pan) lined with baking parchment and leave to set. If you want, you can drop the freshly coated truffle into a bowl of cocoa powder, finely chopped nuts or biscuit crumbs and roll until coated. This method gives the thinnest coating of chocolate.

Method 2

Spoon the tempered chocolate into a small bowl and, one at a time, drop a truffle into the chocolate, using a fork to submerge it completely. Use the fork to lift the truffle from the chocolate, tapping the fork on the side of the bowl to encourage any excess chocolate to drip back in. Carefully transfer to a baking tray (pan) lined with baking parchment and leave to set, or roll in a secondary ingredient, as above. If using this method, try not to use truffles that have been pulled straight from the refrigerator, as they will lower the temperature of the tempered chocolate, eventually making it too thick to use.

Truffles coated in tempered chocolate can be stored in a cool spot for up to two weeks.

CHOCOLATE SWIRLED PEPPERMINT MARSHMALLOWS

Who says marshmallows in a mug of steaming hot chocolate is just for kids? These big fluffy peppermint marshmallows are swirled with dark chocolate and are the perfect way to make a mug of homemade hot chocolate even more special.

MAKES 30

Marshmallow

10 sheets gelatine
100 g (3½ oz) dark chocolate, finely chopped
400 g (2 cups) caster (superfine) sugar
1 tablespoon liquid glucose, or corn syrup
120 ml (½ cup) water
2 large egg whites
pinch cream of tartar
½–1 teaspoon peppermint extract

Coating

25 g (scant ¼ cup) icing (confectioner's) sugar
25 g (scant ¼ cup) cornflour (cornstarch)

1 Lightly grease a 20 cm (8 in) square cake tin (pan) and line with two strips of baking parchment so that the paper hangs over the sides of the tin. This will make removing the marshmallows easier. For the coating, sift together the icing sugar and cornflour, ensuring there are no lumps.

2 To make the marshmallows, put the gelatine in a bowl, cover with ice-cold water and set aside for 5 minutes.

3 Put the chocolate in a small heatproof bowl and melt, using either a bain-marie or a microwave (see page 24). Set aside.

4 Put the sugar, glucose and water into a medium saucepan, place over a medium heat and cook, without stirring, until the sugar is fully dissolved and the syrup reaches 121°C (250°F). Meanwhile, put the egg whites and cream of tartar in the bowl of a stand mixer fitted with the whisk attachment. When the sugar syrup reaches 115°C (240°F), start whisking the egg whites on medium speed. Once the syrup reaches its final temperature of 121°C (250°F), remove the pan from the heat and, with the mixer on medium speed, carefully pour in the syrup, down the side of the bowl, avoiding the whisk. Once all the syrup has been added pour in the peppermint extract. Working quickly, remove the gelatine from the water, squeezing out as much water as possible, place it in the now empty sugar syrup pan and, using the residual heat, stir until melted, then pour into the egg white mixture and increase the speed to high.

5 Continue to whisk until the side of the bowl has cooled just enough that you can rest your hand on it. It should still feel hot. Remove the bowl from the stand mixer and pour in the melted chocolate and gently fold into the marshmallow. Do this briefly as you want a nice, swirled appearance, you don't want to fully work in the chocolate. Scrape the marshmallow into the prepared tin and gently level out using a lightly greased offset spatula. Dust with a little of the cornflour and icing sugar mixture and leave at room temperature for at least 4 hours or until fully set.

6 Turn out the marshmallows and use an oiled knife to cut into cubes. Toss in the remaining cornflour (cornstarch) mixture.

7 Kept in an airtight container these will keep for up to a week.

A DUO OF CHOCOLATE SPREADS

I grew up loving Nutella; roasted hazelnuts and chocolate, what's not to like? As an adult, my tastes have changed and I now find it too sweet. I also don't love that the main ingredients are sugar and palm oil. These days I prefer to make my own homemade versions. These spreads have more texture than the commercial variety and are closer to the French *pâté à tartiner,* a spreadable paste that gets its crunch from little flecks of caramelised hazelnuts. Roast your hazelnuts before using, to really unlock their flavour. Even when I buy 'roasted hazelnuts', I find they've barely seen a whisper of heat and are nowhere near the toasty brown I aim for. Roast your nuts, people!

White Chocolate Hazelnut Spread

Makes about 400 g (14 oz)

200 g (scant 1½ cups) blanched hazelnuts
50 g (¼ cup) caster (superfine) sugar
30 ml (2 tablespoons) water
large pinch flaked sea salt
2 tablespoons hazelnut or a neutral tasting oil
150 g (5½ oz) white chocolate, melted
1 teaspoon vanilla bean paste

Dark Chocolate Hazelnut Spread

Makes about 500 g (1 lb 2 oz)

200 g (scant 1½ cups) blanched hazelnuts
100 g (½ cup) caster (superfine) sugar
50 ml (3½ tablespoons) water
large pinch flaked sea salt
4 tablespoons hazelnut or a neutral tasting oil
200 g (7 oz) dark chocolate (60–70% cocoa), melted
1 teaspoon vanilla bean paste

1 Preheat the oven to 180°C/160°C Fan (350°F).

2 Scatter the hazelnuts on a rimmed baking tray (pan) and roast in the oven until the nuts are a warm golden brown and have a nutty toasty aroma, 10–12 minutes. If the nuts still had their skin, tip them onto a clean tea towel and fold over the fabric to make a little parcel. Leave for a few minutes (the trapped heat will help loosen the skins), then rub with the towel until as much of the skin has been removed as possible.

3 Tip the nuts into a large saucepan along with the sugar and water and cook over a medium heat, stirring occasionally, for 3–4 minutes or until the water has evaporated and the sugar mixture is thick and syrupy. Remove the pan from the heat and stir until the syrup forms a white crust on the outside of the nuts. Place the pan back on the heat and continue to stir until the white crust has melted and turned into rich brown caramel colour. Tip the nuts out onto a baking tray (pan) lined with baking parchment and leave to cool to room temperature, about 30 minutes.

4 Once fully cooled, tip the caramelised hazelnuts, salt and oil into the bowl of a food processor fitted with the blade attachment and process until a loose peanut butter-like texture has been formed. Initially, it will be matte and thick. When it is glossy and loose, almost liquid, you will have reached the desired texture.

5 If making the white chocolate version, add the white chocolate and vanilla and process for a further minute, just until fully combined. Pour into a sterilised jar and seal.

6 If making the dark chocolate version, add the cocoa powder once the hazelnut paste is the desired texture and process for a minute, then add the dark chocolate and vanilla and process for a further minute, just until fully combined. Pour into a sterilised jar and seal.

7 Stored at room temperature both versions will keep for up to a month. They can also be stored in the refrigerator, but the texture will be hard to spread.

HOMEMADE HOT CHOCOLATE MIX

When the weather turns even a touch colder my partner starts craving a warming mug of hot chocolate and I am more than happy to fulfil those cravings. I used to make it from scratch, each and every time, but to make things easier I now have a homemade hot chocolate mix on hand, which means a hot chocolate is always within easy reach when desired. Hot chocolate can vary from thinner 'hot cocoa'-style drinks all the way up to incredibly thick and rich Parisian hot chocolates; this blend fits nicely in the middle of the two styles. Should you want a thicker version, add a little extra finely chopped chocolate as the milk heats up.

MAKES ENOUGH FOR 10–12 MUGS

100 g (1 cup + 2 tablespoons) cocoa powder (dutched or natural)
150 g (⅔ cup, packed) light brown sugar
10 g (1½ teaspoons) fine sea salt
250 g (9 oz) dark chocolate (60–70% cocoa solids)
50 g (7 tablespoons) non-fat milk powder
1 tablespoon cornflour (cornstarch)

To Use

200ml (¾ cup + 1 tablespoon) milk of your choice
5 tablespoons hot chocolate mix

1. Put all the ingredients for the hot chocolate mix in a food processor and pulse until the chocolate is finely ground and everything is evenly combined. Do not leave the food processor running for too long as the blades will generate heat that will eventually start to melt the chocolate. Spoon the mixture into a couple of large sterilised jars and store in a dark, cool spot.
2. To make a mug of hot chocolate, put 5 tablespoons of the mixture in a small saucepan and whisk in the milk. Place the pan over a medium heat and cook, stirring constantly, until the milk is steaming. Remove from the heat and pour into a large mug.
3. The mixture will keep for a couple months if stored in a dark cool spot.

VARIATIONS

Peppermint Hot Chocolate

Add a couple drops of peppermint extract to the milk as it heats up.

Malted Hot Chocolate

Combine 4 tablespoons of the hot chocolate mixture with 2 tablespoons malted milk powder and make as above.

Spiced Hot Chocolate

Add ¼ teaspoon ground cinnamon, ⅛ teaspoon ground nutmeg and a pinch of cayenne pepper to the milk as it heats up.

ICED CHOCOLATE

If hot chocolate is perfect for the winter months, then this frozen chocolate is perfect for summertime, when something altogether more refreshing is required. Somewhere between a granita and a slushy, it is equally at home being eaten with a spoon as it is being drunk with a straw.

SERVES 6

150 g (5½ oz) milk chocolate (40% cocoa solids)
150 g (5½ oz) dark chocolate (70% cocoa solids)
325 ml (1⅓ cups) whole milk
225 ml (scant 1 cup) whipping (heavy) cream

To Serve

250 ml (1 cup) milk of your choice
250 g (9 oz) ice

1 Put the two chocolates in a large jug and melt in the microwave (see page 24). Pour the milk and cream into a saucepan, place over a medium heat and bring to a simmer. Pour a third of the milk mixture over the chocolate and stir together. Add the remaining milk mixture in two additions, stirring to form a silky, smooth ganache. Pour the chocolate mixture into ice cube trays, then freeze for at least 4 hours until solid. (You can freeze the chocolate in any mould, but if frozen as a single block it will need cutting up before using.) At this point the chocolate mixture can remain frozen for up to 3 months.

2 When ready to make the drink, simply add the frozen cubes of chocolate, the milk and the ice to a blender and pulse until a slushy-like texture is formed. Pour into glasses and serve immediately.

ACKNOWLEDGEMENTS

This is a book I have dreamt of writing for many years, with multiple publishers rejecting the idea as too niche (can you believe!) so the first thanks must go to the team at Quadrille, specifically Issy and Judith for believing in the idea and shepherding it through its inception all the way to publication. Specific thanks to Judith for being part of my writing career for the best part of 15 years, thanks for bringing me into the Quadrille family. Thanks also to the wider team at Quadrille, there are many hands that works on bringing a book to life and helping it reach its audience and I couldn't have done it without all your hard work.

Big thanks to Katherine for looking after me this past decade and getting this book across the line, thanks for always believing in my ideas and championing them.

Working on this book was, of course, an incredibly delicious endeavour and I was lucky enough to assemble an absolute dream team to join me in that adventure. Matt, your images are incredible, you've elevated the book and really understood what I was hoping to achieve. Thanks for making the shoot a relaxed and incredibly collaborative environment. Holly, the most organised and diligent food stylist, you helped keep my messy mind in check which meant we could achieve so much in such a short amount of time, a huge thanks goes to you for your incredible styling but also your attention to detail. To the army of assistants – Federica, Phoebe, Bella, Emma and Maria – thanks for all of your help and especially your energy keeping the shoot fun and on track. Claire, you went above and beyond nailing down the design for this book. I don't think I have ever seen so many cover concepts but you kept plugging away until we landed on the winning formula (apologies if I am hard to please!). I absolutely adore the design! To Anna, your props and your vision are the perfect companion to the recipes in this book and you just nailed the brief, thank you.

To all of my chocolate colleagues and friends, thanks for the advice, the feedback, the chocolate samples, the help with history. It was all so appreciated. Special thanks to Jennifer for your expertise and feedback on the manuscript, to Amy at Guittard and Jo at Pump St for the constant supply of chocolate.

Thanks to Mike and Simon for the constant support, and Wesley for being my writing companion.

And, as always, my biggest thanks go to the readers. I have been lucky enough to have written multiple books over the last two decades and it is down to the folk that buy and bake from my books that allows me to continue, so thanks! I will be here providing you with a constant supply of deliciousness for as long as you'll have me.

Thanks

EDD

ABOUT EDD

Edd Kimber is a bestselling food writer and baker from London. He is the author of multiple books, including the critically acclaimed *One Tin Bakes* and the *Sunday Times* bestseller, *Small Batch Bakes*. Edd writes for numerous publications including as a columnist in *Olive Magazine* and *Bake From Scratch*. His work can also be found on Substack, @eddkimber, and Instagram, @theboywhobakes. Edd has appeared on multiple TV shows with appearances on shows such as *Good Morning America*, *Saturday Kitchen* and *Sunday Brunch*, as well as on the inaugural series of *The Great British Bake Off* of which he was the winner.

CHOCOLATE RESOURCES

A selection of my favourite chocolate and cocoa makers.

Guittard Chocolate
www.guittardchocolate.co.uk
Chocolate + Dutched Cocoa Powder

Pump Street Chocolate
www.pumpstreetchocolate.com
Chocolate + Batons + Nibs

Islands Chocolate
www.islandschocolate.com
Chocolate

Bare Bones Chocolate
www.bareboneschocolate.co.uk
Chocolate + Batons + Nibs

deZaan
www.dezaan.com
Dutched and Natural Cocoa Powders

Valrhona
www.valrhona.com
Chocolate + Dutched Cocoa Powder + Batons + Nibs

Original Beans
www.originalbeans.com
Chocolate + Nibs

Dandelion Chocolate
www.dandelionchocolate.com
Chocolate + Nibs

Fruition Chocolate Works
www.fruitionchocolateworks.com
Chocolate

WHAT TO MAKE WITH LEFTOVER EGG WHITES

S'mores Cake (page 56) – **2 egg whites (+3 eggs)**

Chocolate Orange Jaffa Cakes (page 82) – **2 egg whites**

Chokladbiskvier (page 108) – **6 egg whites**

Chocolate Orange Meringue Tumble (page 129) – **5 egg whites (+3 egg yolks)**

Chocolate Swiss Meringue Buttercream (page 231) – **4 egg whites**

Chocolate Swirled Peppermint Marshmallows (page 244) – **2 egg whites**

WHAT TO MAKE WITH LEFTOVER EGG YOLKS

Chocolate Gâteau Basque with Sumac Cherries (page 62) – **5 egg yolks**

Passion Fruit Milk Chocolate Bars (page 86) – **2 egg yolks (+ 4 eggs)**

Chocolate and Absinthe Canelés (page 88) – **5 egg yolks**

Milk Chocolate Speculoos Cookies (page 101) – **2 egg yolks**

Milk Chocolate Crème Brûlée with Lime Blackberries (page 120) – **4 egg yolks**

Milk Chocolate Liquorice Ice Cream (page 121) – **6 egg yolks**

Coffee and Tahini Pots de Crème (page 128) – **4 egg yolks**

Irish Cream Trifle Pots (page 139) – **4 egg yolks (+1 egg)**

Dinner Party Cake (page 145) – **6 egg whites leftover**

Chocolate and Passion Fruit Semifreddo (page 147) – **2 egg yolks (+2 eggs)**

Tahini Milk Chocolate Paris-Brest (page 163) – **2 egg yolks**

Black Bottom Coconut Cream Pie (page 166) – **3 egg yolks (+ 1 egg)**

Vanilla Pecan Tart (page 176) – **3 egg yolks**

Earl Grey Milk Chocolate Millefeuille (page 179) – **3 egg yolks**

Sour Cherry Custard Buns with Cocoa Streusel (page 185) – **4 egg yolks (+2 eggs)**

Vanilla Custard Buns with Milk Chocolate Glaze (page 190) – **3 egg yolks (+2 eggs)**

Chocolate Pastry Cream (page 232) – **3 egg yolks**

Chocolate Crémeux (page 236) – **3 egg yolks**

INDEX

Quadrille, Penguin Random House UK, One Embassy Gardens, 8 Viaduct Gardens, London SW11 7BW

Quadrille Publishing Limited is part of the Penguin Random House group of companies whose addresses can be found at global.penguinrandomhouse.com

Published by Quadrille in 2026

www.penguin.co.uk

A CIP catalogue record for this book is available from the British Library

ISBN 9781837833535
10 9 8 7 6 5 4 3 2 1

Managing Director: Sarah Lavelle
Publishing Director: Kajal Mistry
Commissioning Editor: Judith Hannam
Editor: Isabel Gonzalez-Prendergast
Copy Editor: Tara O'Sullivan
Designer: Claire Rochford
Photographer: Matthew Hague
Props Stylist: Anna Wilkins
Food Stylist: Holly Cochrane
Head of Production: Stephen Lang
Production Manager: Sabeena Atchia

Colour reproduction by F1 Colour Ltd

Printed in China by C&C Offset Printing Co., Ltd.

The authorised representative in the EEA is Penguin Random House Ireland, Morrison Chambers, 32 Nassau Street, Dublin D02 YH68.

Penguin Random House is committed to a sustainable future for our business, our readers and our planet. This book is made from Forest Stewardship Council® certified paper.